What happened to the Jews in Germany in the 1930s and to the Rwandans in the 1990s is happening to Christians in Iraq and Syria today while the United States does nothing. *Again*. And again U.S. journalists are ignoring it, the story of our generation. But thank God one journalist has not ignored it. In fact, Mindy Belz has lived through much of it, and in *They Say We Are Infidels* she has produced a searing, journalistic tour de force. It is a courageous, absolutely fascinating book that tells us how this has happened—and how it is happening now, this minute. *Tolle lege.*

ERIC METAXAS
New York Times bestselling author and nationally syndicated radio host

To be a Christian in Iraq and Syria is to live in mortal danger. Churches are bombed, pastors murdered, children kidnapped. Families whose ancestors have survived two thousand years in the region where Christ and his disciples walked now risk elimination by Islamic terrorists. Journalist Mindy Belz has spent more than a decade covering persecuted Christians in the Middle East. *They Say We Are Infidels* is her brilliantly reported account of what it means to be a follower of Jesus there. It is the harrowing and often inspiring story of men and women of unshakable faith.

MELANIE KIRKPATRICK
Author of *Escape from North Korea: The Untold Story of Asia's Underground Railroad*

This sensitive, informative, and beautifully written book possesses all the immediacy and emotional power of a novel. Yet it combines meticulous reporting of real people with an enormous knowledge of the contemporary Middle East. Belz reflects a deep concern for the courageous Christians suffering persecution there, and her writing is engaging and wrenchingly intimate. Insightful, lucid, and irenic, this book will do much to dispel the fog of misunderstanding that prevails among so many concerning the extent of suffering there. Her moving and gripping account could not be more urgent and timely. After finishing this book, readers will immediately want to pray for our brothers and sisters in this troubled region of the world. I know I did.

MICHAEL CROMARTIE
Vice president of the Ethics and Public Policy Center, Washington, DC

Mindy Belz has earned respect for reporting on world affairs with accuracy and insight for over twenty-five years. In *They Say We Are Infidels*, Belz chronicles the rise of Islamic extremism and the worsening plight of Christians in the Middle East since 2003 through the eyes of the Iraqi people. The narrative is informative, powerful, and beautifully written. This book is a must-read for all who are concerned about what is happening in the Middle East.

FRANK R. WOLF
Member of Congress, retired (1981–2014); senior distinguished fellow,
The 21st Century Wilberforce Initiative; Wilson Chair in Religious Freedom,
Baylor University

Mindy Belz's book should be nominated for Book of the Year! The world cannot continue ignoring the genocide and persecution in the Middle East. Read this, then buy copies for all your friends.

DR. RICK WARREN
Author of *The Purpose Driven Life*

THEY SAY

WE ARE

INFIDELS

On the run from ISIS with

persecuted Christians

in the Middle East

MINDY BELZ

TYNDALE®
MOMENTUM

An Imprint of
Tyndale House Publishers, Inc.

Visit Tyndale online at www.tyndale.com.

Visit Tyndale Momentum online at www.tyndalemomentum.com.

Tyndale Momentum and the Tyndale Momentum logo are registered trademarks of Tyndale House Publishers, Inc. Tyndale Momentum is an imprint of Tyndale House Publishers, Inc.

They Say We Are Infidels: On the Run from ISIS with Persecuted Christians in the Middle East

Designed by Dean H. Renninger

Library of Congress Cataloging-in-Publication Data

Names: Belz, Mindy, author.
Title: They say we are infidels : on the run from ISIS with persecuted
    Christians in the Middle East / Mindy Belz.
Description: Carol Stream, IL : Tyndale House Publishers, Inc., 2016. |
    Includes bibliographical references and index.
Identifiers: LCCN 2015049191 | ISBN 9781496411471 (hc)
Subjects: LCSH: Persecution—Middle East. | Christians—Middle East. | IS
    (Organization) | Islamic fundamentalism.
Classification: LCC BR1601.3 .B45 2016 | DDC 956.9104/2—dc23 LC record available
    at http://lccn.loc.gov/2015049191

ISBN 978-1-4964-1388-8 (International Trade Paper Edition)

Printed in the United States of America

22   21   20   19   18   17   16
7   6   5   4   3   2   1

For Mom

....

*Man is that being who invented the gas chambers of Auschwitz;
however, he is also that being who entered those gas chambers
upright, with the Lord's Prayer or the Shema Yisrael on his lips.*

VIKTOR FRANKL

Contents

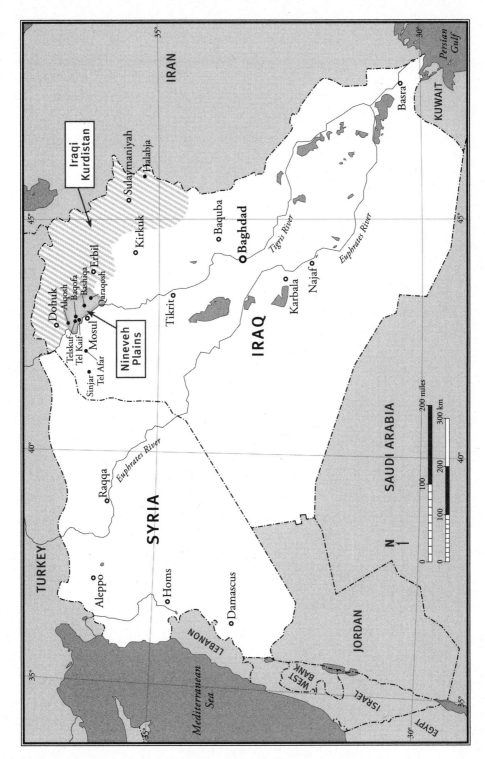

Preface
PAY MONEY

Odisho Yousif choked on baked dust and felt gravel tear into his cheek. His chest throbbed where the man his captors called "Commander" had kicked him. Odisho's breath came in sharp heaves as he looked up at the Commander towering over him, holding his identity card.

Like all Iraqi IDs, Odisho's had a line indicating his religion, and his was marked *Christian*. The Commander, who never removed his black face mask, paced to and fro in the gray dawn, turning the tattered card over and over. "You are an agent with the Jews of Israel!" he exploded.

"No, no!" Odisho protested. "I am a Christian from Iraq."

Odisho was pummeled once more by the Commander's boot, and by a sense of the helplessness of his predicament.

The irony didn't escape him. His job, after all, was to carry money—the funds raised by church members to pay ransom for Christians kidnapped by Islamic militants. As often as he had helped other victims, Odisho never dreamed he might become one himself.

The year was 2006—eight years before the Islamic fighters known as ISIS launched strikes into the center of Iraq's Christian heartland. Everywhere militants were blowing up Christians—their churches, grocery stores, and homes. They threatened them with kidnapping. They vowed to take their children. The message to these "infidels": *You don't belong in Iraq. Leave, pay the penalty to stay, or be ready to die.*

✦   ✦   ✦

Much of the world didn't grasp the deadly dangers for Iraq's Christians until 2014, when a group calling itself the Islamic State of Iraq and Syria, or ISIS, took Iraq's second-largest city, Mosul, in a lightning-fast overnight strike. From that moment genocide unfolded—with rapes, shootings, and beheadings—as ISIS fighters forced thousands of Christians and other non-Muslims to flee.

Long before, Odisho was among thousands who could testify to a decade of such brutality. The ultimatum ISIS handed Mosul's Christians in 2014—pay *jizya*, convert to Islam, or be killed—was too familiar to believers like him.

Paying ransom came as part of the commerce of war. Christians knew that it financed more bombings and more terror, yet they had no choice but to pay. Given Odisho's connections and his ability to raise money and direct it to families who needed it, he naturally became the conduit of funds for kidnapping victims and bombing survivors.

"Fight those who believe not in Allah nor the Last Day, . . . [even if they are] of the People of the Book, until they pay the Jizya with willing submission, and feel themselves subdued," reads the Quran,[1] and the ancient church leaders historically paid the jizya mandated by Islamic law. Modern infidels were paying it just the same: paying special taxes to hold public events and to serve Communion wine. In other words, it was the price to live among Muslims in the Christians' own homeland. In times of war, it was the price to survive.

The decimation of Christians and their communities in the Middle East looks at first like a problem "over there." While sad, it appears too complicated, too tied up in the complex politics of the region, and too big to solve. For me a tragedy held at arm's length over time has become personal. As a reporter covering international events, I've made multiple trips to the region over the past twenty years. While I'm supposed to remain an objective observer, many of these "infidels"—ordinary people committed to raising families and finding work, often after being forced from their homes and losing everything they own—are not merely sources or subjects. They have become friends.

+ + +

For fifty-year-old Odisho, the second of July had begun like so many others. Temperatures rocketed past 110 degrees as he left Dohuk, the city in the far north where he lived, in the company of his driver, a distant relative. By morning he had collected four thousand dollars from churches in Mosul and the surrounding villages of Nineveh Plains; by afternoon, he was making his way along a stretch of good highway south to Baghdad.

Halfway along the five-hour route, the car broke down. As his driver went for help, Odisho, a wiry man with dark hair and tinted glasses, paced and smoked, kicking up dust with the toe of his black leather shoe.

Minutes later a black Opal drove up. Four men wearing black masks stepped out. Before Odisho had time to react, they pulled handguns from their belts and surrounded him. They shouted and wagged their weapons to hustle him into the backseat of their car, but Odisho resisted, backing away. One of the gunmen shot him in the leg. He tumbled into the car, his leg grazed by the bullet, bleeding. After rounding up Odisho's driver, the abductors forced both men, facedown and crouched, into the back of the car. A gunman perched between them.

The car sped off into the desert. Odisho couldn't see, but he guessed they were heading toward Baquba, a town forty miles north of Baghdad that seethed with violence. A month earlier outside Baquba, U.S. forces had killed Abu Musab al-Zarqawi, the head of al-Qaeda in Iraq. The area remained a hotbed for terrorism.

"We have been watching you ever since you left Kirkuk," one of the kidnappers said. But Odisho hadn't traveled through that city. Perhaps his captors were gang members or simple thugs, Odisho thought, rather than trained al-Qaeda militants. He guessed they might be looking for money or prestige by turning hostages over to al-Qaeda.

Shoved onto the floorboard next to a gunman, Odisho felt shock and fear settle over him. *I am a prize hostage,* he realized. *A prominent member of the Assyrian Patriotic Party with visible access to money.* As he considered the impossible burden his kidnapping would impose on others, a heavy dread that turned his stomach spread through him. His body shook all over at the thought of the gunshot to his leg. He couldn't see anything; he could only listen to the whine of wheels just beneath his head and feel the cool metal of the gun pressed to his temple.

The sound of asphalt turned to that of dirt and gravel. Around nightfall the car made a final turn and came to a stop. After being pulled from the car, Odisho stood and looked around. Dirt roadways etched a path lined with fuel tanks, old equipment, and some dilapidated army vehicles. *A deserted military depot,* Odisho thought as his kidnappers began to rearrange corrugated metal sheets and scrap into a shelter. In the distance Odisho saw the Hamrin Mountains in the east. As he had guessed, they were near Baquba.

Odisho lay on the bare ground but couldn't sleep. As the air turned brisk, the sweat of the day cooled against his skin. He shivered uncontrollably. He stood up, paced, sat for a while, then got up and paced some more. When he thought of his two sons at home with his wife, he had to fight not to cry. His driver dozed, and the gunmen kept a lookout. Just before dawn the Commander arrived and began questioning Odisho.

After making accusations, the Commander stormed away with Odisho's belongings, leaving him in the dust. Odisho collected himself but didn't try to stand, and he waited. Hours passed as the Commander talked on a cell phone and argued in Arabic with the gunmen about what to do with the pair. Meanwhile, Odisho and the driver spoke to each other in low tones in Syriac. This ancient language, a dialect of the Aramaic spoken by Jesus Christ, was still spoken by Iraq's Assyrian Christians.

By daylight the Commander told Odisho his ransom had been set at $300,000. It was impossibly higher than the usual demands. Odisho shook his head.

"Kill me," he told the Commander. "It is better."

+ + +

Even as Odisho waited at the abandoned military depot, the seeds of ISIS were forming as a breakaway group from al-Qaeda. In 2006 the Islamic State of Iraq vowed to plant "the flag of the state of Islam" in Iraq, while the West remained transfixed by elections and a budding democracy there.

That same year, an Assyrian clergyman in Iraq gave me an itemized list of Christians who had been killed and kidnapped since the 2003 invasion. It ran to twenty-four pages. It cataloged car bombs at universities and targeted killings at cosmetics shops or outside homes. Christians were killed for joining Christian-affiliated political parties, for being related to clergymen, for owning factories or businesses and refusing to pay jizya—in effect, bribes—to Islamic militants. Many of those who were kidnapped turned up dead.

About six thousand Iraqi Christians had by then fled Baghdad and other major cities for safety in the north. The threats and bloodshed should have been a warning of the terror to come—but few paid attention to what was happening to the Christians three years into the war.

When they did see danger signs, Western leaders were reluctant to get involved. The U.S. leaders in particular, starting with George W. Bush's administration and continuing through the Obama presidency, traded an American legacy of standing up for minorities who faced annihilation—Holocaust survivors, Russian Pentecostals, Rwandans, Congolese, and many others—for a political advantage that never manifested itself. American leaders exchanged the lives of those targeted by sectarian militants for the supposed advantage of appearing nonsectarian.

The reluctance of Western leaders to intervene seemed to stem in part from a tragic misunderstanding. Few diplomats and military commanders appreciated the unique history of Christianity in Iraq; they assumed it was an import of British colonial rule or an invention of American evangelicals.

Nineveh Province was, in fact, the seat of the Church of the East, a church begun at the time of Pentecost when "residents of Mesopotamia" received the Holy Spirit, according to the Book of Acts.[2] The apostle Thomas and others planted the seeds of Christian faith in Iraq, and the church that grew was astute and ardent enough to send two delegates to the Council of Nicea in 325.

That history was forgotten as the terror directed at Christians in Nineveh and the province's capital, Mosul, began. Soon after the United States toppled Saddam Hussein's regime in 2003, a missile struck a convent in Mosul. Christian schools came under attack, as well as Christian-owned businesses—especially beauty salons, stores selling liquor or music, and clothing shops. In August 2004, militants bombed five churches in Mosul and Baghdad. The coordinated attacks happened on a Sunday evening as all the churches held worship services, killing twelve people and injuring about sixty.

As thousands of Iraqi Christians fled the country after the church bombings, one deacon complained that his congregation had to spend more time filling out baptismal forms needed to emigrate than they did in worship: "Our community is being decimated."[3]

Lacking protection and support, about two-thirds of the Christians living in Iraq in 2003 had disappeared by 2011. With the start of Syria's civil war that year, the pattern of targeting Christians expanded. Islamic militants moved across the border from Iraq to join the fight against Syrian president Bashar al-Assad. Early on they killed more than two hundred Christians living in the old city of Homs, including entire families with their children. They kidnapped churchgoers there, too, demanding a ransom similar to Odisho Yousif's.

The militias made no secret of their intention to establish a Sunni caliphate stretching from the Mediterranean Sea to the Iranian border, and perhaps beyond. Unstopped, they eventually would bleed back into Iraq to finish their work.

Yet as threats against non-Muslims were increasing in 2011, the United States military went home. Church leaders in Iraq told me that by 2014 the number of Christians had shrunk to perhaps 250,000 believers, a fraction of what it had been before the United States "liberated"

Iraq. That July, President Barack Obama appointed an envoy to the Arctic region while ignoring pleas to name an envoy to monitor and protect religious minorities in the Middle East.[4]

The prospect of Christian extinction in Iraq spurred Islamic jihadists to act globally, pursuing their goals in Nigeria, Mali, and far-flung places like Indonesia. As one leading journalist wrote, "The most undercovered story these days is the sustained assault by Islamic terrorists on Christians."[5]

As a reporter, I began covering international events for *World* magazine at the end of the Cold War, and throughout the 1990s I saw Islamic extremism rising in communism's place to menace the West. In Sudan I passed just south of Osama bin Laden's training camp and saw the ravages of Islamic terrorism directed at southern Sudan's Christian community.

For many reporters like me, 9/11 changed everything. I found myself covering the Middle East nonstop, discovering that lurking beneath bin Laden's "war on America" was an ongoing assault on Christians wherever they were found. During a trip to Damascus in 2002, I discovered that Sudan was trafficking Sudanese Christians to Syria, where they would be tortured and ordered to convert. In Egypt, the country with the largest population of Christians in the Middle East, believers came under increasing pressure to leave their faith or leave the country.

I didn't go looking for Christians in Iraq; I stumbled upon them when I went to cover a U.S.-led war. But the vitality of the Christian community there would draw me in, and their underreported plight would compel me to return again and again.

PART 1

WAR AND PEACE

1
INSAF'S JOURNEY

Amman, 2003

....

Your statutes have been my songs in the house of my sojourning.

PSALM 119:54

....

Insaf Safou had ten thousand American dollars to give away. They were measured in tens, twenties, and fifties and distributed among dozens of white envelopes. Each bore the name, penciled in soft lead, of a family in Iraq. Some were written in Arabic, some in English. None of them meant anything to me.

"You will take how many thousand through customs for me?" Insaf asked.

We had known each other for maybe one minute and were riding in the backseat of a two-door sedan belonging to a mutual friend, wedged together with luggage tumbling over our shoulders and jammed at our feet. After my overnight stay in Amman, our mutual friend, an American living in Jordan with her family, had collected us one after the other from different street corners. Arab drivers flew past, honking their horns. We were on our way to Amman's Queen Alia International Airport on the outskirts of the city, then on to Baghdad in Insaf's homeland.

Insaf's question hung in the air, close. She stared at me, unblinking. I wasn't sure I'd met an Iraqi Arab Christian before, certainly not one so bold. Her round face and pronounced cheekbones were welcoming. But her dark eyes flashed, demanding.

The white envelopes fanned before me like a royal flush, and I wondered what I'd gotten myself into. I stuttered in reply, then looked back to Insaf's face, a moment ago taut with the power of a just cause, now giving way like glass across a floor. She laughed.

"I am only thinking business before pleasure, and forgetting we must first become friends."

It was December 2003. Nine years earlier, Insaf, her husband, and their two small children had left Iraq. Like many Iraqis who faced threats under Saddam Hussein, they made their way to Jordan, then to Turkey. After seven years as refugees in Istanbul, they immigrated to Canada.

When I first met Insaf, Iraq had been liberated from the grip of Saddam Hussein, and she was on her way back to Baghdad for the first time since her departure. From a compact red carry-on case at her feet, she retrieved a thin notebook with a flowery cover and handed it to me. Inside, written in a careful hand, were the names of families in Iraq who were to receive a portion of the money she carried, and the amount. She had arranged the list with space for each recipient to sign his or her name, so that when she returned to Canada she could show the donors that their money had been signed for and delivered.

The families in Canada who donated the money were Protestant, Orthodox, and Catholic Christians—Iraqi exiles whose roots extended from the mountains of the upper Euphrates Valley to the plains of Nineveh and down to the southern desert.

Before I met Insaf in Amman, we had talked once by phone—a kind of interview to see whether she would permit me, a reporter, to accompany her on this homecoming. I learned then that Insaf had been born into a Catholic family in Kirkuk. As a young woman, she started attending the Kirkuk Evangelical Church, an Iraqi-led congregation established by Scottish Presbyterian missionaries in 1941. She considered herself a born-again, evangelical Christian.

Now I leafed through her flowered notebook, impressed. We were perhaps ten minutes into our relationship, nearing Queen Alia airport, when I agreed to take several packets of money across the border. I folded the envelopes and buttoned them into a leg pocket of my cargo pants, wondering whether I might have been too quick to trust the enterprise of this petite yet sturdy Iraqi.

Insaf was a woman both weighed down by the world and freed from it. The weight showed in the slump of her shoulders and in her pale, creased face. She was forty-five years old, and two years in the West hadn't erased the physical toll of a lifetime living under the regime of Saddam Hussein. Her country was at war, Saddam and his loyalists were hiding somewhere, and Insaf knew only a little of what lay ahead for her when she reached Baghdad. Would she find her extended family, her friends, her old neighborhoods? Yet when she spoke, she was full of confidence and her eyes glistened. They darted over me during our conversation with the passion of a free spirit, of a girl.

Insaf was a refugee who had made countless homes in four different countries with her husband and two children. Her cloistered upbringing included Catholic schools in tenth-century abbeys. She knew privilege and poverty; she knew what it was like to wake up with a missile embedded in her kitchen wall; and she knew four languages as a result of her sojourning.

I'd spent my life wholly in the United States, living on the Eastern Seaboard in two different states not far from where my forebears had arrived in America in the 1600s. I'd had a charmed childhood where church came in brick buildings with white steeples and the Middle East appeared only in the burlap and hay used to make a Nativity scene each year for the baby Jesus. Together, Insaf and I had to bridge chasms that were wider than the ocean we'd crossed to get to the Middle East.

I had seen war before, in Bosnia and in Sudan, and had made one trip to Iraq before this war, but I knew little about what to expect.

Working for a small independent publication like *World* magazine, I had no bureau awaiting me in Baghdad, no hired translator or bodyguard. As most journalists would do, I would spend a few days as an embed at a U.S. military base north of Baghdad, seeing how the war was going from the perspective of American servicemen and women. At a combat hospital, I would witness the hard labor of Americans working around the clock. I would watch the helicopters ferry in the wounded, including an eighteen-year-old Marine with his face blown off by an improvised explosive device (IED). I would see how the doctors and nurses rose from their cots and headed to the operating room at any hour to bind up the wounds of war.

Insaf had her own combat mission, and I made the journey with her to witness an exile's homecoming and a family reunion as once-displaced Iraqis were returning in the months after Saddam was toppled. I came to see through her eyes how the U.S. invasion transformed her ancient homeland and to witness life outside the protection of soldiers, where Iraqis encountered the war every day. But by crossing the border with money in my pocket, I had become, in a sense, her accomplice. We would embark together, find out how much her country had changed, and discover the high cost of going back.

+ + +

Once at the airport, Insaf and I climbed aboard the small Beechcraft plane that would fly us to Baghdad. Captain Chris Erasmus and copilot Rudolph Van Eeden sipped thick coffee out of squat paper cups as they waited for permission to take off. December mornings in Amman break overcast in a cool, dull haze. Erasmus was less concerned about the weather and more about military clearance. His twin-engine turboprop was a workhorse in war zones. But flying into Iraq's capital city, nearly nine months into the U.S.-led invasion, had just gotten hairy.

Erasmus and Van Eeden had started piloting humanitarian flights over Baghdad in November. Their carrier, Air Serv International, had been founded in the 1980s for just this type of mission. Each flight before takeoff, they waited to get a slot from air-traffic controllers a thousand miles away, operating out of the U.S. air base in Doha, Qatar. Receiving a slot meant they could enter Iraqi airspace knowing that they had some U.S. military cover.

A week earlier, slots had grown scarce after militants fired a shoulder-to-air missile that had hit a DHL cargo plane during takeoff, forcing it to make an emergency landing with one wing on fire.

After that, aircraft dodged attacks every day from the ground near the newly reopened Baghdad International Airport. Commercial airlines grounded passenger flights in and out of Baghdad. U.S. Central Command clamped down on available slots, reserving the Iraqi airspace for military flights. Humanitarian flights by Air Serv International were the only option left for civilians. As we blew on our coffee and waited, the pilots explained to me that permission to fly into Iraqi airspace, when it came from Doha, now came with a disclaimer: Fly at your own risk.

"In other words, you might get shot down," said Erasmus.

"And don't come crying to the U.S. military if that happens," added Van Eeden.

In May, Air Serv took three hundred passengers a month into Iraq. By November, its manifests were running a thousand a month, so it added another Beech1900D, a nineteen-seater, and brought on Erasmus and Van Eeden. Demand for seats stayed high as travel by car went from dangerous to out of the question. The road from Amman to Baghdad was a shooting gallery, especially if a Westerner was caught traveling on it.

None of it worried Erasmus or Van Eeden, who had flown in other wars, most recently the one in Afghanistan.

"Ever been shot at?" I asked.

"We don't know because we've never been hit," Erasmus replied.

+ + +

Many Americans expected the U.S. forces to come home after they watched on-screen as Marines pulled down the statue of Saddam Hussein in Baghdad's Firdos Square. The Coalition Provisional Authority settled in under Paul Bremer, embracing the call of President George W. Bush to oversee a "global democratic revolution" in the Middle East led by the United States: a mission with a breathless urgency similar to the Berlin Airlift that began in 1948 or the defense of Greece in 1947.

Eight months later, as I headed to Iraq in December 2003, the country was in disarray. Saddam and his sons were on the run, along with most of the disenfranchised officials from his Baath socialist party, but no successor government had been properly stood up. The streets of Baghdad overflowed with sewage. Roads remained blocked, cratered from U.S. bombings during the invasion. Electricity flickered. In some areas, running water ceased.

Americans didn't appreciate how war-weary Iraqis were from the start. Bremer and others entered Baghdad energized, confident they could put abstract ideas about democracy and freedom to work and full of zeal about their own skills in political engineering. Iraqi statesmen who had been exiled during the Saddam Hussein years, having spent the previous decades in London or Washington, had similar thoughts. Iraqis who had stayed in their homeland had struggled to survive two wars in the past decade, not to mention the daily crush of life under a dictator. They were ready for change, but Saddam had conditioned them to expect order, not the chaos that ensued.

While the Americans tried to figure out Iraq, the jihadists came with a plan. From Saudi Arabia, Yemen, Jordan, Syria, and elsewhere, they came to fight the occupation. Some militant groups offered three thousand dollars for every U.S. soldier killed. Coalition casualties numbered between thirty and fifty a month, then suddenly spiked to 110 in November. The word on the street was that Saddam himself was directing the resistance, sometimes disguised as a taxi driver, a woman, or a nomad.

+ + +

From the air, the midday December sun cast long shards of light. We made our way from the chalk-white hills of Amman to the flat, burnt desert city of Baghdad. The flight took us east across a six-hundred-mile stretch of desert. Insaf settled in to talk with two aid workers from Germany, both of whom were heading to Iraq to teach the logistics of holding elections. My seatmate was a consular-affairs officer from the U.S. State Department, just transferred from Cairo to the newly reopened embassy in Baghdad.

What was the hardest thing about serving in Iraq? I asked him.

"Working the overnight desk," he replied, "and the late-night phone calls from American women who married Arab men and want out."

He invited me to visit his office, located inside the military-protected Green Zone, after I settled in.

The plane cabin was spartan, with bottled water in a cooler as the only refreshment. But conversation was lively, full of the kind of diverse interests and perspectives that everyone hoped to see take root in the "new Iraq." The nineteen passengers included the aid workers from Germany, an Egyptian pastor, an American teacher who lived in Jordan, relief workers from Sweden, and a couple of U.S. diplomats wearing suits.

Below us lay the border between Jordan and Iraq, a literal line in the sand. Border checkpoints were visible from the air, the sunlight glinting off razor-sharp concertina wire marking a fence line that stretched in both directions. We neared the Euphrates and saw the wide lines of irrigation canals first built by the Babylonians. Dirt tracks in the barren desert gradually became paved roads, then highways. Date groves dotted the sandscape, walled compounds surrounded flat-roofed houses, and finally the city came into view. At ten thousand feet, Erasmus leaned the controls left for the corkscrew landing we'd been briefed about in Amman.

High over Baghdad International, Erasmus steered the plane into concentric circles down to a quick, stomach-churning dive onto the runway to avoid heat-seeking missiles. As the plane spiraled, it took us over the presidential palaces. Each sprawled like a vast oasis in the desert. Al Faw, nearest the airport and surrounded by aquamarine water, was built by Saddam Hussein after the Iran-Iraq war and had sixty-two rooms plus twenty-nine bathrooms. Then As-Salam came into view, a six-story palace already taken over by the U.S. military and visibly damaged from the U.S. "shock and awe" bombing runs. From As-Salam ran underground tunnels to other palaces, to government offices in central Baghdad, and to the airport. We made another circle, and there below was the Republican Palace, where the United States and its Coalition Provisional Authority had their headquarters. This vast complex reached into the city itself. Saddam had reportedly built eighty-one palaces while he ruled Iraq, and U.S. military commands had taken over nearly all of them. Inside, they created barracks and chipboard office cubicles, running cables for Internet and phone service across patterned marble floors.

From my bird's-eye view, the palaces formed outsized symbols of the excesses of the now-deposed regime. They made for odd bunkers to garrison U.S. forces. Iraqis thought the Americans might be repeating history. As one journalist pointed out, "If you're trying to convince a population that you have liberated them from a terrible dictator, why would you then sit in his throne?"[1]

Iraq was a different place since my first trip. Eighteen months earlier, I had crossed the Tigris River in an outboard motorboat with help from the Syrian security directorate and Iraqi Kurds. That way I avoided Saddam's media minders, but I couldn't stray outside the northern region of Iraqi Kurdistan, where a U.S.-led no-fly zone made it possible to maneuver without the regime's oppressive scrutiny.

Unlike those furtive comings and goings, this time Insaf and I would enter Iraq legitimately and with stamped passports. She was chatting it up with other aid workers on the plane while secreting her cash and steeling her nerves for this, her first trip back. With her coming and her thousands of dollars, Insaf sought a resolution, not only from decades under Saddam but from centuries under Islamic rule.

2
RIGHT OF RETURN
Baghdad, 2003

....

The bricks have fallen, but we will build with dressed stones; the sycamores have been cut down, but we will put cedars in their place.

ISAIAH 9:10

....

They say the fate of exiles is to dream and wait. For Insaf, the dreaming and waiting were almost over. As our plane taxied toward the passenger ramp, she gazed out the window at an exhausted version of the once-busy Baghdad airport. Jetways hung useless like broken arms off the main terminal. Large windows loomed dark: holes without electricity to light them. As the winter afternoon turned overcast, everything looked olive drab, blending with the desert camouflage worn by the UN and American soldiers we saw. Theirs was the only movement as they manned sandbagged checkpoints along the airport perimeter.

In the distance we could see soldiers patrolling near the tent barracks of Camp Liberty. If this was a war zone, it seemed at first a slow-motion one: The only other signs of movement were Apache and Black Hawk helicopters landing and taking off from an adjoining airfield. Insaf launched from the plane as soon as the stairs touched the tarmac, red case in one hand and passport in the other.

Inside the terminal Insaf stopped short, looking down at her passport. It was more than a decade old, faded green with tattered pages the color of coffee stains. Denied a right of return for years, she'd told me that she had clung to that passport from the time she and her family had crossed the border to Jordan, then to Turkey, then to Canada. It had been unwelcome in many countries, including the United States, and useless until now. Mindful of all the rejections, she handed it over slowly to an American officer who stood by a metal detector.

Apparently he'd seen her hesitation before. He took her passport from her and took her by the hand in one gesture. "Your passport is old, but we will make it new again," he said, smiling. With a thump he stamped the booklet with an entry visa marked "Iraq-CPA," signifying the joint rule of the U.S. Coalition Provisional Authority and the formative Iraqi government. "Welcome to Baghdad."

Her eyes filled with tears. She beamed back at him. "Canada is okay," she said, "but Iraq is good."

Another Air Serv turboprop, this one from Erbil in Iraqi Kurdistan, had just touched down, and its passengers hurried through the terminal to catch our plane out on its return leg to Amman. Most of those in transit were Americans and Europeans. One, a tall strawberry blonde, looked familiar. A mutual acquaintance had told me Heather Mercer might be on one of these flights, and there she was, making her way through the airport.

Heather Mercer was the twenty-four-year-old U.S. aid worker arrested in Afghanistan only weeks before the 9/11 attacks. She and colleague Dayna Curry, along with six other workers with the German charity Shelter Now, had been arrested for proselytizing Muslims. They were in a Taliban cell in Kabul when al-Qaeda launched attacks on the United States. Once the United States went to war in Afghanistan, the Taliban fled Kabul with the prisoners, who hid in a metal shipping container. Their guards abandoned them when the U.S. attacked, and they were finally freed by anti-Taliban forces and evacuated by U.S. Special Forces. That had been just two years ago, and here was Mercer, again scouting for aid work in a war-torn, terror-ridden country.

We introduced ourselves. Heather's smile broadened, especially when she learned of Insaf's journey to reunite with family and friends. Heather asked us not to tell others we had seen her. The publicity following her liberation and return to the United States had been overwhelming—and not all positive—and she wasn't eager for a journalist to report that she was trying to set up aid and relief work in northern Iraq.

Insaf nodded as she pulled her Arabic Bible from her red case. I watched as she flipped to Jeremiah 29, which contains the text of a letter the prophet sent from Jerusalem to the surviving exiles carried into captivity in Babylon. Insaf began reading the passage in a soft, steady voice:

> This is what the LORD says: "When seventy years are completed for Babylon, I will come to you and fulfill my good promise to bring you back to this place. For I know the plans I have for you," declares the LORD, "plans to prosper you and not to harm you, plans to give you hope and a future. Then you will call on me and come and pray to me, and I will listen to you. You will seek me and find me when you seek me with all your heart. I will be found by you," declares the LORD, "and will bring you back from captivity. I will gather you from all the nations and places where I have banished you," declares the LORD, "and will bring you back to the place from which I carried you into exile."[1]

The breeze kicked up dust around us, and the prophecy sounded as if it might have come from one of Insaf's forebears in some Babylonian courtyard at dusk. After Insaf finished reading, she said simply, "I am praying for God to bless my people." Heather smiled and embraced her, then turned to catch her plane.

+ + +

Before U.S. occupation, before Saddam, before Baghdad's ancient caliphate, and before the Babylonians, "the LORD God planted a garden in Eden, in the east."[2] The Scriptures of Jews and Christians speak of four rivers watering that garden. Today we can follow the course of only two. The Tigris and Euphrates pour from the Taurus Mountains of Turkey across Syria and into Iraq. They watered the ground from which God drew mud to form a man.

Adam, with Eve, his wife, lived only for a time in the Garden, but the civilizations that grew in the fertile plains of the Tigris-Euphrates river system—starting with Sumerians, Assyrians, Chaldeans, and Babylonians—formed the earliest cities and empires in the world. This land came to be known as Mesopotamia, which means "between two rivers."

Travel along the rivers and the network of inland canals in the Tigris-Euphrates Valley was commonplace when Terah, the father of Abraham, took flight with his family from Ur of the Chaldeans, a city on the Euphrates in southern Mesopotamia. Terah and his people headed north to Haran, following the irrigated lands of this Fertile Crescent. Thanks to the waterways, the land was rich in crops, fruit groves, and pasturelands.

Abraham settled with his family in Paddan-aram, an important crossroads and commercial center for Assyrian traders—not far from today's Turkey-Syria border near the city of Aleppo. Clay tablets discovered in Syria in the 1970s confirm the Abrahamic settlements, including Sodom and Zeboiim, two cities highlighted in the book of Genesis. The tablets predate biblical texts and refer to Canaan, the biblical Promised Land to which Abraham continued his pilgrimage.

This time, Abraham's journey led him south and west toward the Mediterranean. His party skirted the Arabian desert, passing through the coastlands of modern-day Syria, Lebanon, Israel, and Palestine until they reached Egypt and the Sinai Peninsula.

Yet Mesopotamia would pull on Abraham's descendants like a lodestone. First his son Isaac and then his grandson Jacob returned to Paddan-aram to find wives and amass fortunes. There they likely spoke an early form of Aramaic: the common language that united the diverse peoples of the Fertile Crescent, the trade language spoken in the time of Jesus, and the language of the early Christians. In the ancient but still-active churches of northern Iraq and Syria, Aramaic (also called Syriac) is spoken even today.

In Canaan the Jews would persist in building a nation, eventually separating into a northern kingdom known as Israel and a southern kingdom called Judah. Conquered and brutalized, they would one day retrace the Fertile Crescent routes as captives. The Assyrians captured Samaria in 722 BC, and the Babylonians captured Jerusalem in 597 BC. Each conquest, in effect, carried the Jews back to where they had first begun.

In a similar way, Insaf was back where she began, carried by events beyond her control to depart and return, standing in the terrazzo-floored arrival hall of the airport and reading aloud from a Jewish prophet who had foretold his people's exile and capture.

I hadn't accounted for the layers of history that informed the Iraqis' outlook and in some ways predicted the looming divisions—divisions even the Western experts would fail to see. In subtle ways, the Sumerian, Babylonian, Assyrian, and Persian empires—bedrocks of pagan, Jewish, and Christian tradition—lived on, all established before the prophet Muhammad ever had a dream or the eighth-century Abbasid caliphs made Iraq the center of the Muslim world.

+ + +

At the start, Insaf's journey represented for me a way to report on what was happening to everyday Iraqis in time of war. Her reunion with family, I thought, would be a touching, symbolic reentry. She would guide me through the ancient streets of Baghdad, deciphering the war and the place for Americans back home.

Beyond that, I saw Insaf as a little-understood emblem of war at the dawn of the twenty-first century: the global refugee. Already I had spent most of a decade trekking from Bosnia to similarly troubled countries in Africa, and now Iraq and Afghanistan, observing how civilian casualties, wartime survivors, were moving across the globe, reshaping the places they left and the places where they resettled. In many ways they were instigators of change, determined to persevere even as they were the victims of forces beyond their control.

But Insaf hadn't returned to explain "the meaning of Iraq" to a novice like me. She wasn't back in Iraq to explore dusty souks. She was there to help Christians—some of them actual relatives and others strangers whom she considered brothers and sisters in her faith. Together they had lived through persecution, and the experience had formed in them a fierce attachment, even among Christians who'd never met one another. I would meet many like her—such as Odisho Yousif—who thought nothing of spending all their time and savings to help a fellow Iraqi, whether friend, relative, or stranger. Now they saw a window of opportunity to gain equal footing in what everyone was calling "the new Iraq." Their stories would be the lure pulling me back, when State Department warnings and the needs of my growing family all called me to remain at home.

After Heather Mercer's departure, Insaf and I gathered our luggage to hustle out the airport's front doors and onto a waiting bus. I had only a black knapsack that held rolled-up clothes, a laptop, a recorder, and notebooks. Insaf corralled her several suitcases, eyeing the road ahead. The late-afternoon sky was a dull gray, giving no cues on its horizon as we rode out through a zigzag of sandbags and concertina razor wire to our first checkpoint. Even as the air cooled into evening, traffic kicked up dust thick and acrid through the bus's open windows, making us cough and squint.

As we neared a car lot, Insaf and I saw Iraqis standing around, some waiting for returning family and others for strangers, foreigners they'd agreed to meet. When the bus slowed, Insaf locked sights on her sister, waiting on the dusty pavement. She'd had no way to see Angham in nine years.

Across the lot Angham raced to Insaf. Though younger, Angham looked older, several teeth capped and a mottled birthmark at her cheekbone. The two women, who'd parted as young mothers, now reunited as they approached middle age, grinning at each other with the same wide smile and shining eyes.

For a few moments they had no words, falling together into a tight embrace. The cares of a decade seemed to fall away, and I simply watched them—unmindful of our bags, our stashed envelopes of cash, or the perimeter of Iraqi police and U.S. servicemen. The two sisters moved about as if on some gyroscope spinning in the prearranged motions of a war we were now seeing up close: Men in sunglasses and desert camo, weapons ready, crisscrossed the parking lot, questioning the taxi drivers and bus drivers, looking under the wheels, eyeing the traffic chugging through the serpentine paths of each checkpoint.

For a moment the hubbub receded, along with the uncertainty of what lay ahead. There stood two people in the middle of dusty Mesopotamia retracing the rites of exile and return. Watching Insaf weep on her sister's shoulder, I thought of Abraham's feisty grandson Jacob, who departed Canaan to journey back to Mesopotamia. There he labored twenty years in another's land. Even after amassing his own fortune, Jacob couldn't escape the inward fears born of rootlessness, the quest to be home again. "With only my staff I crossed this Jordan," he said, "and now I have become two camps."[3]

Like so many forced to flee under Saddam Hussein, Insaf had one foot in Iraq and one foot in the West. Now I looked to her as my escort into this unfamiliar camp.

3

NO GUARANTEES

Baghdad, 2003

....

[Mesopotamia] will be a wonderful country some day, when they regulate the floods, and dig out the irrigation ditches. Yet it will never be a really pleasant country, or a country where Europeans can live a normal life.

T. E. LAWRENCE IN A 1916 LETTER TO HIS MOTHER

....

Muthafar Yacoub grabbed a box cutter from the coffee table and sliced into an electric cable snaking away from him in the dark. He worked at the guts of the cable, finding colored wires and stripping them, threading each piece into copper conductors for a new plug.

As he worked, his neighbor sat at his shoulder, holding a penlight. It was after nine, and around them the living room was black, chilling fast in the cold night air. Light and shadows from three scattered oil lamps traced across the walls. Insaf and I, a few days into our stay in Baghdad, joined Muthafar in the dark room, but he was one man at war in Iraq, fighting for his lights.

With the war, electricity in the capital was at best unpredictable. On some days, Baghdad residents had power all day; on others, only a few hours. Today's schedule called for power on a three-hours-on/three-hours-off rotation. But after two hours in the afternoon, it quit. At seven in the evening, it came back on, only to shut down again almost immediately.

"*Ma fe dhaimaan*," Muthafar muttered as he worked. No guarantees.

Insaf was not the only returnee. All over the city Iraqis were coming back to their homeland, crowding in with family members; and Insaf's sister had a full house. Muthafar and his wife, Ghada—both friends of Insaf—had just returned from Jordan. They agreed to take us in.

They had moved back only ten days earlier, into a two-story home on a quiet street in Rasafah, a neighborhood in central Baghdad. Insaf and I shared a small room just off the living area, barely big enough for two twin mattresses. This bedroom was usually occupied by the Yacoubs' two girls: eleven-year-old Lydia and five-year-old Roda. During our stay the girls slept on pallets in their parents' room. Upstairs were the other houseguests: a professor from Jordan; an Egyptian pastor; and a young man, a former Shiite who had recently become a Christian.

Every day since the Yacoubs' return to Baghdad had its own tale of improvisation. With guests in the house, Muthafar was eager for light and heat. So that afternoon he'd paid $225 for a household generator. At home he discovered that its box had already been opened, and the generator wouldn't start.

He returned to the store carting the generator, a unit about the size of a compact refrigerator. "It's yours now," the store owner said, and he would give Muthafar only $100 on return. Out $125, Muthafar then paid the same store owner full price to buy another generator.

Back home, its engine sputtered and caught, only for Muthafar to discover that he didn't have the right cable to connect the generator to the fuse box and power his home. Once again, he returned to the store, and then a nighttime retrofitting of cables, wires, and plugs began. When he finished splicing and reconnecting, Muthafar yanked the generator's engine to life and flicked a switch inside. Lights flooded the living room at last. Though the hour was late, Ghada fired up the stove and served tea all around. As I did with everyone, I asked them to tell their story of flight and return.

Like Insaf, Muthafar's family had been forced to flee their home despite having good educations and thriving careers in Baghdad.

Muthafar was a biochemist who'd worked in the oil industry before taking up teaching. Ghada had worked as a dentist for ten years. "Suddenly that was all taken from us," she said. When I asked them what had happened, they were reluctant to explain.

Lifelong Baghdad residents and Chaldean Catholics, they had left for Jordan. In Amman, away from the watchful eye of the Saddam regime, they had more freedom and took up Bible study and evangelism training. By the time they were ready to return to Baghdad in the autumn of 1993, they considered themselves evangelical Christians. "From Catholic background we are accused of leaving our religion when we become evangelical Christians. Imagine how much harder it is for Shiite converts," Ghada said, motioning upstairs where the young man was sleeping.

Back in Iraq, they met opposition from family members and their Catholic church, but it didn't deter them. Muthafar and Ghada worked with several churches, organizing Bible studies to meet in homes. They taught new believers and received a stipend through a prominent American evangelism and discipleship group.

"We avoided all associations with foreigners," Muthafar told me, but the work drew suspicion anyway. When President Bill Clinton launched air strikes on Iraq in 1998, the regime singled out nearly anyone working for U.S.-affiliated groups, including nonpolitical ones. Muthafar and Ghada were forced to disband Bible studies and other meetings.

Baathist heavies still followed Muthafar's activities. They showed up at his home one evening, warning him he could be thrown in jail. The family made a quick getaway to Lebanon, but after two months, the head of Lebanon's security bureau ordered them deported. Instead of returning to Baghdad, they went to Jordan (their second stint there), where a number of Iraqi Christians—like Insaf and her husband, Shawki—had migrated by that time. For five years they lived in relative security; Muthafar studied the Old and New Testaments at a school in Amman, and Ghada took care of their young girls. But the couple viewed the interlude as exile.

As we drank tea in their new Baghdad home, I asked, "Couldn't you have stayed in Jordan, a more stable, prosperous place?"

Together they quickly said no. They knew they would come home once the United States toppled Saddam. The family was still getting used to the mostly Muslim neighborhood, the shortages of electricity and other items, and the persistent sound of attack helicopters overhead. But they preferred those challenges to living outside Iraq.

In later years, as bombings in Iraq became commonplace and a new kind of dictatorship—Islamic terrorism—took hold, I would hear Iraqis say that life had been better under Saddam. By then they had simply forgotten. In the months following his ouster in 2003, all present hardships—the challenges and chaos of life in U.S.-dominated Iraq—were preferable to life under Saddam. That winter I did not meet a single Iraqi whose life had not been upended by Saddam in some way, often brutal and scarring. I met Christians who'd been imprisoned in lightless closets not big enough to sit down, who were forced to defecate and urinate in the same place standing for weeks on end. I met Muslims who'd been forced to clear date-palm groves outside Baghdad in the searing midday sun, left to watch helplessly as older prisoners collapsed in the heat.

Under Saddam, everyone lived on a knife's edge of fear—Muslims, Christians, and others. No rules for the road mattered, only Saddam's pleasure, which became more elusive and unpredictable as the world closed in around him. As Saddam's son Uday once said, "My father's right shirt pocket doesn't know what is in his left shirt pocket."[1]

It wasn't only President George W. Bush who called the Iraqi dictator by his first name; all Iraqis referred to him simply as Saddam because the way he dominated all of life, not only political life, was personal. The regime was everywhere all the time, expected. Before Saddam's defeat, Iraqis lived as if he might stop by the house at any moment, asking Muthafar where he bought the generator and how much he paid for it. No one would be able to predict whether Saddam would blame the store owner for stiffing Muthafar with a broken generator or would punish Muthafar for going along with being stiffed.

"Under Saddam, a Westerner could not come to my table and eat like you," Muthafar said quietly.

But Saddam was gone. Every morning during my stay in his home, Muthafar took a sack from the kitchen and headed to a nearby market. While Ghada put on water for tea, he bought a wad of greens as big as a man's head, along with tomatoes, cucumbers, parsley, onions, and purple figs, or maybe dates and fresh cheese. He returned with the sack overflowing and dumped its contents on the counter.

At this Ghada would smile, pleased above all to put a real Iraqi breakfast on the table for her guests. She put the greens in a pan of water to soak by the sink, and by the time the tea had steeped, she had filled the round kitchen table with dishes: *gaymer*, a rich buffalo-milk cheese drizzled with date syrup; a slightly harder cheese served in a braid that Ghada poured milk over before serving; fig jam and honey; yogurt drizzled with oil; olives; cut cucumbers with tomatoes; and plates of fresh flatbread.

One morning after breakfast, Insaf and the other guests left to visit Christian families, to see what churches had opened (or reopened). Insaf was eager to begin handing out her envelopes of money to designated families. I had a meeting in the Green Zone, the headquarters for American military and government offices; Iraqis called it "the security complex" or, more straightforwardly, "the bubble." Muthafar had agreed to take me there, showing me the city along the way.

We drove in his Toyota sedan toward Firdos Square, where in April Iraqis watched triumphantly as the statue of Saddam came down. The square teemed with traffic, and a sign in its center read in Arabic, "Lift up your heads—you are Iraqis." Threading through the traffic circle and its swerving lines of cars, we saw another sign proclaiming, "The dictator will not be back."

Central Baghdad hummed with activity despite being broken, like a lame man who couldn't stop hustling no matter how crippled his hands and feet. U.S. bombing runs in March and April had left craters on side streets. They remained unfixed, filled with foul standing water in places where exploded sewer pipes bubbled over enough to flood a whole road. The Americans were busy elsewhere, but in the massive de-Baathification program, they had cut loose government workers who could have taken care of the streets. Traffic jammed everywhere as returning Iraqis joined Arabs who'd come looking for business, all of them driving new sedans with Jordanian and Persian Gulf license plates and competing with U.S. military convoys for the roadways.

Men clogged the sidewalks, pushing boxed refrigerators or generators or loitering by the money changers and kebab sellers, fingering their prayer beads. Unemployment was climbing to 25 percent or more, and with American dollars suddenly hitting the economy, prices were rising by the hour.

And there was the fuel shortage. Everywhere stretched lines for gasoline, which Iraqis called benzine. On most days fuel prices skyrocketed to compensate for shortages, and sometimes Muthafar waited most of a day to buy a half tank. We passed lines that were a mile or more long, sometimes with cars parked two deep. That same week customers would set an all-time record, with one gas line involving 670 vehicles. Bootleggers managed to buy enough fuel to set up roadside tables lined with two-liter soda bottles of gasoline. For a premium—about ten times the normal price—drivers could purchase a few liters, wait as a young boy dumped them in the tank, and drive on.

Was it like this before? I asked Muthafar.

No, he said. Iraqis found the postwar fuel shortages galling, sitting as they did atop the world's second-largest oil reserve. "We are like a camel who goes hungry while carrying all the food," Muthafar said, waving at the gas lines in exasperation.

Having worked in the oil industry, Muthafar recognized, as did most Iraqis, that looters and terrorists, not the advance of U.S. forces, were hurting their oil supply. But the Americans frustrated him.

"When they came to change the situation, they should have been ready for the next step," Muthafar said. "They should have been ready to supply hospitals and to fix electricity. They should have trained people for security. If they had been ready, they would not have given an opportunity for Islamic parties."

As he said this, we were driving past SCIRI headquarters with its four burly guards carrying heavy machine guns standing post. SCIRI, or the Supreme Council for the Islamic Revolution in Iraq, was a political party with direct backing from Iran. It had scant support among Baghdad's majority Shiites, but the United States had given SCIRI a seat on the Iraqi Governing Council anyway. The Americans couldn't— or wouldn't—see that parties like SCIRI sought a theocratic government, in direct contradiction to what President Bush was pledging at home and what U.S. forces were trying to protect and establish here.

Under Saddam's Sunni-dominated regime, Shiites had had little to no political power, though they made up 60 percent of the population. Iraqis whom I spoke to, especially Christians, wanted an inclusive government but feared the rise of political Shia movements, with their ties to the ayatollahs in Tehran. The Americans' manipulation of the governing council felt more like dictatorship than democracy to them.

Already the terrorists were striking with increasing success, pushing casualties higher by the month. Some of these extremists were Sunni militants affiliated with al-Qaeda; others arose from the Shia movements doing Iran's bidding. In November, coalition casualties leapt to 110, up from 47 in October. "The next six months in Iraq," wrote *New York Times* columnist and Middle East expert Thomas Friedman that November, "are the most important six months in U.S. foreign policy in a long, long time." The war, he said, "is the most important liberal, revolutionary U.S. democracy-building project since the Marshall Plan."[2]

American planners would be dogged by two errors in judgment: underestimating how dangerous the terrorists truly were and ignoring the subtle differences dividing Islamic jihadists.

Muthafar dropped me off across the traffic circle from the Green Zone, afraid to approach the American soldiers standing watch at the entry. When I asked him why, he only pointed to the width of their shoulders and the length of their guns.

In those days the gateway to U.S. headquarters in Iraq was a five-foot-high wall of stacked sandbags, with tall poles protruding from the stacks to support desert-beige tarpaulins that formed a kind of tunnel ushering all the foot traffic into the Green Zone. Concertina wire stretched in a mass of razor-sharp spirals over the sandbags. Inside this tunnel was a labyrinth of armed guards, metal detectors, and checkpoints. Iraqis milled about outside, eager for entry to plead a cause or ask for a job. But a press badge, an American passport, and an appointment were all that I needed to get in.

Once inside the complex, an area of about four square miles, wide paved roads fanned out to palaces and government buildings that housed offices for American workers. The streets were closed to traffic. I walked past a combat hospital, where a triage unit treated the sick or wounded outdoors beneath white tents. The cordoned-off enclave also included Iraq's parliament building, where American officers held daily press briefings on the conduct of the war, and the Al Rashid hotel, where more officials and diplomats worked in the converted rooms and where many diplomats and American journalists lived. Downstairs, a lobby area of the hotel was serving as the dining facility.

Inside the Green Zone everyone looked purposeful, busy. Unless you dug beneath the surface or looked at the city outside the enclave, you had the idea that the United States had a plan for running this "new" Iraq. Anyone working inside, though, could tell you that chaos reigned among the policymakers.

Over lunch with a friend from the State Department, I told him about the craters and broken sewer pipes untended in the streets of Baghdad. They were left over from U.S. bombing raids almost nine months earlier, I pointed out, and businesses along those streets had to close, families had to move. Why didn't the United States repair the streets? I asked. How hard could it be?

"I have no idea," he said, "because we aren't allowed to go out to inspect those streets, or much of anything else."

Nine months after liberation, the United States was already operating at a disconnect from the lives of the Iraqis. Hope, even among supporters of the U.S. effort like Muthafar, was turning to fear and suspicion. Walking the streets inside and outside the Green Zone, as I was doing, made that plain. Too few Americans were doing both. The occupation had cleaved the governing authority into a two-headed entity, military and civilian. Neither had a coherent, much less coordinated, strategy to recruit Iraqi leaders to deal with the developing insurgency. No one at the top seemed to understand the religious diversity I was discovering—or the depth of brokenness and cruelty most Iraqis had experienced.

Back in Washington each morning, top aides briefed President Bush. Using an easel, they displayed the deck of cards carried by soldiers in the field showing the fifty-two most wanted men in Iraq. American forces were tracking and taking them down, but all the while the insurgency was growing. Iraq on the ground was more than the deck of cards. Through borders left wide open, insurgents were coming from all over the Arab and Muslim world, and their attacks were becoming more sophisticated, more determined. Yet not only did the United States dissolve the 400,000-strong Iraqi army, it sent home 40,000 U.S. Marines.

The Americans were ousting Baathists, but they failed to comprehend something Insaf or Muthafar could have told them: Under Saddam, even a teacher had to be a member of the Baath Party, the Arab socialist party of the dictator who had dominated Iraq's politics for more than thirty years. Comedians registered as members of the party and earned a monthly stipend from the Ministry of Culture. It was like a security badge, the cost of doing business in Saddam's Iraq. At its core were virulent strains of nationalism and oppression, but it included many who joined simply to keep their jobs.

What the Baathist ouster meant was that Iraq now had no army, no central government, no local provincial governments, and no bureaucracy. Further, terrorist attacks on the UN headquarters in Baghdad that August, followed by another a month later outside the Canal Hotel, had succeeded in driving out the top international experts working there.

The United Nations sent home more than six hundred personnel, and many private aid workers followed their lead.

In hindsight it should have been no surprise that an insurgency rapidly filled this vacuum, a potent mix of discontented Iraqis and determined foreign jihadists. What the Americans had going for them in 2003 was a heady rush of gratitude from most Iraqis: Brigade commanders under Gen. David Petraeus in the north acted for a time like local governors, settling land disputes and funding development projects. In the Shiite south, Lt. Col. John Mayer was invited to sit with the local council, and in Karbala, about sixty miles southwest of Baghdad, locals wanted to elect Lt. Col. Matt Lopez mayor.[3] In the north, Kurds opened the George Washington restaurant in Erbil, and American flags flew from buildings all over the city.

Under the Coalition Provisional Authority led by Paul Bremer, the goodwill vanished with the winter wind that first year as hardships set in. The CPA postponed local elections, halted development projects (even those that included fixing what the American invasion had destroyed), and forced Kurds and other powerful factions to funnel their every move through Baghdad and the Green Zone. What that left, in communities across Iraq, were Muslim imams as leading community figures, many of whom preached violence from the seclusion of their local mosques.

What's perhaps more surprising is that so many Iraqis held on to their optimism, their soaring expectations of what the Americans could do. They clung to their hopes, confident that life in Iraq would get better.

+ + +

"There are so many rumors that are not true," Ghada told me later that week as we sat again at her table for tea. It was just after four in the afternoon, and the sky was beginning to darken. "You cannot unlock your doors? All day my door stays open! I can go to the store; I can walk in my Muslim neighborhood. It's very safe." Then she added, "We are afraid from explosions more than thieves."

Outside, shadows fell across the tiled courtyard, and soon Ghada's neighbors would begin grilling lamb over small charcoal fires on their own patios. The electricity had been off for an hour; Lydia and Roda, Ghada's daughters, appeared with flashlights they waved around the long, narrow room, throwing more shadows across its walls as they darted in and out of the bright beams.

"Every day you see people going to school and going to the store. They are fighting for their way of life. They are wanting to be normal," Ghada observed. Just over five feet tall, Ghada was thickset but youthful in her face and in the way she spoke in clear but careful English, all the while tossing correction to the girls in soft, almost offhand Arabic. Her hair was slightly wavy and layered just above her shoulders, with streaks of henna running through it. Since my arrival she'd worn only black—casual black trousers with a black turtleneck. A relative in her family had died, and this was the customary way for women to show respect during a period of mourning.

Ghada, I had learned in a week of living in her home, was a progressive, smart woman who outwardly seemed bound by tradition. I wondered whether this was by choice or by habit. She seemed content to meet each day of uncertainty with confidence, and I wanted to learn from her. Wanted, honestly, to find the crack in her calm joy and startling welcome of strangers.

How has your life changed since you returned to Baghdad? I asked. Is it different than you imagined?

She said she could see that life for women in Iraq was changing after the invasion. "More Muslim women are wearing coverings since the war," she said. "It's a way to say they are different from the Americans. Many women actually want to protect themselves from the gaze of the U.S. soldiers. It's also a way to assert our identity as Iraqis."

Hijab not only refers to the coverings worn by Muslim women but also comes from the Arabic verb *hajaba*, meaning "to veil." With it comes submission to the custom of full covering in public (including wrists and ankles), as well as symbolic acceptance of the trait that Muslim society expects of all women: invisibility. In most Muslim countries, a woman's property rights and court testimony legally amount to half of a man's. Even in Muslim countries where the laws are less extreme, often a husband can beat his wife for disobedience, divorce her at will, and deprive her of custody of children without facing severe repercussions himself.

All the Christian women I'd met walked boldly in the streets with no head coverings and in simple Western dress. Most of them covered their heads only in church, often using a square of lace netting they pinned in place or simply laid across their hair. Theirs was a direct contrast, purposefully so, to the Muslim women who went covered in the streets but wore Western clothes in the privacy of their homes. In the Shiite neighborhoods nearby, women walked in full black burqas, revealing their faces but not their hair and wearing long, black leather gloves to cover their hands and forearms. They hurried past, their garments swishing the ground and creating plumes of dust as they walked.

I wore jeans, sweaters, and dusted-up boots, with my blonde hair pulled back, sometimes tucked into a turtleneck or the collar of my shirt, occasionally beneath a dark ball cap. Americans were everywhere and easily recognized, but I kept a dark blue scarf tucked in my bag, which was essential if I went into a mosque or Muslim home, or if the people I was with felt more comfortable when my head was veiled. American women, especially living and moving among Iraqis, were rare. Often I was mistaken for a German or Scandinavian, which could be useful: I wouldn't be asked for money.

Like other Arab countries, Iraq was patriarchal, a society controlled by men. It was more progressive than other Muslim-dominated countries, such as Afghanistan or the Gulf states. Women could vote, attend school with men, and hold jobs of all kinds, including political office. Yet in many Muslim homes, men and women ate separately. Muslim men could and did have multiple wives, and divorced them at will.

Sometimes the limits for women could be confining for a female reporter. Mostly I embraced them, trying to see them as an advantage. I may have been barred from some meetings, but this happened rarely in Iraq. More often, I was treated as another strange Westerner, welcomed but also asked—despite being in my forties—why my father hadn't accompanied me.

What this discrimination gave me was access to the world of women. Welcomed to join them at their kitchen tables, to walk with them in the market, to pray with them, and to attend their Bible studies, play groups, or civic meetings, I had access to a realm that few men and fewer outsiders troubled themselves to enter. At first not realizing my good fortune, I later discovered I had a window into an under-explored world, the opportunity to see a perspective sometimes lost in larger venues and more powerful halls. The concerns, hopes, fears, and opinions women voiced in those settings sometimes cut across ethnic and religious lines. They held a pulse of popular opinion no one was polling.

With Ghada at her twilit table, that meant returning to the topic of electricity. Outdoors you could hear the two-cycle engines of generators screaming to life, but Muthafar and Ghada's new generator sat silent. It needed fuel. Muthafar had to limit use of the generator, given the shortage of gasoline to run it. The family could rely on it only at certain crucial hours of the day—to make dinner, do homework, and knock off the evening chill. At first Ghada was disappointed, but she readily accepted Muthafar's plan.

Ghada also wanted to talk about her girls and her own altered life. Upon returning to Baghdad, Ghada and Muthafar had placed Lydia in school. It was traditional, she said, "like we are used to," where Muslims and Christians learn together and education is largely secular. Christians could exempt themselves from the religious classes required of Muslims.

Lydia was an eager learner and was already full of ambition. Every night that I stayed in her home, she met me after supper for English lessons. She constantly asked me to pronounce words she knew and to name ones she did not. She wanted to perfect an American accent, not the British dialect commonly taught.

Roda did not go to school. She could have been in kindergarten, but

Ghada told me the school was "Muslim and insecure, the teaching heavy Islamic." Ghada was happy to have Roda at home during the family's transition to life in Baghdad, and she told me she was confident that— with American influence, the passage of a new constitution, and new elections in the next year—pressure for Islamic education would fade.

In the meantime, Ghada watched her own years of study and a decade working as a dentist become a vanishing memory, as war and displacement seemed to make continuing her career impossible. In the days I lived with her, it was easy to see that she was a thrifty, immaculate housekeeper and an excellent cook. She told me she enjoyed those roles. But what is the place for a displaced Arab woman who is an educated professional and a Christian? she wondered.

Christian women in Iraq had fewer straightforward sets of rules than those to which women submitted under Islam. Ghada had no interest in wearing coverings like Muslim women or in outward rule keeping, but she was seeking a zone of safety and acceptability nonetheless. She longed for a clearer picture of her identity as a Christian woman living in post-Saddam Iraq. Even though their life in Jordan had offered more options for her—more freedom and possibilities—she told me she had found it unsettling, too.

In Jordan she'd become acquainted with American Christians who invited her to a weekly women's Bible study held in the home of a U.S. diplomat. But after several weeks of the meetings, Ghada said Muthafar asked her to stop going. "You become dissatisfied with our home and our family as you spend more time with Westerners," he told her.

Ghada said she knew he was right. The meetings took place in a hilly neighborhood of expensive white homes with covered entryways. Outside were trellised bougainvillea, rosemary hedges, and citrus trees. Inside the diplomat's residence was a tasteful collection of Arab rugs, shirred drapes, brocade chairs, and fine china. Even as she found the women smart, engaging, and attentive, she knew that their Western affluence warred with her family's life as refugees, living in a simple apartment of curtainless windows and borrowed furnishings, and dependent on others for many things. She grew to resent her circum-stances—something that contradicted what she was learning from the Bible. Looking at Muthafar, Lydia, and Roda convinced her she was wrong to be discontent. She never went back to the meetings.

The experience made Ghada more at ease with Westerners but also more determined to preserve her roots as an Arab Christian. Upon returning to Baghdad, she mostly stayed at home, more conscious of speaking Arabic with her daughters and teaching them to make the dishes and appreciate the customs that she herself treasured. Coming home also meant spending more time with extended family, a way for her daughters to connect with the heritage Ghada feared they had lost in Jordan.

4

FIRE LIKE COLD WATER

Kirkuk, 2003

....

Everyone has the right to freedom of thought, conscience and religion; this
right includes freedom to change his religion or belief, and freedom, either
alone or in community with others and in public or private, to manifest
his religion or belief in teaching, practice, worship and observance.

ARTICLE 18,
THE UNIVERSAL DECLARATION
OF HUMAN RIGHTS

....

The Americans were hunting for the King of Clubs as the December
cold settled in, and I left Baghdad and the warmth of Muthafar and
Ghada's home to meet more Christians and see the liberation elsewhere.
Along the road north toward Kirkuk, city slums gave way to sheep
pastures and tilled fields. Cars dodged tractors and slow-moving military convoys, only to halt and wait while passengers presented identity
papers at the many checkpoints along the way.

The search for Izzat Ibrahim al-Douri—the King of Clubs—was
on, said my companions in the car, and he would be a tough one to
catch. Douri was number six in the United States' "deck of cards,"
with a $10 million reward for information leading to his capture or
killing. A lifelong friend of Saddam who was widely regarded as his
most trusted deputy, he had been vice president and deputy chairman
of Iraq's Revolutionary Command Council. Douri grew up poor not
far from Saddam's own birthplace near Tikrit but a long way from his
privilege. As a boy, Douri had worked for an ice seller, and while still

35

young, he had joined the revolution that would become the ruling Baath Party.

For decades the redheaded Baathist commander worked side by side with Saddam, carrying out violent mass killings against the Marsh Arabs in the south and the Kurds in the north. He built his own patronage network based in north-central Iraq, and now rumor had it that he was using that network to direct the growing insurgency.

Seven of us had squeezed into a small sedan for the trip—our driver; Insaf; me; Sabri, who lived in Erbil; and the three guests who had stayed upstairs at Muthafar's house: the Egyptian pastor, the professor from Jordan, and the Muslim convert, whose name, I learned, was Mustafa. I was never sure what brought us all together, except that everyone knew Insaf.

We halted behind traffic piled up at a checkpoint not far from Samarra, an ancient city about eighty miles north of Baghdad on the eastern bank of the Tigris. Westerners were coming to know it as the heart of the "Sunni Triangle," but historically it held a mix of Sunnis and Shiites, the two major but divergent branches of Islam.

Date groves and fields planted with plastic-shrouded crops stretched toward a gray-blue haze, where bluffs rose in the east. The cars crept past Kurdish soldiers inspecting passengers and vehicles along a stretch of road muddy with rain. Despite being dressed to blend in with the Iraqis, the American officers weren't hard to spot. They were usually taller and more muscular, and some wore mirrored Ray-Bans.

At one checkpoint I got out of the car and walked over to talk to some of them as our car waited to get through. They were friendly, asking where I was from and whom I worked for, but their eyes stayed fixed on the cars inching past them. Behind them by the side of the road sat Bradley armored fighting vehicles, hidden but for their turrets and gunners behind a sandbagged berm and razor wire.

We stopped in Tuz, a city a little more than halfway between Baghdad and Kirkuk, at a desolate intersection where a date grove met the banks of the Aksu River. We went into a roadside restaurant that

Insaf knew served excellent kebab. She was making up for lost time by eating Iraqi food, especially kebab, wherever we could find it. We ate lunch inside and continued the journey after Insaf bought warm pistachios and baked watermelon seeds from a produce stand next to the restaurant. The fruit seller spoke Turkish, but when I paid him for pomegranates and dates, he said in perfect English, "You are welcome. Please come again."

Tuz had a large population of Turkmen, but it marked the entry point to the Kurdish north. Iraqi Turkmen, I learned, were the third-largest ethnic group in Iraq, behind Arabs and Kurds, mostly descendants from Turks and Persians under the Ottoman Empire with their own Turkic language. Just outside the city was a large air base that had been seized by U.S. forces in March. After converting it into a forward operating base, the Americans battled the insurgents, launching north toward Kirkuk and Mosul, west to Tikrit, and south to Baquba and Baghdad.

When President Bush came to Baghdad for Thanksgiving with the troops a week earlier, an Arab newspaper showed him handing a turkey, caricatured to look like Iraq, on a platter back to Saddam. Our trip north coincided with a visit by defense secretary Donald Rumsfeld, who also traveled to Baghdad and Kirkuk.

Before we reached Kirkuk, we smelled the burning sulfur from the oil refineries, a pungent odor that pricked the nose, stung the eyes, and even pinched at the taste buds. Coming into the city, we could see the oil fields stretching endlessly west, the flare stacks from one of the largest petroleum deposits in the world shooting flames of excess raw gas skyward. It was a strange backdrop to the now-familiar sight along the roadside: gas lines, endless rows of cars waiting for fuel.

"Twenty-five years ago, Kirkuk was very different," Insaf said. "It was clean, and business was good." She explained that her family had moved to Kirkuk from Mosul in 1947 when her father landed a job working on the pipelines. She had been born in Kirkuk and mostly lived there until 1990.

Insaf married Shawki Abdulahad in 1985, the same year she met him. When I asked how it all came to be, she said, "Okay, you should be writing this down to understand."

Insaf's aunt was married to Shawki's uncle. In other words, her father's sister was married to Shawki's father's brother. So while they weren't related by blood, Insaf had cousins who also were Shawki's cousins. Shawki and Insaf knew each other but distantly. He was born and reared in Basra in the southeastern tip of Iraq, while she was born and grew up in Kirkuk, five hundred miles away.

As Insaf continued, I was writing down the details.

Insaf's aunt and uncle arranged the marriage. "When it is time, they called my parents and asked, 'What do you think of Shawki?'" Before Insaf knew anything about it, Shawki had traveled to Kirkuk, spent three days with Insaf and her family, then asked her to marry him.

"I said, 'I don't know you enough.'"

Shawki's mother was Armenian, and his father was Arab. Insaf grew up in the Chaldean Catholic Church in an Arab family. One year before Shawki proposed to her, she had become a new believer, discovering anew, she said, what the life, death, and resurrection of Jesus Christ meant for her life. She began attending the Evangelical Protestant Church in Kirkuk and filling her spare time with prayer meetings and Bible studies. Shawki was a musician and went to parties.

"We were in two different worlds," Insaf said. "I told him, 'If I want to go to a prayer meeting, you'll want to go to the cinema. If I want to be in a Bible study, you will go to parties.' Shawki responded, 'I am tired from that life, and that is why I ask you to marry me.'"

Insaf said she could not say no. Ten days later they were engaged in Kirkuk, and five months after that they married in Basra. After the wedding ceremony and feasts surrounding it, they traveled to Kirkuk to live. Insaf taught high school physics, and Shawki remained in the military. The Iran-Iraq War came to dominate their lives, as it dragged on for eight years.

One day Insaf and Shawki learned that the Iranians had captured one of Shawki's cousins. They returned to Basra to await word of him with their family. (As it turned out, he would be held for twelve years before the Iranians released him.)

On the train back to Kirkuk, Insaf asked Shawki, in a manner I imagined was similar to the way she'd asked me how much money I wanted to carry across the border, "When would you like to give your heart to the Lord?" Shawki said he was ready. They prayed on the train for new life together as Christians. Until that time, Insaf admitted, she had prayed, "Lord, I don't want any children from this man before he gives his heart to God." Soon after they returned to Kirkuk, Insaf learned she was pregnant. She said, "God kept that his secret until the right time for me to learn it."

The Iran-Iraq War would lead almost seamlessly into the Gulf War, and Shawki remained in the army until 1992. He was stationed in the south, but Insaf remained in Kirkuk, caring for their small children, Peter and Nour.

"I never went to bed before 2 a.m. in those days, waiting for the bombs to stop," Insaf recounted. The family lived near the airport and a military base. "Every night the sky lit up red and orange. We couldn't sleep."

By day Insaf loved teaching high school physics. She enjoyed her students and was a natural at cajoling them through the subject. She teased them with questions too hard for anyone but her to answer, all the while setting high standards and making the classroom come alive. But Insaf refused to give undeserved grades. Eventually some high-up members of the Baath Party complained about their children's low grades in her classes. She came under mounting pressure from the school to show favoritism. Instead, she resigned.

Some menaces can arrive without a sound, and a missile often isn't heard until impact. Shawki had returned to Kirkuk, and one morning the couple awoke as a missile swerved into their home, embedding itself in the kitchen wall. It was clear—they could no longer stay. Their home in Kirkuk had become uninhabitable. They feared Shawki being redrafted into the military, and they worried that Insaf would never teach again. Insaf said they decided that moment to move to Baghdad, and they began to discuss leaving the country.

That same week they left with their two children for Baghdad, where Insaf took up tailoring and Shawki found jobs in construction. Shawki's mother was from Turkey, and the family as a whole talked of moving back there to escape the Saddam regime with its unending wars.

Insaf told me the story of her life's upheaval, of the dangers she had braved with and without Shawki's presence, as though they were routine. Isn't this what every young family goes through? her soft voice seemed to say, never changing its lilt or pitch as she described bombs, missiles, and POWs in her own family. With her quiet tone, we could have been two moms going over the challenges of switching preschools. In those days I had been a young mom too, safe and secure while she was enduring a life of war. When Saddam Hussein invaded Kuwait, Insaf worried over her husband on the front line and stayed awake to watch over her children living beneath bombardments. I was at home deciding what sort of cake to bake for my daughter's fourth birthday, worrying over whether the icing would hold up in the August heat.

When I asked Insaf what happened next, she said matter-of-factly: "In September 1994 we decided to go."

She would always be reluctant to talk about the details of their departure or her feelings about leaving everything she knew behind, but the days remained etched in her mind. "We drove to Amman on October 15, and thirteen days later left for Istanbul."

The family would live as refugees in Turkey for seven years until Canada granted them asylum. They moved to Toronto in 2001.

Insaf's story of exile would be one among many I heard from Iraqis about those years. During the Iran-Iraq war and again after the Gulf War, the Iraqi government forcibly expelled more than 120,000 Kurds, Turkmen, and Assyrians from northern Iraq, most of them from Kirkuk. It was part of a forty-year Arabization program, a lengthy chapter in a long saga of the determination to rid Iraq of Kurds and other minorities and solidify control by Saddam's Baathists.

At first the government paid compensation to home owners when they forced them out, while moving Arabs from southern Iraq to live in the city's vacated houses and elsewhere—hardly hardship duty, given the oil boom. Later, the Arabization plan turned violent when the poorest families were also evicted. These included about one thousand Kurdish and Turkmen families who had deeds dating back to the Ottoman era for housing inside Kirkuk's old walled citadel. Many were forced out without compensation, and their homes—even whole neighborhoods—were bulldozed. In 2003 large tracts of empty space still testified to the ruin.

As recently as the 1960s, about half the city's residents had been Kurds. A 1965 census did not enumerate non-Islamic minorities but listed the presence of Assyrian and Chaldean Christians, Yazidis, and a "small colony of Jewish merchants."[1] As the oil boom caught hold, the leaders of the Baath regime moved more and more Arabs into the city.

+ + +

Just before we entered Kirkuk, Insaf pointed to a railway that connected Kirkuk to Baghdad and then followed the Euphrates to Basra. It was the same line she and Shawki had taken to Kirkuk as newlyweds. Rail cars, now defunct, sat on rusting tracks stretching north and south. Seeing them, she said, took her back to the days before her marriage when she traveled to Basra and back.

She had attended Catholic schools and Catholic churches with her family then, but she first took part in the Kirkuk Evangelical Church as a teenager. Even then she didn't break ties with her Catholic upbringing or her many Catholic friends. But in the evangelical church she heard for the first time that she could know Jesus Christ as her own Savior and have a lasting relationship with him. Under the evangelical church's teaching, she grew in her understanding of the Bible and in her zeal to tell others what she was learning. She recalled the impact friends like Yousif Matty, the church's pastor at the time, had on her burgeoning faith.

Yousif, too, she explained, grew up in the Catholic tradition, but he became a Christian while serving in the military during the Iran-Iraq

War in the 1980s. A geologist, he had no formal biblical training but read the Bible plus every theological book he could find. His brother-in-law Maher Tawfiq—"the first of us to know Christ," Yousif said—had a great influence on him, as did Maher's wife, Saher. From 1985 through 1990, Yousif served as pastor of the Kirkuk Evangelical Church, which had dropped the "Presbyterian" from its name after affiliation with its founding Scottish counterparts faltered.

Yousif was passionate about the importance of education in the life of the church and in Iraq generally. He was passionate, too, on the subject of old traditional churches in Iraq. "We have more roots than fruits," he was fond of saying.

Yousif opened three bookshops in Iraqi Kurdistan, and in 1992 he moved to Dohuk in northern Iraq. In 1996 the Dohuk bookshop was bombed, and Yousif barely escaped. An Iranian-backed group, he later learned from Kurdish authorities, had targeted him for assassination. He would face more attacks in the future.

None of that stopped him, as he worked with Kurdish authorities to gain permission to open an evangelical church. He also founded the Classical School of the Medes, first in Sulaymaniyah, then in Dohuk, and in Erbil. Iraqis, led by Yousif, ran the schools using a classical curriculum formulated in the United States. The students were mostly Kurds and nearly all Muslims.

If Iraq's Christian community had the equivalent of a New York City taxi driver, it was Yousif. He was passionate, argumentative, blunt. He had the survival instincts of the self-taught church leader that he was, the confidence of a man who'd faced enough of his own life-and-death situations. He challenged Kurdish authorities to send their children to his schools as a test of how good they were. The officials did, and the schools gained legitimacy once elite Kurdish families began to champion them.

+ + +

When we turned the corner to the entrance of Kirkuk Evangelical Church, we met several guards wearing badges and carrying automatic weapons. They were expecting us, so they pulled open the gate and let us into the church's walled compound.

Inside, a multistory building was under construction, and the grassy swath of church property buzzed with sounds of activity—groundskeepers working, women sweeping the walkways, and children singing from inside the church building. In addition to its sanctuary, the church owned a home where the pastor, Haitham Jazrawi, lived with his family. The church property also contained a school building and a unit of housing for widows, poor families, and others in need. Insaf and I would stay in an apartment there.

We sat with Haitham in a large reception room rimmed with sofas and deep upholstered chairs, its walls lined with bookshelves. We were joined by Yousif Matty and his wife, Alia. It was part of Haitham's home next door to the church, and as we talked, Haitham's wife, Mayada, brought us tea in small, clear glasses, with sugar visible as a bright lump at the bottom of each. Then she returned with a spread of delicious food—mezze-style dishes like hummus, flatbread, and homemade soup.

"Many more people are attending the church now, who at the time of Saddam Hussein were afraid to join the evangelical church," said Haitham. "Before, many people said about the church, 'They are Americans,' because we are supported by American missionaries. Many people think we belong to Americans, but that is not true. This church belongs to Iraqis."

Haitham believed that more Iraqis would return to the church—refugees returning from Jordan and countries overseas. "We expect them," he said with confidence. "After change, many people join us in church."

Yousif was also outspoken in his frustration with the old churches. "Centuries of domination under the Islamic yoke created a survival mentality," he said. "The bargain was this: 'We'll keep the gospel to our own racial groups, if you will let us exist in your Muslim society.'"

Yousif said a Chaldean bishop opposed him when he brought Muslims to be baptized, telling him, "We should not be evangelizing Muslims. That will just get us into trouble."

Haitham told us that he planned to baptize a few Muslim Kurds in two weeks and that they would join regular services, something Haitham would have considered reckless and unwise under Saddam Hussein. Others with Christian backgrounds but who had not attended church in many years were also coming. "Now the hall of the church is not big enough."

Presbyterian and other mission societies established churches in this part of Iraq in the nineteenth century, but the Evangelical Presbyterian churches won permission to open under British rule at the end of World War I. In addition to the congregation in Kirkuk, the largest in northern Iraq, Evangelical Presbyterian churches in Mosul, Baghdad, and Basra were all organized in the early twentieth century.

But Christianity had a long and unusual history in Kirkuk. The Persians in the fifth century had persecuted Christians, beheading hundreds inside the city citadel. A commander overseeing their deaths was himself moved to become a Christian because of the faith and trust of the believers in the midst of massacre. His conversion prompted his own martyrdom, which sparked widespread conversions among the ruling Persians. The Red Church was built over the site where he and the other believers were martyred, and Chaldean Christians commemorate the executions with a courtyard mass there every year.

Today the fortress walls of the citadel still stand in central Kirkuk, a medieval city-within-a-city visible on a plateau high above the Khasa River. Some sources say the tomb of the Old Testament prophet Daniel, who was governor of Babylon when the region was ruled by King Nebuchadnezzar, is contained within the citadel walls.

+ + +

In September 2003, Haitham told me, the Kirkuk Evangelical Church had organized a conference for all evangelical churches nationwide. More than 430 Iraqi Christians attended, coming from all parts of the country. The success of the gathering was remarkable, given the violence in the country at the time. Haitham invited Americans to the conference from the U.S. base on the edge of town, and twelve chaplains showed up. Others didn't attend for fear of drawing unwanted attention, so Haitham met them at the base and began holding a regular Bible study there.

Only days before our arrival, soldiers had defused a bomb just outside the church entrance. The same week, an oil engineer in the church—a man with a wife and a thirteen-year-old daughter—had been killed by a roadside bomb.

None of that stopped Insaf, who immediately launched into nearby neighborhoods, going door-to-door to visit church members and old friends. In between long conversations with Haitham, Yousif, or others, I would sometimes join Insaf on these visits. I met up with her one afternoon after she met with the engineer's widow, Joanne, and her thirteen-year-old daughter.

They talked for a while about financial needs. Joanne worried how she and her daughter would survive without her husband's income. Joanne, who looked to be in her forties, said she did not know how to face the future, and she wept.

"I am burning from inside, burning and burning," she cried out, her words choked in sobs. Insaf wrapped her arms around Joanne and held her in a tight embrace. Then quietly she said, "I can pray with you."

Insaf continued, "My pocket is empty, my hand is empty, but I can pray for you and be your voice and be your heart and talk with my mouth and see how God provides." She prayed for Joanne's broken heart to be healed, for her needs and her fear of the future, and for her daughter.

Joanne continued to cry, but Insaf could feel the woman relax in her arms. After a few moments Joanne said softly, "Please come back again."

"I start to cry with her," Insaf told me later, "and I start to pray again, for the power of the love of God to make this fire inside Joanne to be like cold water."

+ + +

Insaf had not traveled to Kirkuk in more than ten years. She was eager to revisit the neighborhoods and acquaintances of her childhood and young married life. Our walking tours brought her face-to-face with the reality of how much had changed. Streets where she had grown up were now dirty, gutters lined with trash. Neighbors in some cases were gone, forgotten. She pointed out where she had eaten oranges from a tree here, reminisced about playing ball in that driveway there. We walked up and down many streets of her bygone Kirkuk—two women in jeans with heads uncovered, talking loudly like Westerners in hushed streets where we found more houses abandoned than lived in.

We did receive surprised welcomes at a few of our stops. One of the homes we visited belonged to a childhood playmate of Insaf's. The Ramez family home was like a museum to Kirkuk's glory days, when the expansion of oil fields had employed nearly everyone, lifting residents into an expanding, prosperous, and literate middle class. There was a small courtyard of orange trees and olive trees, with laundry hanging between them. When we knocked at the front door, a stranger asked us to come in, and we waited in the living room.

Inside, real Persian rugs covered terrazzo-tiled floors, and the windows were draped in brown velvet. Brass lamps rested on hand-rubbed furniture reminiscent of the British colonial era. A coffee table held a basket of cigarettes, a pot of flowers, and a box of tissues. A "Siko" wall clock hung above bookshelves full of knickknacks. Other walls held somber portraits of the Virgin Mary, their frames festooned with rosary beads.

Mama Ramez appeared through a doorway from the kitchen in a printed housedress, navy cardigan, white hose, and plastic slippers. Then her daughter rushed into the room, thrilled to see Insaf, near tears.

"We were playmates," Insaf told me as she introduced us, "playing house to house in the afternoons after school."

"The best days of our lives," the daughter added.

Insaf eyed family photos. The Ramez family had six children—four girls and two boys—and one grandson. The three women chatted over one another, but as in other homes we'd visited, the hosts were so intent on showing hospitality that they kept disappearing into the kitchen. Mama Ramez returned first with a sweet juice to drink, then with pistachio-laced pastries, and finally Arabic coffee. With each new item, the women eased into chairs to talk and reminisce. They asked about Insaf's sisters and her brothers.

At one point, Karam Ramez, the grandson, entered silently and watched Insaf closely. Finally he spoke. When he was seven years old, Insaf had given him cassette tapes with Christian songs and Bible verses, he said. He always wondered, *Who was the woman with the tapes? Where did she go?* That had been nearly fifteen years ago, but he recognized Insaf immediately.

"Now I am a Christian," the young man told her with a smile, patting his chest. He recited from the tapes from memory, then fetched his Bible to read to Insaf.

When I asked how their lives had changed since the downfall of the Iraqi government, a somber spirit overtook the jovial atmosphere of moments before. No one answered, until Karam finally replied, "We believe God is controlling everything in Iraq. Who could believe the Saddam statue would fall one day?"

Insaf told me later that they were reluctant to speak freely to an outsider. "There is a fear inside every Iraqi that built for thirty years. It is not easy to get away from it. They are still afraid of retribution."

+   +   +

In the evening we attended a Kurdish wedding. We'd been invited by Insaf's friend Assam, an Iraqi refugee living in Canada who also was visiting family and friends in Kirkuk. Assam picked us up in a cab, and our route took us toward the oil fields. In the early evening darkness, the flares shone in brilliant hues of red, orange, and pink, edged in purple and sapphire—a glow of colors low on the horizon that left us with the impression of driving into a sunset. Plumes of smoke and flares shot high into the night sky.

We arrived at a large community hall, where the wedding was already under way. Young men stood smoking by the doorway, thin as rails and youthful but dressed in black pants, nice shirts, and leather jackets. Light and music flooded from within.

Insaf and I didn't know the family, but they ushered us into the hall like honored guests. I was the only blonde in the place, obviously an American and hopelessly underdressed in olive cargo pants and boots. The children, wearing brilliant dresses and bold-colored scarves, crowded around me. "Hi, buddy!" they shouted, thrusting thumbs-up signs into my face. They ended sentences I didn't understand with "That's nice."

After the wedding, Assam, Insaf, and I found another taxi and headed into town. At the Abdullah Restaurant, we climbed from the cab to see soldiers from the 173rd Airborne hanging around outside an Internet café. Based out of Italy, they had parachuted into Kurdistan on March 26. Within weeks, the entire brigade—two thousand military personnel, plus vehicles—had dropped into northern Iraq from C-17s, ready to advance. They worked alongside Special Forces and other units to secure Kirkuk's oil fields and nearby air bases, ultimately seizing control of Kirkuk, taking out Republican Guard units defending the city, and dismantling four Iraqi infantry divisions. They also battled forces connected to Ansar al-Islam, a militant group that had been operating in the north with leaders trained under Osama bin Laden.

In the restaurant, just two tables away, I noticed another group of Americans with Iraqis. The men wore turtlenecks and leather jackets. They laughed and talked easily but kept a constant surveillance of the room, their eyes darting warily. The Iraqis at our table insisted that these men were CIA officers or members of the Special Forces. Assam said, "Maybe they will find Saddam," and we laughed.

Insaf was reinvigorated by every story she heard, every acquaintance she encountered, and every friendship she could resurrect. Her thoughts kept coming back to widows like Joanne. "On the inside, so many are tired. They need a touch of having Jesus listen to them, and us listening to them, just giving ourselves," she said.

Terrorizing the infidels—the so-called enemies of Islam—was at the heart of the jihadists' work. "It is the end itself," declared a short treatise distributed to Ansar al-Islam fighters and recovered from the breast pocket of one who was killed in battle. "Terror is not a means of imposing decision on the enemy; it is the decision we wish to impose on him."[2]

+ + +

Insaf and I shared an upstairs room at the church, and at night before bed we talked and prayed, thinking about our children at home and the families we were meeting, most of whom had overwhelming needs. So we prayed for them all.

In Canada Insaf's son, Peter, was looking for work. At home my oldest, Emily, was preparing to graduate high school and studying Arabic in her free time, and I wondered if these seemingly intractable wars would become a fixture in her life, our lives. I was missing her last Christmas band concert (she played the oboe) and wouldn't be able to see her off to her final high school Christmas formal.

I was learning to let go as a parent, and in Iraq I was seeing that lived out tenfold. Everywhere I turned, families young and old were showing me what it looked like to let go of kindred and possessions, to leave and return, to take nothing for granted about their futures. So late into the night I wrote a long letter to my daughter, convinced that our separation and this faraway place somehow would grow us as a family at home. "What a thrill for me to sit in a war zone, somewhere at the outer edges of my own experiences, and know that you will run further ahead of me always."

It was hard to sleep, the noise of the sky too close. Nearby was the U.S. military base, and with Secretary of Defense Donald Rumsfeld in town, plus patrols, helicopter traffic was constant. So were gunfire and small explosions. Rumors that the regime fugitive Douri was hiding nearby had the army on the alert.

From the balcony I watched the glow of the oil fields, saw the Black Hawks moving purposefully, crawling over the sky above the city with the stars behind them. I listened to the gunfire, wondering how near the dangers were. I found myself thinking of Joanne, her daughter, and others who had lost so much in these young days of so-called freedom.

Insaf took advantage of her insomnia to plot a future ministry. "People are strong here, but they have a lot of pain. I hate to leave when the needs are so great and when I need to listen more." Mindful of her family, too, she was particularly drawn to the hurts and desires of Iraqi women. "They need support," she said, and she began planning ways to work with pastors' wives to develop ministries for women.

Insaf believed that many of the Christians we'd met gave the outward appearance of being strong while inside they were suffering, burning. She wanted to tend to those needs, even as she longed to see more Iraqi exiles, including her own family, return to stand with them. In spite of the danger, her thoughts returned to her own children at home in Toronto. She wanted them to have a part in rebuilding Iraq. She hoped that one day soon her whole family could move back there, could have a part in its new beginning.

"I want their hearts to be here, not to be cut from this."

5

THE WAR BEFORE

Tigris River, 2002

....

These terrorists kill not merely to end lives,
but to disrupt and end a way of life.

PRESIDENT GEORGE W. BUSH,
SEPTEMBER 20, 2001, ADDRESS TO CONGRESS

....

No one in the West wanted to admit it, but the emerging terrorist groups in Iraq found their roots in Afghanistan amid the Taliban and al-Qaeda, and they existed long before the 9/11 attacks on the United States. Their presence was the undercurrent to the early days of war in 2003, and Iraqis everywhere knew that terrorists were behind the checkpoints and violence unfolding around them.

In September 2001 a number of jihadist militants had come together under the name Jund al-Islam (Soldiers of Islam), changed it to Ansar al-Islam (Supporters of Islam) that December, and set up a base of operations at the Iraq-Iran border. They congregated in villages near the city of Halabja, the site of Saddam's most deadly chemical weapons attack on the Kurds. Was the timing for a terrorist base outside Afghanistan coincidental or part of a larger strategy? No one knew.

Operating in the remote mountains of Kurdistan, they exerted Taliban-like control. They declared Islamic law and harsh punishments over the area, including amputations for offenses like stealing. They barred women from schools and from jobs outside their homes and forced them to be veiled in public. They confiscated musical instruments and banned all music, satellite dishes, and television. They declared a jihad against the "secular and apostate forces that are waiting for an opportunity to overpower Islam and the Muslims of Kurdistan; and waiting to implement the sinister plans of the Jewish, Christian, and all other apostate leaders."[1]

At the forefront of the campaign was Ansar's founder and leader, Mullah Krekar, a Kurd. Krekar studied law under Abdullah Azzam, the same professor who once mentored Osama bin Laden and his deputy Ayman al-Zawahiri, who assumed leadership of al-Qaeda after bin Laden's death.

Azzam gathered foreign fighters into the al-Qaeda fold, the so-called "Arab Afghans" who fought the Soviet invasion of Afghanistan. Krekar likely was one of them. Somehow Krekar managed to gain asylum to Norway in 1991, giving him leave to travel freely to both the East and the West.[2]

From the al-Qaeda Afghanistan hideouts, across the steppes and mountains of Iran, and to the remote peaks of Iraqi Kurdistan, the road was long but not unfriendly. In October 2001, following the invasion of Afghanistan by American forces, jihadist fighters who had been recruited from Iraq fled home and found a new base of operations with Ansar in the Zagros Mountains of Iraq, near the Iranian border. Insurgents from other Arab nations arrived too, including Abu Musab al-Zarqawi, the Jordanian lieutenant of Osama bin Laden who would one day lead al-Qaeda in Iraq.

Snow-capped peaks in the Zagros reach nine thousand feet in elevation, not unlike the Afghan hideouts the fighters had known. In Iraq the Arab Afghans could find sanctuary and regroup. Saddam Hussein welcomed them; they would torment the Kurds for him.

Ansar wasted no time launching attacks in Kurdistan. They struck first in villages made up of small religious minorities. In late September 2001, Kurdish officials discovered that the group had massacred twenty

Kurds in one village, their throats slit and some of them beheaded. "They used swords and machetes. They were speaking Arabic and Persian," said one of the women in the village.[3] Later they used the same brutal methods to kill forty-two Kurdish soldiers sent to fight them.

The group penetrated Kurdish cities, too, where assassins targeted and killed political leaders, including Franso Hariri, an Assyrian Christian and the popular leader of the KDP, a prominent Kurdish political party. Only weeks before my May 2002 visit to Iraqi Kurdistan, Ansar al-Islam had tried to assassinate eastern Kurdistan's prime minister, Barham Salih. They failed but in the attempt managed to kill five of his bodyguards.

+ + +

Anthrax attacks the week after 9/11 fostered the widespread feeling that the United States remained under a strategic attack, which ushered in a new era of vigilance. It wasn't enough to carry gas masks, plastic bags, and a quart of bleach. Nearly everyone wanted to hunt down terrorists, and President George W. Bush soon turned the focus to Saddam Hussein's Iraq.

Seven months after the 9/11 attacks, I left a conference in Damascus on Christian-Muslim dialogue, flying in a Soviet-era plane to Qameshli in northern Syria with a number inked on my hand. The number was from Syrian intelligence, received by them and delivered to me by Iraqi Kurds in Damascus, thus guaranteeing my river crossing to Iraq. It was one of the only open channels that Kurds in northern Iraq had to the outside world, hemmed in as they were by a no-fly zone and by a border closed off by Saddam Hussein. In the Middle East such a balancing act was normal: Syrian president Bashar al-Assad kept up ties to Saddam Hussein, while some in his intelligence service were allied with the Kurds.

Qameshli felt like a frontier town with dusty streets and fleabag hotels. When I landed at the airport, my Kurdish contact wasn't there. Instead I was surrounded by Syrian cab drivers offering to give me a ride. I watched the throng and wondered what to do, listening to Kurdish and Arabic swirl around me and bereft of my one and only English-speaking contact in a city of 150,000. My contact had given me clear instructions on where he would be, along with descriptions of him and his car. Yet he simply was nowhere to be seen. In desperation, I simply spoke the name of my missing contact, and one of the cab drivers spoke up in broken English, "I know him."

The cab driver called him on his cell phone and found out he was at a family birthday party. (Apparently I was a day early.) So my newfound contact, the anonymous cab driver, agreed to take me to a hotel. At the desk, I greeted a hotel clerk who spoke no English. I was beginning to worry—aware I was in completely strange territory preparing to make an illegal border crossing, and my plan for meeting contacts was fading to nothing before me.

I thought of returning to the airport to fly back to Damascus and start over. But I had contacts awaiting me in Iraq, and that side of this odyssey might disappear also if I didn't persevere. As I chewed my lip in indecision, a nine-year-old boy appeared, walking down the hall.

"May I help you?" he said. As I later found out, he was the son of Kurds returning to Iraq from Sweden, and he spoke perfect English. One of the hotel workers, seeing an American woman enter the hotel and recognizing my predicament, had gone to find him. With complete comprehension of my English, he translated my situation to the clerk, who gave me a giant skeleton key to a room upstairs.

Once inside the bare room, I lay on its thin mattress, stared into a brown fan making loping circles overhead, and listened to the sounds of markets reopening on the street below. It was Friday, and shops that had been closed until dusk for the Muslim day of prayer now opened. The clatter of their roll-up doors and the sounds of raucous bargaining filled the block. The smell of lamb kebabs mixed with that of pungent herbs over outdoor coals and rose from the street to my room. I thought of going outside, thought better of it, and slept.

In the morning I met my nine-year-old translator and his family in the lobby downstairs. For one twenty-four-hour period I dangled between countries, moving from the Middle East where Americans were welcome to the Middle East where America and Americans were the enemy—Iraq. Cut off from my Kurdish contacts who had made transit across this divide possible, I had as my guide only a nine-year-old stranger who had learned English as a refugee in Europe, thanks to his family's hardships at Saddam's hands.

+ + +

The Kurds are an ethnic group whose roots are in Iran but whose homeland is divided among Turkey, Syria, and Iraq as well. Two hundred years ago the Kurds were twice as populous as Egyptians; today Egyptians outnumber Kurds two to one.

With the end of the Iran-Iraq War in 1988, animosity toward the Kurds spiraled into full-blown genocide. Saddam was victorious in that war but not magnanimous; he instigated payback for Kurdish solidarity with Iran. In a systematic campaign run by Ali Hassan al-Majid (whom the Kurds dubbed "Chemical Ali"), Iraqi forces rounded up and killed as many as 100,000 Kurds. They used chemical weapons against dozens of Kurdish villages, the first time such weapons had been used against a country's own people since the Holocaust. Saddam's forces destroyed and bulldozed about four thousand towns and villages; and they leveled so much infrastructure that the Kurds' agricultural base, and virtually all their economy, collapsed. Kurdish Iraqi soldiers and POWs returning from the long war with Iran discovered their homes destroyed, their families gone. A generation of victims of mustard gas and nerve agents, including sarin, was maimed and blinded, and women were left infertile or gave birth to babies who quickly died.

Saddam invaded Kuwait in 1990, provoking the U.S.-led Gulf War in 1991; and on the war's heels, the Americans came to the Kurds' rescue in a dramatic way, opening a corridor for humanitarian aid to millions of displaced Kurds. They also offered security to allow the Kurds to return and rebuild what Saddam had destroyed, even as the United

States left Saddam in power at that time. Under the United Nations' postwar treaty with Iraq, a no-fly zone patrolled by U.S. and British air forces would continue to protect three Kurdish states in the north, and a much smaller no-fly zone would protect the Shiites in the south.

The Kurds had an expression: "The mountains are our only friends." But American protection resurrected their will to thrive. Where Saddam had plowed up ground to destroy the Kurds' villages, the United States made it possible for developers to regrade land for condominium developments. Supermarkets with gourmet food and imported clothes opened; Internet and cell phone service quickly caught on and expanded.

In the decade following Kurdish genocide in Iraq, and under benign U.S. protection, the Kurds rebuilt about three thousand villages destroyed by Saddam.[4] That renewal, plus talk of another American war on Iraq, gave many Kurds in the diaspora a reason to return, with up to four hundred a day traveling through the northern Syrian town of Qameshli.

+ + +

Trucks built to carry cabbages now were being used to help ferry returning Kurds and others to the border. Under a gray dawn the morning after my arrival in Qameshli, I piled my luggage into one of those trucks. Then I crammed myself into a minivan, along with the family of my nine-year-old interpreter and other returnees from Sweden and Germany. Several minivans would follow the trucks in a convoy for the two-hour journey to the Iraqi border.

Out of Qameshli, the road crossed rich, grassy plains green with spring. This was Hasakah Province, where a fertile valley nursed by the Kharbur River and the Tigris fed Syria—and, one could say, the entire world. Most of Syria's wheat, rice, vegetables, and cotton were grown here. Our route also took us near the old Silk Road, built to facilitate early trade between China and the Roman Empire. In the distance were the hills where men first domesticated wild grasses, where wheat originated from the first farmers in the upper reaches of the Mesopotamian valley.

Before reaching the Tigris, we stopped at a roadside open-air restaurant for a breakfast of tea, roasted eggplant with tomatoes, yogurt, and flatbread. We drove on in our convoy, halting again only when we reached the riverbank. After leaving the trucks and minivans, we hiked up a narrow clay path to a small shack manned by Syrian security. Inside, an officer held a ledger for everyone to sign. Next to my name I filled in the number I'd kept penned on the side of my hand. I scrambled alongside others up over the riverbank, my bag in hand, to an awaiting outboard motorboat. We crossed the Tigris in twos and fours, a fast journey of only a few minutes over placid water with a hostile Turkish border upstream and Saddam Hussein's troops only a mile or two downstream.

A sign read "Welcome to Kurdistan" on the other side of the river, where families were having their photos taken and a reception center was under construction. Inside the government offices, I had tea with Sadi Ahmed Pira, a visiting Patriotic Union of Kurdistan official on hand to greet me, and then awaited a driver to take me into the interior of northern Iraq. Tea and greetings with officials have long been part of protocol, a key to so-called Arab hospitality, which actually is common among all groups in the Middle East, I would learn. These rituals were an essential initiation for me, a reporter entering new areas, before I met with other contacts and set out to explore the region.

Despite their hospitality, the Kurds weren't natural peacemakers. From 1994 through 1997, the two leading Kurdish parties—the Kurdistan Democratic Party and the Patriotic Union of Kurdistan—had fought each other for control of the region. The following year they reached a ceasefire and agreed to a unified government. The cease fire held, but plans to unify their regional government did not. The two parties governed separate and carefully delineated regions of Kurdistan: the KDP in the northwest and the PUK in the northeast. The Barzani family controlled the KDP, and the Talabani family headed the PUK. With the coming U.S. war, they would coalesce.

After crossing the Tigris, I traveled to the Kurdish cities of Dohuk and on to Erbil, the region's capital, with the help of the KDP. At an empty and arid expanse of high desert east of Erbil, a car arranged by the PUK awaited, and I was handed off, essentially, from one side to the other. Coming toward me was Ala Talabani, a tall, friendly woman in her thirties. She was a niece of PUK leader Jalal Talabani and had agreed to be my translator.

The Kurds took seriously patrolling their region against outside foes. They had recognized the terrorist threat long before anyone else. "The battle for post-Saddam Iraq is already under way," Qubad Talabani, son of PUK leader Jalal Talabani, told me as the United States inched toward war.

+ + +

Barham Salih, Kurdistan's prime minister, supplied an armed escort to pick me up for our meeting in his expansive office in Sulaymaniyah. Heavy drapes covered the windows, blocking bright midday light.

"We live in a tough neighborhood," he told me. The attempt on his life two weeks before had "served notice we were facing something very serious."

Salih included deputies in the meeting and was generous with his time; not many Americans sought his viewpoint then, but I was hearing from lawmakers and others in Washington that he was the type of leader the United States should be supporting in Iraq. That was why the meeting with him, despite the security risks, was important to me. The Kurds had firsthand knowledge of Saddam Hussein's ability to deploy chemical weapons and commit atrocities, so it was never hard for them to believe that the Iraqi regime was capable of supplying weapons of mass destruction to terrorist groups bent on destroying America.

The Kurds knew the blunt end of Saddam Hussein's anti-Arab ethnic-cleansing programs, and they had some sympathy for other beleaguered minorities. But there was more, I learned during the visit.

Barham Salih and other Kurdish leaders saw the threat of Islamic militancy readying to fill the vacuum left by a dictator.

"These Islamic terrorists want to change our way of life, our way of government," he told me. Attacks like the one he'd just narrowly escaped "should if anything reinforce our commitment to civil society, to the rule of law and to justice." Salih wanted a future Iraq to be modeled on the secular government of largely Muslim Turkey, with constitutional protection similar to that enjoyed by Americans.

Kurdish leaders like Salih wanted attention and felt they had earned it by what they'd endured. Salih made it clear that they wanted to fight the war on terror alongside the Americans. Few outside the region seemed to pay attention to the terror activity of Ansar al-Islam and to its link to Baghdad. The attacks on the Kurds, some believed, suggested training exercises for something bigger.

By early 2002 the Kurds had acquired evidence to make their case, capturing some of the Ansar fighters bleeding back from Afghanistan. At a security prison in Sulaymaniyah run by the intelligence service of the PUK, detainees were being held who had confessed to working with al-Qaeda in Afghanistan.

Haqi Ismail was one of them. He usually wore the customary beard of the Afghan mujahideen, but on the day I interviewed him in prison, he'd decided to shave. He'd also exchanged traditional Afghan clothing (a tunic with loose-fitting trousers) for drawstring pants and an American T-shirt with a logo for a "Tri State Martial Arts Tournament."

Security officers at the prison told me they had detained Haqi when he tried to cross the border from Iran. He was from Mosul in Iraq. He told me he went to Afghanistan in 1999, frustrated by the lack of what he called "religious schools" in Iraq, and in Kabul he met a man named Ahmed who took him in a pickup truck to an al-Qaeda training camp.

Haqi had drawn a map of the camp and traced over it for me as we talked. At the center was a mosque surrounded by tents, a clinic, a weapons storehouse, guest quarters, and a main house for commanders. He also penciled in underground entries and exits.

Haqi said he had stayed in Afghanistan at the camp until the "accident," the word he used for the 9/11 attacks in the United States. "Then I left."

By the time I saw him, Haqi had been detained by the Kurds for six months, along with at least four other suspects. All of them seemed to have had contact with top-ranking al-Qaeda leaders in Afghanistan, suggesting that they, too, may have been sent to Iraq on high-level missions. Several had smuggled arms to Afghanistan overland and met with members of Saddam's inner circle.

Haqi's father was a retired officer in Iraq's air force, and an uncle of his was a senior official in Saddam Hussein's Mukhabarat, or security service. The PUK had compiled a fifty-three-page dossier on Haqi and had videotaped his testimony. Haqi was willing to talk freely about his activities during his first days in captivity, thinking he would be released quickly once he shared what he knew. But as the weeks dragged on and the PUK officers took time to investigate and corroborate his story, he grew wary and said less. I was the third or fourth American journalist to show up to interview the detainees, and by that time he would not say whether he had been involved directly in terrorist attacks.

+ + +

In the opening hours of the war on Iraq in March 2003, U.S. air strikes targeted the Ansar al-Islam compound near Halabja. But the United States showed little interest in the captured jihadists. Months later when I checked back with the prison officers by phone, they told me the United States had made no effort to learn information from the jihadists about Saddam's possible ties to al-Qaeda.

Unlike the prisoners, Mullah Krekar, the Kurdish founder of the jihadist militant group Ansar al-Islam, steadfastly denied any connection to al-Qaeda or bin Laden, but ample evidence supported such a link. Krekar had spent time in Kabul and the al-Qaeda training camps of Afghanistan.

My weeks of travel in Syria and Iraqi Kurdistan were followed by months of keeping track of what was happening from afar. Back at my desk, I spoke with sources like Yossef Bodansky, director of the Congressional Task Force on Terrorism.

"Is Krekar worth watching?" I asked Bodansky.

"Yes, definitely yes," he said. Bodansky was one of the first analysts in Washington to profile Osama bin Laden, writing about him in a 1999 book.

Between my 2002 and 2003 trips to Kurdistan, the Netherlands took Krekar into custody as he traveled in Europe and promised to deport him for his suspected involvement in suicide attacks in northern Iraq. But the Dutch faced a dilemma: The only countries to which they could deport him were the United States and Iraq. Both had extradition orders for him, but both also used the death penalty. Norway and the Netherlands had a policy of not deporting even suspected terrorists to countries where they might be put to death. The Dutch set Krekar free, so he traveled to Norway. At one point I was told by a public affairs officer at the State Department, "Norway is to deport him at 3:55 p.m. to the United States." But it never happened, and Krekar was to remain a menace for years to come.

For Kurds who lobbied intently for Krekar's extradition, the incident was unsettling. A spokesman at the Justice Department told me that "the United States obviously is interested in speaking to those taken into captivity" by Kurdish authorities, but the Justice Department also faced legal hurdles to extradite terrorists like Krekar and have them stand trial. The CIA never investigated the terrorists in the PUK's custody.

United States policy was to spread democracy in Iraq, but in reality, the U.S. government held at arm's length democratic groups with long-standing opposition to Saddam Hussein, such as the KDP and the PUK. Meanwhile, the U.S. government supported Shia groups because it saw itself as being allied with popular Shiite exiles in the West like Ahmad Chalabi, a leading advisor to the Bush administration. Chalabi and others like him came to U.S. attention for their opposition to

Saddam Hussein and for the intelligence they provided to the United States during the 1991 Gulf War.

Before the war, PUK deputy Qubad Talabani told me he feared "large terrorist plans" would accompany a U.S. invasion. "This would be catastrophic, not just in the Kurdish region but in the whole country. Such an incursion will be like waiting for a pin to drop—when you are dealing with very, very unhappy people, they will not tolerate occupation."

What did all this mean for Iraq's Christians? Krekar and Ansar al-Islam threatened to turn Iraq into an Islamic caliphate and along the way ensure the demise of Christians. Saddam Hussein had no qualms with the jihadists' aims if they helped further his own. Before the U.S.-led war began, the Christians stood on the periphery of political life—yet at the center of the terrorists' crosshairs.

As I began to see the country through the eyes of people like Insaf, Muthafar, and Ghada, I wondered how much had really changed.

6

WINDOW OF OPPORTUNITY

Erbil, 2003

....

The cloud of the LORD was over them by day,
whenever they set out from the camp.

NUMBERS 10:34

....

Snow was falling as we entered Kurdistan. In the dry air the flakes floated, fine and soft, forming a gauzy, pristine blanket. Insaf and I had said good-bye to Haitham Jazrawi at the end of our stay at his church and were headed north to Erbil, the capital of Iraqi Kurdistan and one of the world's oldest continually inhabited cities, its Christian roots dating to the first century.[1]

We continued our journey with the same group that had left Baghdad together. The trip from Kirkuk to Erbil was only sixty-five miles, but it was momentous for our traveling group. Under Saddam Hussein the road north had been blocked, a militarized border closing off Kurdistan from the rest of Iraq. This was the first time since 1991 that anyone in our car had traveled this stretch of highway.

As we headed north from Kirkuk, a wide plain opened before us, the Zagros Mountains frosted with snow in the distance. Life-sized posters of Saddam, mounted at entrances to every town and government installation, were all defaced, the dictator's profile scratched out or torn to shreds. Large empty buildings, including two prisons to the east from which Kurdish and Iranian political prisoners had been freed, had "USA" spray-painted in tall letters across their walls.

We passed abandoned depots where tanks and military transports sat just as U.S. bombing runs had left them, burned to twisted crisps of metal. Along a bluff to the west, redoubts—defensive lookouts once manned by the Republican Guards—were occupied by U.S. soldiers or sat abandoned. In some fields, cabbage and lettuce appeared in long rows broken by an occasional stray sunflower soldiering against the snow. In others, marker flags warned of recently discovered land mines. Sabri, who was from the north, told us that the prisons had been land-mined by Saddam to prevent prison escapes and intrusions. The landscape sobered us, and our conversation faltered. In the backseat, Mustafa, the new convert, cracked his knuckles.

Mustafa was among a growing number of Christian converts trying to find their own way in the new Iraq. He grew up near Salaheddin but would not be returning to his family home. Since his conversion, he was not welcome there. Instead, he planned to stay with Sabri and his wife for a few days. Then he hoped to persuade some distant relatives to take him in. He smiled briefly when I told him I'd been to Salaheddin, then resumed rubbing his hands and wrenching his knuckles into loud pops that we heard the whole trip.

Sabri was one of the Iraqi returnees taking advantage of relative freedom in Kurdistan. He and his wife, Nahla, had resettled in Erbil in 2003 after studying in Jordan. They found a home in Ankawa, a traditionally Christian suburb of the city, and invited Insaf and me to lodge with them. I was never sure how Insaf knew them, but I was learning that Iraqi Christians found connection points with one another even when they were strangers.

Checkpoints were fewer in the north, and we made the trip from Kirkuk to Erbil in under two hours. We were glad for Sabri and Nahla's hospitality as the snow gathered and chill, damp air settled over us. Their house was bare and nearly as cold as the outdoors, but Sabri and

Nahla offered us their large bedroom with its small kerosene heater and thick, king-size mattress. Insaf and I laughed at our luxury. We'd been sleeping on the equivalent of camp mattresses, or just about anywhere we could.

Nahla cooked on a small kerosene burner set in the middle of the kitchen floor. The back door stood open, the doorway framing random snowflakes and chickens wandering in a muddy yard.

Nahla and Sabri were newly married, and Nahla's light-brown eyes had the clear radiance of a bride's, even though she'd spent all her young marriage as a refugee, moving from place to place and scraping together an income. She betrayed no weariness and readily agreed to help me run a few errands. We left the house as Insaf began her visits to local families. After crossing two streets to reach a main thoroughfare, we quickly caught a cab downtown. Nahla took me to a money-changing shop in an area of old covered walkways and stone buildings. We exchanged dollars for dinars and activated a satellite phone someone had loaned me in Baghdad.

Next we swung south of town, taking a wet dirt road to a poor neighborhood where the lines of houses were shacks with open doorways and corrugated tin roofs. The paths leading off the main road were filled with pedestrians, children clutching their mothers' skirts, and young men and women standing in groups, talking and waiting.

At a muddy intersection, we picked up two young women whom Nahla had invited to a Bible study that Sabri would lead that evening. We headed back into town, where we climbed the dimly lit stairs of an apartment building. Nahla led us into a carpeted room with no furniture. About a dozen men and women sat cross-legged on the floor, their shoes tossed in a pile by the door. We joined them as Sabri warmed to the young men and women and introduced several of us who were there for the first time. Then, after asking us to turn to a passage in the New Testament, he asked, "What is the most important thing needed to be in service to God?"

His students had each brought a Bible that sat open in their laps.

They stared into the pages, unsure of the right response as they scanned the selected passage. After a long silent pause, Sabri answered his own question. "Repentance," he said. "Repentance teaches you obedience and patience."

Some people think that to repent means to say you're sorry, he said, but for the Christian it is an action verb, meaning to turn around and walk in the opposite direction. It means to have a new start and a new life, leaving behind the old way.

The meeting lasted about an hour and was conducted mostly in English—a reflection of the eclectic mix of returned exiles. There were Kurds who'd always lived in the north and spoke Kurdish, Kurds who'd managed to live in Baghdad long enough to have rusty Kurdish but good Arabic, and several Kurds coming back from exile. In this way, a slow rekindling of Christian gatherings was emerging in the northern provinces under Kurdish control. The Christian message moved in a season of turmoil as it always had, transcending the barriers of language, geography, ethnicity, and economic standing.

After Sabri finished teaching, the group broke into easy conversation and laughter. One woman served tea, and a young man led the group in singing. Then, prompted by Sabri, the men and women offered their concerns and challenges for prayer. One wanted prayer for a son living in Australia who hoped to return to Iraq. Another asked for prayer for a Muslim neighbor suffering from an undiagnosed ailment. Together they stood and held hands to pray for one another, then slowly retrieved their shoes from the pile and filed out into the cold darkness.

+ + +

Americans and Iraqis alike wanted to think that freedom was on the rise in Iraq, but protection and security proved elusive. Ansar al-Islam was giving a foothold to al-Qaeda in Iraq and would again and again demonstrate its ability to attack without warning.

My meeting with Fawzi Hariri convinced me that, less than a year after the U.S. invasion, cautious optimism was in order. Fawzi was the son of Franso Hariri, the leader of the Kurdistan Democratic Party who'd been killed by Ansar assassins. Following his father's death, Fawzi had returned to Kurdistan from London, where he had become an executive with British Airways. This Assyrian Christian was making his way into the patriarchal politics of the KDP, which included some Assyrian Christian, Turkmen, and Yazidi communities. The KDP dominated politics and the economy, but opposition political parties had been formally licensed. More than twenty had become part of the regional government in Erbil.

The Kurds were making a stab at granting rights and freedoms under a rule of law. In Zakho, a town north of Erbil near the Turkish border, authorities had convicted a Kurdish Muslim man who had brutally murdered a Christian in early 2003. In the old days he would have walked away from his crime; instead, he was serving fifteen years in prison.

"We were an endangered species," Fawzi said of Christians in Kurdistan. "But the last ten years have reinvigorated our existence."

+ + +

After several days in Erbil, Insaf and I returned to Baghdad. She wanted to spend more time with family and friends there; I tagged along because I wanted to see how freedom was working for some of the new churches in the capital. Once again, Muthafar and Ghada were our hosts, and on our first Sunday back, Insaf and I crossed the Tigris River so we could attend services at the Christian and Missionary Alliance church. When it had opened four months before, sixty-three people attended. Church attendance grew to 150, then 400, then 500. In the next year it would mushroom to 800 worshipers.

The church's pastor, Ghassan Thomas, was Insaf's cousin. As she greeted him, along with other old friends and distant relatives, I made my way to a pew near the front. I smiled at the older Iraqi women in dark dresses and lacy head coverings who sat around me. They spoke no English. In the front row, I spotted Americans—military, I guessed, judging by their clean shaves and close haircuts. The latecomers sat in white plastic lawn chairs wedged at the back of the sanctuary, or in two overflow rooms off each wing. Nearly everyone entered with a Bible in hand.

The congregation sang contemporary worship songs in Arabic, accompanied by a keyboard and a drum set. Then American evangelist Gary Haines spoke to the congregation. With him were missionaries from Brazil who told the congregation that a prayer movement for the Iraqi church was under way in South America. A Pentecostal evangelist from South Korea also came forward. He said women in Seoul were selling chocolate in the streets to support the church and that the Koreans hoped to help start a seminary in Iraq. As he finished speaking, the power went out.

The Alliance church was more eclectic than I had anticipated. Sudanese Christians were leading a study group, and on my way out I met young men who'd served in Saddam's Republican Guard.

"Please come back," a smiling Pastor Thomas told me as Insaf and I left, "but we don't have room."

We had lunch that day with Younan Shiba, a tall pastor in his midthirties, at his home in Baghdad's Sumar district. Insaf had taught Younan physics in high school, and their families had left Iraq for Turkey at about the same time. In Istanbul, Younan had pastored an Iraqi congregation of Presbyterians where Insaf and her family attended. They had not seen one another since.

By the time we reached Younan's home, electricity had been out for a few hours. Younan's wife, Layla, managed to cook anyway. On the dining room table sat round platters heaped with food: lamb patties flavored with anise seed, chicken, rice, flatbread, and a dish of cooked tomatoes and eggplant called *mahldoon*.

The dining room had no windows, so we ate in the dark. Conversation grew more animated, it seemed, in the absence of seeing one another's faces and expressions. It was as if we were talking over the phone instead of sitting across the table from one another. I was learning to love these kinds of encounters, Arabic and English mingling in the room. I enjoyed hearing the odd English constructions that came from those whose first language was Arabic. It forced me to concentrate to understand each voice and inflection.

As we ate, Younan told me more of his story. He and Layla had returned from Istanbul to Baghdad in May 2003. Younan had traveled the country, he boasted, to see the state of churches for the first time in a decade. "With Saddam it was very dangerous. If I had contact with anyone in the north, he could kill me," he said.

Younan then started a church, which he described as "Assyrian evangelical." Within a few weeks of its opening, ninety-six worshipers attended, coming from Chaldean, Armenian, Orthodox, and other backgrounds. Younan was an Assyrian—"old, from the Church of the East, but evangelical," he said.

Saddam had legally recognized the old-line churches—Assyrian Church of the East, Syriac Orthodox, Chaldean Catholic, and Armenians. He'd let stand their legal status, held over from the British Mandate era for the Evangelical Presbyterian churches and the one Anglican church in Baghdad.

Younan dismissed these old congregations. In his view they had accommodated the Baathist regime under Saddam, forsaking evangelism and gospel messages. Like Insaf and others born into these old churches, Younan grew to resent the liturgies and rituals of his childhood, which he and others felt were missing the message of new life offered in Jesus Christ.

What I and the returning Iraqi Christians overlooked was that by holding fast to their liturgies and ancient Scriptures, the old-line churches had clung to an orthodox view of Christian teaching. In the West many old-line denominations were busy deconstructing those texts. In Iraq, the old churches used ancient Syriac and Arabic translations of the Bible. Because both Syriac and Arabic are Semitic languages closely rooted to Hebrew, they often were more true to the original writings than modern translations that are commonly used in the West.

Younan was excited to learn that the old churches were looking for ways to revitalize worship and Christian life in Iraq now that Saddam had been removed. Tensions simmered between the older churches and the newer evangelical churches like his that were siphoning Sunday worshipers, but Younan said, "We are learning to have unity."

Before we left Younan's house, we moved to a sitting room near the front door, where the sun cast soft, filtered light through thin curtains pulled over the windows. Layla made tea and brought us oranges and apples. The couple's two young girls listened to our talk in English and giggled.

All the time I'd been speaking with Younan, Insaf had been focused on Layla. "I feel in my heart Layla needs encouragement," she said suddenly to everyone. "I would like to give her money to buy Christmas presents for the ladies in the church."

Younan and Insaf discussed the amount as Layla listened. They settled on helping thirty ladies with $200. Insaf asked if she also could give Layla money to buy clothes and stuffed animals for about a hundred children, many of them orphans whom Younan's church had begun to care for. Insaf reached into her bag and pulled out several envelopes, handing money to Layla as we all looked on. Layla agreed to organize the gifts for the women and children before Christmas.

Back at Muthafar and Ghada's house that evening, Insaf crouched in the dark between our two beds, bent over her knees with her face to the ground. She prayed by name for everyone she had met that day. She prayed for the pastors and their wives. She prayed for the churches. She prayed for the broken pipes beneath the street and for the busted power grids no one seemed able to fix. She prayed for the children afraid to go to school; for the widows like Joanne; for the newly arrived like Younan and Layla; and for the long-suffering people in Kirkuk such as Yousif and his wife, Alia, as well as for Haitham and Mayada.

When she finished, none of the burdens of prayer showed in her face. The youthful glint in her eye that I first saw in Jordan hadn't been erased by the reality of life in Baghdad.

When Younan had asked her, How do you find Iraq? she'd responded, "I find my answer from Moses. He sent out spies to Canaan, and most of them came back and said, 'It is terrible.' But two said, 'It's good. It's full of grace. We can have it.' That's how I find Iraq. I am one of the two. The Lord gave me that answer."

It was simple: The people had come to live in their houses again, while Saddam had been kicked out of his palace.

+ + +

On a rainy evening I visited one of the Pentecostal charismatic congregations that had sprung up in out-of-the-way residential areas of Baghdad. With the lights out and rain beating down on streets already covered with standing sewer water, a group of 120 had gathered to worship in a large rented house, led by a thirty-year-old single pastor from Eritrea named Joseph. They were singing Handel's "Hallelujah Chorus" when I arrived.

After the service, one of Joseph's associates lit a candle, dripped wax into a pool on the bare table between us, then set the candle into the hot wax for light. Rain thudded against the roof, and music from the next room drifted over us.

When I asked him about his congregation, Joseph told me, "All are new believers," meaning most were Muslim converts. Only months before the U.S. invasion, Joseph and others had been jailed for sharing the gospel with Muslims.

"The reason for being thrown into prison is we were doing house groups," he said. "And the problem with that is we had Muslims coming and converting."

The Republican Guard arrested Joseph and fourteen other Christians, including one woman who had converted from Islam. They were sent to the main Mukhabarat security prison in Baghdad. Guards and fellow inmates beat them. The men said that for days they were stuffed into a room, more like a closet, six feet long and three feet wide. It had no windows and only a hole in the middle of the floor for a toilet. To endure the smell, they inhaled soap. They were allowed to leave the room only for questioning.

Rumors of an American invasion traveled through the prison, and a few days before it began, the other fourteen jailed Christians were released. Joseph was left behind.

When U.S. soldiers attached to the Third Infantry Division reached the prison on April 4, they freed Joseph along with five hundred other prisoners. "We were praying for Americans to come, not only to free us but to free our churches," he said.

+ + +

All across the city, congregations were springing up spontaneously, but some were organizing strategically: In Iraq's eighteen provinces, regional caucuses to choose representatives for a constitutional assembly were slated for May 2004. Eager to codify their religious liberty in Iraq's new constitution, Christians saw the need for churches to have a more visible role in the community than ever before, to win a real place at the table for the first time. So in the months between the beginning of the U.S. occupation and the elections, church leaders sought to expand their public influence. Given the likelihood that Muslims would control the future government, their effort was risky. These believers wagered that it was better to act now and get permission later.

Iraq's Shiites, once shut out of political life under Saddam Hussein, now marched in the streets of Baghdad, Najaf, and Basra, opposing the formation of a constitutional assembly and demanding nationwide direct elections instead. That way the Shiites, who formed the majority of Iraq's population, could assume power more quickly. The Iraqi Governing Council, formed by the United States to work alongside the U.S.-led Coalition Provisional Authority, was made up of thirteen Shiite Muslims, five Sunni Muslims, five Kurdish Muslims, one Turkman, and one Christian.

Some church leaders remembered when Christians made up one-fifth of Baghdad's population and pressed on to do better, fearing the

U.S. tilt toward Shia political figures. "They should not rule Iraq," one church leader told me, "or we will be like Iran, and no one in Iraq wants clerics to be our rulers."

"The Lord has opened a window of opportunity. If we do not go through it now, we will lose it," said Nabil Haj. "We are in the heart of a Muslim country, where no gospel will be preached. But through living by a good example we will make our place."

Nabil, a Lebanese-American Christian from Ohio, was stationed in Baghdad with the 30th Medical Brigade. He had spent his whole life in the United States but was fluent in Arabic, so he often served as a translator. Nabil gravitated to Baghdad's Christian population and quickly began moonlighting to help the churches.

Besides working with the Alliance church, Nabil had a budding friendship with Maher Dakhil, an Iraqi working to revive St. George's Anglican Church. "We are making it a casual evangelical service," Nabil informed me, "and Maher has eighty families coming, which is about four hundred people."

Nabil saw his role as empowering Maher and others to stand up for churches "because we [the Americans] are not going to be here forever." When I saw him visiting churches, he was usually with other servicemen but always engrossed in conversation with Iraqis, his laughter traveling across the room. When we both attended a service at the Alliance church, he smiled broadly and flung his arms wide, telling me, "These are my people."

Nabil would change from his army fatigues and body armor into street clothes and wait outside an army checkpoint near the Republican Palace. A plain, beat-up sedan driven by an Iraqi friend would arrive, and Nabil would slip into the backseat and make his way to the churches.

Working with Iraqis and Americans, Nabil already had organized a Christmas charity event: U.S. soldiers joined forty orphans for a day, bringing gifts and playing, eating, and coloring with them. Later, he collected two busloads of Iraqis, all wearing Santa hats, from one of the churches to sing carols for U.S. Marines standing guard at the Green Zone gates.

Not far away lived Maher Dakhil, another risk-taking Iraqi pastor. When I entered the home of Maher and his wife, Mona, he greeted me loudly as an American would, and in good American English. He'd been collecting slang while working as a translator for the U.S. military, he said. He was a stocky, gregarious man in his forties. He was like a teddy bear: his greetings boisterous, his face a perpetual ready smile, and his conversation full of easy laughter.

Maher was born a Sabaean-Mandean, an ancient Arab sect found primarily in southern Iraq and mentioned in the Old Testament and the Quran. Sabaean-Mandean worship draws on elements of Judaism, Christianity, and Islam, and the sect particularly reveres John the Baptist.

While working as a scientist, Maher had been coerced into becoming a member of the Baath Party. He was important enough in the party structure, he told me, to have his name read in a televised Security Council session when the United Nations debated Saddam's refusal to cooperate with UN weapons inspectors. Maher was on a list of five hundred scientists provided by Iraq to UN weapons inspectors in January 2003, men and women whom Saddam apparently was willing to name in hopes the UN would drop its sanctions and the United States would end its threats of war. Maher insisted he didn't work with weapons of mass destruction. "Saddam had a lot of scientific programs," he said. "He controlled it all."

Though dutifully ensconced in the Baath Party, Maher lost his job after making his conversion to Christianity public. He wrote booklets covering Christian living, understanding the Bible, and the writings of the church fathers. On just about any evening, Maher could be found on a street corner in Baghdad, handing out booklets and telling stories. His cheerful demeanor drew attention and questions about his faith.

When I asked Maher to tell me about his life under Saddam, he threw open the doors of tall built-in cabinets in his living room. "Under Saddam, men came to my home by night, and when I returned, they had torn everything from these shelves—everything—smashed things in my house, and taken away my papers. Why? Because they worked for Saddam." They imprisoned Maher for eighteen months. Once freed, Maher printed more booklets and headed out to share them again. Then Saddam Hussein was toppled.

He laughed at the memory, paused, and took a dramatic breath. "But you see, I am here," he concluded, "and Saddam is gone."

By the time I met Maher, he had refilled the shelves in his living room. They held rows of neatly stacked cassette tapes and Bibles, plus small booklets with clear plastic covers that he had photocopied and collated.

During the U.S. invasion, Maher went to work with military personnel, serving as an interpreter for various units working out of the Green Zone and later from Baghdad's Olympic stadium. He met Col. Frank Wismer, a U.S. Army Reserve chaplain and an Episcopal priest. They worked together to reopen St. George's Church. The British had built St. George's in 1936, and it held services, largely for Brits and other members of the Commonwealth, until Saddam Hussein closed it in 1991 as retaliation for Britain's part in the Gulf War.

St. George's was only minutes away from the U.S.-held Green Zone and just across the street from Iraqi government buildings. In early 2003 it sat ignored, looted, and thick with dust, its stained-glass windows broken and its pews and other fixtures destroyed. Maher supervised a clean-up crew, and by the time I visited St. George's, congregants—nearly all Iraqis, with a few uniformed Americans and Brits—filled white plastic chairs arranged on a bare floor.

Maher led singing and worship, the sound glancing off the tall Romanesque walls, while Wismer conducted baptisms and the Eucharist. Few attendees had an Anglican background, but the church received supervision from the See of Canterbury and Coventry Cathedral in Britain. Since World War II, Coventry had operated a reconciliation center with work among Christians and Muslims. Canon Andrew White, the center's director, had worked with many churches in the Middle East and made regular visits to St. George's.

The church grew rapidly, and soon overflow seating had to be set up in a courtyard garden. Even Maher with his unbounded optimism had not dreamed that a church like St. George's could come back from the dead. As the sanctuary filled Sunday after Sunday, it seemed more and more possible that Christianity would again flourish in Iraq.

+   +   +

One balmy night, Insaf and I drove to Baghdad al-Jadida, the largely Shia neighborhood where Insaf's sister Angham lived. We could see cars burning along the Tigris as we crossed the 14th of July Bridge, and gunfire popped around the city.

Angham's son Sarmad was celebrating a birthday, and the house was full of family and guests. As we entered their living room, an explosion thundered close enough to shake the room.

"Was that a bomb?" I asked.

"Yes," came several voices around the room, but no one paused from greetings, kissing cheeks, and conversation. *For all they cared, I could have asked whether it was rain on the roof,* I thought.

For this occasion, Angham planned to serve *masgouf,* a grilled-fish specialty. For Iraqis, preparation of this Mesopotamian dish is as much about the process as the results. Traditionally, fishermen would return in their boats to the banks of the Tigris, where a necklace of lights outlined open-air restaurants waiting to receive the day's catch. The cooks hoisted the fish, usually carp, directly onto a table to scale them, slit them belly up, and gut them. They would then hang them by apricot branches to smoke over hot, glowing ashes in large, round outdoor fire pits. A brine of olive oil, salt, tamarind, turmeric, or other spices coated the fish as it fire-roasted, and it was often stuffed with peppers, onions, and tomatoes. But each restaurant and each family had its own recipe.

Preparing masgouf could take hours—time spent in conversation and storytelling. The prophet Muhammad himself said, "Eat together and do not separate, for the blessing is in the company."

As we waited, I was given a special seat of honor on the sofa next to Insaf and Angham's *jaddah*, their grandmother. Insaf said she was in her nineties, though no one knew her age for sure. Then the two sisters introduced me to Insaf's nephews and cousins, and their spouses and children. These relatives were a remnant of the wider clan: Insaf had a brother living in Moscow, a sister in Sweden, and parents who had emigrated to Istanbul. Angham and her husband alone remained to care for their grandmother.

I was talking to others when I realized Insaf's grandmother was saying my name over and over, patting my thigh. She said something in Arabic, and the room erupted in laughter.

"She said, 'If I have a baby, I will name her after you, if you give me permission,'" Insaf told me.

Insaf added, "My grandmother is very special to me. I was raised up in her arms. My mother was young and in school when I was born, and Jaddah took care of me. She was very generous, always giving good presents and taking good care of me."

Before the main dish arrived, the elderly woman retired to bed, her stooped frame helped to a back room behind a heavy curtain by several great-grandsons.

After several rounds of tea and plates of snacks—including sweets like baklava and *kleja*, a pastry filled with dates—the men came in bearing the outsized platter of masgouf. They had cooked it themselves outdoors, and the large blackened carp lay on a fluffy bed of *biryani*, rice cooked with chopped vegetables. Even though it was Sarmad's birthday, Angham served me first. The fish was buttery and meltingly tender, fragrant after the spices had softened over the coals. Later Angham appeared with a traditional birthday cake, heavy with icing and covered in candles. We sang "Happy Birthday" twice, in English and then in Arabic, before Sarmad blew out the candles and cut the cake.

+ + +

On a morning of low clouds we departed from Iraq. Insaf had spent the night at her sister's house, and Muthafar and I picked her up en route to the airport. As Muthafar stuffed her luggage into the trunk, we said our good-byes. Insaf lingered to hug her sister, to murmur a prayer into her shoulder.

As we climbed into the backseat, Angham came across the sidewalk toward the car carrying a large laundry tub filled with water. In a swift gesture she heaved the water into the air behind us and the car.

"It means we will come back," Insaf said, "like the rain."

PART 2

CHASING PEACE

7

VANISHED

Baghdad, 2005

....

All Christianity concentrates on the man at the crossroads.

G. K. CHESTERTON

....

Nabil Haj phoned me on a warm day in September 2005. Maher Dakhil, the lay pastor of St. George's Anglican Church in Baghdad, had disappeared. He had been returning to Baghdad from a church conference in Amman, Jordan. Nabil said, "He called from the Iraqi border to say he had entered the country. It should have taken three or four hours for him to arrive. But he hasn't been heard from. He just vanished."

Maher had traveled to Jordan with his wife, Mona, who led the church's women's ministry; their son, Yeheya, who also served in the church; Firas Raad, the deputy lay pastor; a church pianist; and a driver. In 2004 Maher told me the church had four hundred attendees. When he disappeared in 2005, it had close to eight hundred.

Nabil's phone call shook me. I hadn't been back to Baghdad since December 2003, but I had exchanged e-mails and kept up steady phone conversations with Maher. Only weeks before his disappearance, he'd sent me photos of the restoration progress at St. George's Church, along with pictures from a baptism he and Col. Frank Wismer had conducted.

Americans were fed news from Iraq daily, but I was becoming more and more aware of the untold story: what was happening to men and women on the streets, in their homes, and with their businesses, not in the halls of Iraq's parliament or the Green Zone offices. That a family could simply disappear on their way home from an ordinary church event in this "new" Iraq left me stunned, certain that they could be located by American or Iraqi forces, by someone. I was sure there simply had to be some mistake or confusion.

As Nabil told me about Maher's disappearance, I thought back to the last time I'd spoken to Maher. I'd asked again about his Baathist affiliation and scientific work.

"I need to close this subject," he told me. "The security situation in Baghdad is such that this type of information might put my life in danger." He wanted to talk instead about the church and its growth, about plans for a school and other programs.

"On a day-to-day basis," I had asked, "do you feel safe?"

"Our Lord is responsible for our security," he said.

+ + +

The disappearance of Maher and his traveling companions again raised questions about the widespread opinion that the U.S. war in Iraq had ended in May 2003. What was becoming clear was that from May to August, the occupying forces had wasted a safe environment where they could have moved forward with real governance, had they not dismantled the army and local bureaucracies. By August, outside fighters had linked up with Iraqi terrorists and with disaffected Sunni holdovers from the Saddam regime, such as the redheaded King of Clubs, Izzat Ibrahim al-Douri (who was still at large). A new war was beginning.

The August 2003 bombings at the United Nations headquarters in Baghdad and at the Imam Ali Mosque in Najaf announced it. The insurgents aimed to destroy not only reconstruction efforts but also whatever remained of the secular state. The Iraq where Sunnis, Shiites, Christians, Turkmen, Sabaeans, and others lived side by side would

soon be a distant memory. In its place was relentless bloodshed and distrust of once-trustworthy neighbors, in a contest to reduce the country
to a monoculture of either Shiites or Sunnis. In that sense, it was the
beginning of a religious war that few leaders in the United States or
among its coalition partners were willing to face, much less talk about
in the religious context it was being waged.

Even in Canada, Insaf stayed determined to help her people however she could, and we remained in regular contact through phone
calls, e-mail, and chats via instant messaging. In 2004 my family had
visited Insaf and her family in Toronto. At that time she couldn't travel
to the United States on her Iraqi passport. So my family and I made a
detour on our way through Michigan to see her and meet her husband,
Shawki, and their children, Peter and Nour.

We all attended their large Arab church for a Sunday service. We met
Iraqi, Lebanese, and Palestinian Christians afterward and asked Insaf
and Shawki to show us their favorite places. They took us to lunch at a
kebab restaurant run by an Iraqi Christian. Arab Christians in Toronto
have outnumbered Arab Muslims for many years (an indicator of how
heavily the need for asylum tilts toward Middle Eastern Christians), but
this restaurant owner hired Muslims from Iran and Iraq so that more
people from both communities would eat there. It helped that the food
was fabulous.

Back at their apartment, Insaf made Arabic coffee, also known as
Turkish coffee: thick espresso served with sugar. She heated water and
fine-ground coffee beans with cardamom in a stove-top pan. It took
thirty minutes to prepare, as is common in the Middle East, where
women stir the coffee until it foams hot. Then they take it off the heat,
returning it to heat to foam again and again—an unhurried ritual that
the Iraqi mothers like to say melts their sorrows away.

As Insaf stirred, we talked of her hopes for an upcoming trip to Iraq.
Down the hall we heard others talking as Shawki hauled a tuxedo from
his closet for Peter to wear to his first prom. We could tell that their
kids were industrious and respectful. Sharing stories about school and

sports, my children gravitated to them as I had to Insaf. Peter worked after school at a gas station, and Nour, also in high school, would be looking for work as soon as the school year ended.

Insaf and Shawki lived in a neighborhood of refugee groups, but they kept to their own community. Arabs didn't mix with the large African community only blocks away. They shopped in stores that displayed signs in Arabic, attended Arabic-speaking churches, and gathered with friends and family from Iraq's diaspora.

"I cannot tell you when I watch the news how I have such peace, such big hope," Insaf said as we sat on her sofa by a large picture window, late afternoon light streaming over us. "The United States captured Saddam. They can capture these bombers. We have a good future."

+ + +

Insaf not only embodied optimism about Iraq's future; she was representative of its deep Christian roots. If you asked her when she came to faith, she (like most Middle Eastern Christians) would likely respond, "When Jesus rose from the dead."

Jesus was a Jew, of course, and the earliest converts to Christianity sprang from Jewish enclaves—those who had witnessed and told others about his life, death, and resurrection. The twelve disciples, all Jews, were known as the "sect of the Nazarenes"—hence, they were called *Nasraye* in Aramaic and *Nasara* in Arabic. The Arabic word for Christians, a sign of their Jewish roots, is used today.

But the earliest Jews to follow Jesus were not confined to Jerusalem and the banks of the Jordan. In fact, during Jesus' lifetime, most of the world's Jews lived outside the Holy Land. At least one million lived in Babylonia.[1]

More than five hundred years before Jesus' birth, Jews had been taken captive, first by the Assyrians and then by the Babylonians. The Jews endured hardships at the hands of King Nebuchadnezzar, but the destruction of Jewish worship in Israel and the diminished life of the Jews in exile became an indelible part of the Jewish story, recorded by scribes in Babylon. Jewish scholarship gravitated largely toward Mesopotamia, where modern-day Hebrew script developed and where the teachings of Moses survived in written books known as the Torah.[2]

Talmudic academies that produced the best translations of Jewish law sprang up near present-day Fallujah, and religious authorities served out justice as the Sanhedrin once did in Israel. Today a professor in Brooklyn teaches Jewish business ethics using the Babylonian Talmud as his primary text, its genesis somewhere near Saddam Hussein's hometown, where it was written in Aramaic along with Hebrew.

The apostle Thomas sent Thaddaeus from Jerusalem to Mesopotamia, and by some accounts they, along with Aggai and Mari, two from the seventy-two sent out by Jesus, made their way there in the first century.[3]

Jewish converts to Christianity carried their message along the Silk Road trade routes to Edessa, a city at the crossroads halfway between the Mediterranean Sea and Mesopotamia. From Edessa ran routes to Armenia in the north, Damascus in the south, and Persia in the east, with India and China beyond.[4]

Whether by commerce, pilgrimage, or exile, the new religion received a welcome among Mesopotamia's large and established Jewish population that rivaled its reception in Jerusalem and Palestine. Archaeologists in the twentieth century discovered the world's earliest known church near Edessa, at Dura Europus.

From that center came the earliest collection of hymns and the first forms of chant, precursors to what would later gain wide acceptance in Christian worship in Latin. In the second century, Abercius, a bishop from southern Turkey, made a trip across the Euphrates into Mesopotamia and wrote, "Everywhere I found Christians with whom to speak."[5]

By the early third century the church in Mesopotamia had substantial communities in what today are the cities of Erbil, Kirkuk, Mosul, Baghdad, Tikrit, Karbala, Najaf, and Basra. Two bishops from Mesopotamia attended the Council of Nicea in AD 325, where a creed for all Christendom was established.

But historians, starting with Eusebius, said little about Christianity in Mesopotamia. The Euphrates was a geopolitical gulf, separating the Roman Empire from the Persian Empire and forming a barrier rarely breached except by merchant caravans traveling the Silk Road.

The story of the Church of the East was recorded chiefly in Syriac and was little accessed in the West. Furthermore, early theological disputes over the nature of Jesus Christ separated its leadership from church fathers in the West. For centuries, the Church of the East existed outside the domain of either Rome or Constantinople. It was in that sense neither East nor West.

Yet throughout the eleventh century, half the world's Christians lived in the Middle East, and much of what later became known as Arabian advances in science, medicine, and philosophy were at first Assyrian, Persian, and Coptic, rising out of the learning sparked by the Christian gospel. For those Christians living in Asia, their understanding was rooted in Syriac or Aramaic writings, their church bound in some ways to Jewish tradition and Semitic culture. Their language became the forerunner of Arabic, the language of Islam beginning as a branch of the language of Jesus. Today, handfuls of Christians still speak forms of Aramaic, from the Mesopotamian heartland to lands as far removed as Tbilisi and Chicago.

+ + +

The overarching history of Christianity in modern Iraq lent no inherent protection to its followers, as being a Roman citizen in the days of the Roman Empire once could. After Maher and his party had been missing for days, the presiding bishop of the Episcopal Church of the Middle East declared, "They are almost certainly dead."[6]

In 2005 there had already been at least twenty-seven attacks by the time Maher and his companions disappeared. In 2004 there had been sixty-three separate attacks on Christians in Iraq. Because of them, Insaf had had to cancel her plans to return to Iraq in November 2004. Even Air Serv stopped flying into Baghdad regularly.

A coordinated attack on six churches during Sunday evening services on August 1, 2004, had served notice on all the churches in Iraq. At six in the evening, explosions tore through four churches in Baghdad and one in Mosul, killing eight Christians attending worship services and five Muslim passersby on the street. The blasts injured about sixty others. The bomb at a sixth church failed to go off and was discovered in time to prevent further casualties.

The churches were heavily damaged—their windows and doors had been smashed, and one church's building was partially collapsing. Glass had sprayed into nearby homes, parked cars had erupted in flames, and massive plumes of smoke rose into the air. Fellow worshipers crawled over the wreckage in search of Bibles, crosses on necklaces, and other tokens to identify the scattered remains of the dead.

Others felt the explosions too. Worshipers were packed into the Christian and Missionary Alliance Church in Karada when a bomb exploded at a Chaldean church two short blocks away. The force of the explosion knocked books from their shelves and left worshipers screaming and running from the building. Ancient and contemporary churches alike began to view themselves as targets, posting guards and changing or sometimes suspending their hours for services.

Now fear rose with the disappearance of the core leadership at St. George's, at that time the largest Protestant church in Iraq. The loss of such an exuberant leadership team devastated what had so recently been a dynamic, reemerging church scene. Baghdad's churches came together to fast for three days and pray for Maher and the others' safe return. Nabil held out hope the five had been kidnapped, not killed, or taken in for questioning by soldiers. But as the days dragged on, no one demanded ransom, and no evidence surfaced that they had been detained or killed. They had vanished.

+ + +

The road from Amman to Baghdad is more than five hundred miles long. It begins in bone-white desert and ends in black soil after crossing the Euphrates River into the Mesopotamian valley. There the desert fades into a patchwork of tilled fields, irrigation canals, and the farmers' earthen dwellings, which blend into the clay dirt of the city of Baghdad. In search of the missing group, family members of the driver traveled the road from Baghdad to the Jordanian border and found a bombed-out car. At first they thought it fit the description of their vehicle, but there were no bodies inside; and as it turned out, the make and model didn't match. For two weeks, members of the church searched portions of the road, asking for word of the six missing people and learning that they likely had disappeared west of Baghdad between Ramadi and Fallujah—perhaps the most dangerous section of highway in all Iraq.

The passage of time didn't make it easier to accept the likelihood of their deaths. Only their daughter, Ronna, remained after the declared deaths of Maher, his wife, and their son. Ronna was in her first year of university studies in Baghdad, studies that had prevented her from making the trip to Jordan. Once her family was declared dead, she emigrated to Australia.

"We are all devastated. This is the very core of our Anglican Church in Iraq," said Canon Andrew White.[7]

The British had built St. George's in 1936 as a memorial to the Commonwealth soldiers who died in the Mesopotamian campaign of World War I. By then Iraq had become an independent state, and the church opened in a rare time of religious freedom. For the first time since Ottoman rule, which had begun in the 1500s, Christians and Jews gained full citizenship alongside Muslims.

The British abolished the Christians' and Jews' *dhimmi*, or "protected," status, which consigned them to second-class citizenship. King Faisal I, Iraq's ruler from 1921 to 1933, declared, "There is no meaning in the words Jews, Muslims and Christians in the terminology of patriotism; there is simply a country called Iraq and all are Iraqis."[8]

The sun never set on the British Empire, and St. George's filled with Anglican believers from the Commonwealth stationed in Baghdad. Christians made up one-fifth of the city's population; Jews a third, or about 120,000 residents. Hebrew was listed as one of the country's official languages, and Iraq's first minister of finance was Jewish.

It was to be a singular era. The British briefly reoccupied Iraq during World War II, but the postwar era brought first Nazi sympathizers, then rising Arab nationalism, and eventually repercussions for Jews living in Arab lands (known as Mizrahi Jews) following the 1948 establishment of Israel—all before the rise of the Baath Party and Saddam Hussein's dictatorship starting in 1979. By 2004 only thirty-five Jews could be counted in Baghdad, and the city fathers shuttered its one remaining synagogue. Some of the Jews, remembering the earlier era, sought protection in the churches, including St. George's.

Christians thought the coming of U.S. personnel in 2003 had pried open a window of opportunity, a time for a multiplicity of churches to operate freely and to grow. They wanted to be the leading edge of pluralistic democracy in the Middle East. By 2005, with increased attacks and the devastating loss of the Anglican church's leadership, many acknowledged that the window might already be drawing shut.

8

CRUSADERS AND THE MUJAHIDEEN

Baghdad, 2006

....

The strength of those who bear the burdens is failing.
There is too much rubble.

NEHEMIAH 4:10

....

When Sunni Muslim insurgents kidnapped American journalist Jill Carroll on a bright Saturday morning in Baghdad, the news made instant headlines in the United States. Carroll was a young but experienced journalist covering the Middle East for the *Christian Science Monitor*. She was captured in broad daylight in Baghdad by militants known to abuse women and decapitate men.

I saw the news flash across the TV screen while sitting in a doctor's waiting room with one of my children. By this time I'd seen U.S. soldiers, including one who'd just had his nineteenth birthday, with parts of their faces or limbs blown off. Like so many Americans, my family had known the loss of dear friends, in our case a twenty-year-old Marine killed in a roadside-bomb attack along with thirteen others.[1] I was repelled in a different way by Jill Carroll's kidnapping. Carroll's lovely open face, her wide American smile, and her hijab showed up everywhere. To my way of thinking, she had done everything right. She was savvy, she'd spent ample time in Iraq, and she knew enough Arabic to get by in tight spots. She made a point to work with locals, living her life out on the streets and entrusting herself to Iraqi drivers, interpreters, and others—not confining herself to the Green Zone press conferences as many journalists were beginning to do.

I didn't pretend to be the intrepid foreign correspondent she was, but I saw parallels between us. Like her, I preferred to do my reporting from the streets of Iraq rather than from official press briefings. I had come to trust the Iraqis I'd worked with more than any foreign security money could buy, and to rely on their sense for danger. Now I couldn't find anyone I trusted who was willing to give an American a ride from the Baghdad airport into the city. I had a daughter in college, a son in high school, and daughters in middle school and elementary school; and with every trip plan, I was including a list of Iraqi and American military contacts for my husband, in case I disappeared or was kidnapped. It was a worst-case-scenario list, but it seemed foolish not to have it. After Jill Carroll's kidnapping, I postponed one trip to Iraq and then another.

For Baghdad residents, kidnappings had become routine, but this one was news because of the death of Alan Enwiya, Jill Carroll's young Assyrian Christian interpreter. When her abductors backed a truck in front of her car and came for her in the backseat of the Toyota sedan, they shot and killed Enwiya, who rode in the front passenger seat. Her driver managed to get away before the kidnappers drove off with Carroll.

Enwiya was known for the popular music shop called Alan's Melody that he'd run in Baghdad's once hip and Westernized A'arasat neighborhood. Iraqis who frequented the shop called him "DJ Alan" and said he had few rivals for expertise in foreign music. He kept *Billboard* hits posted on a sheet of paper near the door, and even in wartime he managed to get CDs shipped in from a cousin who lived in Chicago. Enwiya liked Pink Floyd, and his fans posted lyrics to "Goodbye Blue Sky" as an epitaph.

Enwiya, known widely as a Christian, was an only son and lived with his parents, his sister, and a cousin, along with his own wife and the couple's five-year-old daughter and toddler son. He was the extended family's breadwinner. In 2005, threats to his business, including an unexploded grenade tossed through the music store's window, forced him to close: Selling Western music had become too dangerous.

A trained electrical engineer who spoke excellent English, Enwiya next took up translation work for journalists. He'd worked off and on with Jill Carroll for two years, and the pair were investigating the Sunni community and its tacit support for insurgents when they were attacked on January 7, 2006, by Sunni militants.

Shot twice in the head, Enwiya survived long enough to alert arriving soldiers of Carroll's kidnapping.[2] She was held for eighty-two days, and in that time she learned that her captors had direct ties to al-Qaeda in Iraq and to its head, Abu Musab al-Zarqawi. Some of the intelligence picked up from her abduction may have led to U.S. forces locating and killing al-Zarqawi in June 2006.

After Enwiya's death, his surviving family, including his parents and sister, felt too endangered to remain in Iraq. They left and applied for visas to live in the United States. With the end of Alan's Melody, one more piece of pre-war Baghdad—its culture and cosmopolitan tempo, with one foot in the East and one in the West—was lost.

+ + +

The year Enwiya closed his music business, 2005, seemed filled with promise for the Iraqis. In twelve months' time they would go to the polls three times: in January to elect an interim assembly to draft a constitution, in October to vote on the constitution, and in December to elect permanent representatives to four-year terms in parliament, with Nouri al-Maliki as the country's new prime minister.

The timetable for initial elections in Iraq had been rushed—forced, even—and events in the country plainly were outrunning the government's ability to contain them.

On the surface, each set of votes was a milestone and a success, with high voter turnout, especially in the December elections. In reality, the pace left no time for civil groups to take root and grow in support of a new government. The emphasis on elections masked the absence of functioning security forces and a bureaucracy. Shiites and Kurds pressed the United States to stick with the quick timetable because by sheer demographics they stood to gain the most. Sunnis balked but had little leverage after Saddam's ouster, unless they resorted to stoking terror.

Christians, too, felt sidelined from the political process. The constitution's preamble acknowledged the country's historic diversity, but Article 2 revealed how quickly sectarian loyalties had arisen. It declared Islam "the official religion of the State" and "a fundamental source of legislation." Furthermore, those who were drafting the constitution had watered down the text on individual rights to appease first Sunnis and then Shiites, leaving Christians and other minorities without legal standing. In fact, the new constitution undermined the secular state itself. By guaranteeing "the Islamic identity of the majority of the Iraqi people," the document put religion at the forefront, ensuring it would be the basis for ongoing strife.

"Article 2 is a time bomb for us," one Iraqi pastor told me.

U.S. State Department officials delved into negotiations over the constitution's wording, but they failed or refused to comprehend how it disenfranchised Iraq's minorities, even when Iraqi church leaders sent delegates to Washington to lobby for changes.

I sat in on one meeting during which an Assyrian leader explained why problems for Christians stemmed from the constitution's wording.

"Wait, I helped draft that document," interrupted a surprised John Hanford, the U.S. ambassador-at-large for international religious freedom and a long-standing advocate for persecuted Christians in the Middle East. The new constitution and the rush to ratify it, according to one analysis, became another "stake in the political battle rather than an instrument to resolve it."[3]

When I would ask Insaf about these developments, she'd respond, "I am not a political person; I am a prayer person. So I hear the news and I just pray." Every time she spoke to a church or school group about Iraq, she asked them to pray specifically "against the spirit of bloodshed in my homeland." Yet somehow, the growing violence and hardships had yet to dent her optimism. "God is in control, and I am not discouraged. This is a war, and everything bad you expect in a war."

She did not let up in her own prayers. "God will change all this curse to be blessing," she told me, "and it is time to cry to God, to ask him to release people from fear and from bloodshed. I am praying for women to sleep in peace and to take care of their children."

With each trip to Iraq, she was overwhelmed by more needs she saw in churches, especially for women, and she set about raising funds and devising ways to meet them. She often told me how she and Shawki hoped one day to return there to live and work in full-time ministry.

In the meantime, Insaf helped many pastors' wives start ministries for women at their churches. Together they organized classes and conferences where women could be taught how to study the Bible; how to start home-based businesses; and how to serve others in their communities, which now included bombing victims and growing numbers of displaced families. In Kirkuk she met a Shia convert to Christianity named Usama, who was running a charity for poor Muslims in the city. With him, she began making visits to their homes too, bringing basic supplies—food, clothing, soap, shampoo, and small toys and books for the children.

When she was in Toronto, she kept up with friends and family in Iraq via instant messenger chats and e-mail. Raising money for the work in Iraq kept her so busy that it morphed into a full-time job. Using her skills from working as a tailor in Baghdad and her own designs, she created bags to sell. I bought boxes of them from her and gave them as gifts. She sold them all over Canada and the United States at craft fairs and church mission conferences. She helped several women set up their own sewing businesses in Iraq, teaching them using her patterns to make and sell bags, Bible covers, and other small items.

When Insaf wasn't sewing for Iraq, she was cooking for Iraq. Posters in Toronto advertised banquet-hall dinners she catered as fund-raisers.

From her small apartment kitchen, she cooked up biryani and kebab for 60, 100, or 250 people, often speaking about Iraq at these same dinners and saving the money for her next trip. "I am praying that I may be able to go with a full hand to my people who have so many different needs," she said.

+ + +

By 2006 the violence in Iraq could be described only as unstoppable. After a public outcry and extensively choreographed negotiations involving her government and her employer, Jill Carroll was released unharmed on March 30. Sunni militants, however, appeared determined to destroy Christian communities, particularly in Baghdad and Mosul.

In the United States, news reports of such attacks were overshadowed by the rising level of U.S. casualties: over eight hundred killed in Iraq in 2005 and about the same number again in 2006, all leading up to a midterm election in which President Bush and the Republicans would be thrashed over the bogged-down war. The American public was hardly aware of the toll on Iraqis during that same time period: Official reports in 2006 showed 16,564 civilians killed.[4]

Iraqi Christians faced a two-edged sword. They were infidels whose presence in Iraq couldn't be tolerated; at the same time, they allegedly belonged to the same "crusader army" as the occupying U.S. forces, forces that provided them no special protection. After the murder of one Assyrian Christian in Mosul in 2006, the Mujahideen Shura Council, an al-Qaeda-linked group, posted a statement on the Internet that was typical: "We eliminated him, because this impure crusader offended our noble prophet Mohammed."

Few could continue with the usual business of life after U.S. Marines set to constructing concrete blast walls and checkpoints to keep militants out of neighborhoods. Yet as the streets became more dangerous, the American military presence became scarcer. The one force able to counteract the terrorists was pulling back to bases to protect its own.

Six weeks before Enwiya's death, armed men stormed a home in a Christian quarter of East Baghdad, killing four women inside. Car bombs and gunfire regularly targeted the homes of Christians, their businesses, and churches. The jihadists were turning Dora, another predominantly Christian area of Baghdad, into something almost uninhabitable. They began shoving printed letters beneath the front gates of Christian homes or delivered their threats face-to-face.

Bihnan Rehana had lived since 1975 in Dora, where he owned a spacious home and ran a street market selling produce. "I was approached by terrorist groups and asked how many children I had," he recounted to me. "When I told them five, they said, 'Fine, three for you and two for us.' They wanted us to pay $10,000 a month as a kind of tax for staying in Dora, or they would take my children."[5]

In some cases young people were targeted, and simply getting to school could be the challenge. Ninos Shamuel Adam, a twenty-year-old about to receive his engineering degree from the University of Baghdad, was killed in a bomb explosion in June. He was a straight-A student who had planned to spend the following year studying abroad. Brothers Fady and Bashar, who also attended the university, told me over tea in their home that holidays had been lengthened and classes shortened to lessen the dangers students faced. Fady and Bashar, along with two other Christian students, hired a taxi driver they knew well to take them to and from school every day. "It's not safe, but we know the roads that are safer than other roads, the roads where there are no checkpoints, only Iraqi soldiers and police."

Ghassan Thomas, the pastor of the Alliance Church in Baghdad, told me he and his wife had begun packing pajamas in their children's backpacks as they headed off to school: "We're never sure if it will be safe enough for them to return in the evening." Sometimes it wasn't, and students spent the night with their teachers inside dark classrooms.

Insaf, meanwhile, was not deterred. She returned to Iraq in early 2006, about the time that Jill Carroll was kidnapped. Though Insaf had been twice delayed because of security, the trip was her third since we'd traveled together in 2003. It was too dangerous to fly into Baghdad, so she flew into Erbil in the north, and drove from there to Kirkuk and then on to Baghdad.

The situation was worse than she had imagined, she told me, and Christians felt powerless to do anything to improve their security. She included herself in that account, as her own family felt the intensifying violence.

During parliamentary elections on January 30, 2005, Insaf's cousin Muaayyed and his son Firas decided to go together to vote. They headed to a nearby school that served as their polling station in Baghdad, marked their votes on paper ballots, and pressed their index fingers into purple ink pads to show they were done. As they left, they saw a man hurrying toward the school, which was still full of voters, his loose cloak barely concealing a vest full of explosives. Muaayyed and Firas didn't have to think or discuss what to do; they simply ran forward as one and tried to stop him, leaping atop the man just as he blew himself up. The force of the explosion also killed both of them—two of about thirty-five Iraqis killed on election day.

I had met Muaayyed at the home of Insaf's sister. We ate together at the birthday celebration in 2003, and he offered to take us around the city and help us with our travels. His son Firas had been married for less than a year, and Firas's wife was six months pregnant. Hundreds turned out for their joint funeral at a Baghdad church, calling them martyrs for the cause of democracy.

Insaf said she'd like to think that one day Firas's child would be proud to say his father had died on a special day when Iraqis voted freely, that his death had contributed to some greater good.

Insaf's cousin Akram Almashmos, who was also on hand for the 2003 birthday celebration, ran into trouble too. Militants threatened his cosmetics wholesale company in Baghdad al-Jadida, telling him to close the business. They taunted him, saying Islam forbade women to wear cosmetics. In 2005 a car bomb exploded on the street near the shop entrance, but no damage was done. Then in 2006 a three-bomb attack destroyed his business—and killed sixty-four Iraqis and wounded nearly three hundred. The force of the explosions rocketed Akram's shop assistant forty feet into the air. The bombs leveled the store, collapsing the three-story building where it had been located. The assistant lost a leg but survived.

When I met Akram and his wife, Sarab, in 2003, she had a baby in her arms, a newborn son born during the first waves of "shock and awe" bombing runs. Sarab went into labor as the bombs fell, the family's apartment rumbling and fires going up all around them. Several neighbors in the building were killed.

When her baby was finally born, she thought, *Why are you protecting me, God? What is our purpose?* That night Sarab decided to name her fourth child Yousif, after the Old Testament patriarch Joseph, "because he is not here by accident. God has something for us."

Akram and Sarab became friends with the U.S. soldiers patrolling Baghdad al-Jadida. Sarab slowly came to believe "they are coming to make the area safer, not to fight." But despite military protection, the neighborhood only grew more dangerous. Two weeks after the insurgent bombings destroyed their business, Akram and Sarab packed their four children and some clothes into their car and left Baghdad for the north.

By 2006, Iraqi Christians who had voted at the polls in 2005 were now voting with their feet. By some estimates, forty thousand Christians left Iraq in 2006. A U.S. diplomat admitted to me that Iraq's Christian population, once numbering 1.2 million (from the last official census in 1987), had dropped to about 700,000, maybe less.

At the U.S. State Department, John Hanford told me it was hard to distinguish the number of Christians from the population at large affected by the widespread violence. He said the United States "doesn't want to see ancient Christian communities fleeing." But he added, "We don't think there is a wave of violence against Christians; it's inadvertently happening as a result of the overall situation." The numbers seemed to indicate he was right, but the stories the Christians told—of churches bombed, threat letters received, businesses attacked, and neighborhoods emptying—did not.

Many Iraqis viewed the violence differently. One evening I saw a familiar face on CNN: Fawzi Hariri, one of my first contacts in Iraqi Kurdistan and now Iraq's Minister of Industry. He spoke for many, like Insaf, who believed the struggle in Iraq was between two completely different ideologies, "one that believes in the new dawn of Iraq, the new democracy . . . and an ideology that is determined to stop the people of Iraq from achieving that goal." The latter elements, he said, gained support from "the former regime of Saddam Hussein" and "some regional interferences."[6]

Two months after making those televised statements, Hariri survived an assassination attempt in south Baghdad when two explosive devices targeted his convoy. Three Iraqis in Hariri's security detail were killed, and thirteen others were wounded; but Hariri was unscathed. Fifteen minutes later a booby-trapped car exploded on the same street.

+ + +

Iraqi Christians relied on their own twenty-four-hour news cycle. They met in their churches most days; they talked to their relatives and friends, followed their comings and goings. They knew within minutes about the latest bombing—who was killed, who was injured, whose business was destroyed.

They then shared their news with an army of exiled Iraqis who, thanks to prior conflicts and the cruelties of Saddam Hussein, were spread all over the world. They might have followed the headlines on cable news, but they had their own networks. They Skyped, they instant-messaged, and they called from their multiple Nokia flip phones. Some, like Insaf, went to see for themselves.

And from Australia to Antwerp, from their desks, their shops, their delicatessens, their university offices, their churches, their schools, their mattresses, their windowsill jars, and their kitchen drawers, these exiles sent money to help—thousands of dollars, again and again. For the Assyrian Church of the East and for the central committee of the Assyrian Patriotic Party, Odisho Yousif collected this slurry of funds. It was his job to know where it was most needed and his daily task to get it there.

So in July 2006 when Odisho told the Commander to kill him rather than try to collect a $300,000 ransom, this worldwide network was ready to act. When the kidnappers relayed the ransom demand to clergymen in Kirkuk, they replied flatly, "We don't have that amount of money."

Nonetheless they went to work, tapping the network Odisho had cultivated for others. They contacted party members, Iraqi families who had benefited from Odisho's help, and Odisho's own relatives.

When word reached Chicago, an Assyrian Patriotic Party member named Elias Shamuel started making phone calls to raise money for Odisho's ransom. Elias was an established accountant and a longtime American citizen. He had known Odisho from childhood. The two men grew up in the same village, Bebede, in northern Iraq, a historically Christian town devastated by Saddam Hussein during his long campaign against the Kurds in the 1980s. At that time Elias and his wife, Janet, had to flee Iraq after Elias refused to become a member of Saddam's Baath Party. They walked for fifteen days to Iran, where they discovered Janet was pregnant. They were refugees in Damascus, then in Athens, and Janet gave birth to two children before the couple received resident visas to live in the United States.

As the news of Odisho's kidnapping spread among Iraqis living in Chicago, Detroit, and Canada, the Assyrian exiles understood the gravity of the threat: Odisho could be killed, perhaps beheaded, to spread terror throughout Iraq's Christian community. "Our priority was his release unharmed," Elias said. "We did not care whether the ransom money would be used to fund terrorist groups or not."

Speaking to me from his office in Chicago, Elias told me a story from his childhood in Iraq to illustrate: "In 1975 my father received a threatening letter, saying his children would be orphaned if he did not stop selling alcohol. All he did was to bring the letter to the police station; action was taken—and he died twenty-one years later of old age."

He continued, "Although we did not agree with the policies of the prior regime, there was a rule of law that controlled the fundamentalists. The absence of rule of law following 2003 created a security vacuum and gave fundamentalists, terrorists, and criminals the upper hand to do what they pleased."

After conveying the ransom demand, the criminals holding Odisho and his driver indeed did what they pleased, hopscotching their hostages from one remote locale to another across desert scrub and fields, then back to the abandoned depot. Church leaders and party officials continued to work their mobile phones, negotiating day and night to lower the kidnappers' demands. All the while they were raising money: "The first day we raised $6,000," a party official told me later. "By the end of the second day it was $10,000, so on the third day we told them that's all we had."

The kidnappers would come down just to $25,000. Odisho, aware only of the original demand, had begun to despair. He didn't think enough money could be raised for his release. He didn't think he would see his family again. Whenever he thought of his two sons, he had to fight back his tears.

Unbeknownst to Odisho, church members in Iraq had decided to float a loan for the balance, trusting the cash would arrive. They agreed to the kidnappers' demand and set a time and place to meet to exchange the ransom money for the two men.

Odisho's faith was tested, but he prayed. He worried over the money. He didn't know who was negotiating his release and suspected they were putting their lives at risk by trying to gain his freedom. He told his guards, "You can kill me, but don't ask such a huge amount from the church."

Odisho's captors behaved erratically. One day a motorcycle showed up. The driver asked whether he could help, assuming the group was a pack of vagrants. The kidnappers shot him dead. They also wandered off at times, leaving Odisho and the driver untied. They were jittery, unpredictable, and murderous, and Odisho realized he had to be ready to jump at any opportunity for escape.

The next day the guards left Odisho unbound after he'd made a trip to relieve himself. Odisho started inching from the makeshift shelter where he and his driver had been tied. He moved a meter, then another, then another, then five, and then ten meters. If the guards spotted him, they would shoot him.

Down a dirt track Odisho and his driver could see the approach of a shepherd driving a tractor and followed by lambs. The two went for it, sprinting to reach the tractor. The shepherd pulled them in, heard their story, and turned the other way with his flock following.

No one came after them as they disappeared over the horizon. It seemed incredible, but they were safe—and free.

Just as the two escaped, a party official was speeding to a rendezvous near the Hamrin Mountains. He'd received instructions to deposit the ransom money inside an abandoned tank. Along the way an American convoy blocked the road, forcing him to wait. He eyed his watch, worried he would miss the rendezvous.

Next came a call on his cell phone from an unknown number. He hesitated before answering. On the other end was the shepherd, calling from his tractor. Soon the official heard Odisho's voice, urgently telling him not to make the ransom payment. By nightfall, the shepherd had delivered Odisho and the driver to the party official. They were free. The masked men were never heard from again.

✦ ✦ ✦

In the midst of the mounting violence on the next-to-last day of 2006, the executioners led Saddam Hussein to the gallows. He wore black and carried a Quran. At least one Shiite witness shouted curses at the former dictator after a heavy noose was secured around his neck. They ended in a chorus of "Moqtada! Moqtada!" It was a taunt, cheering for the radical, populist Shiite cleric Moqtada al-Sadr, who targeted Sunnis and opposed Saddam and the secular Arab state he stood for.

Saddam fired back, "Moqtada? Is this how real men behave?" The taunts continued as Saddam began to chant his final prayers. The trap-door beneath him opened suddenly, and Saddam Hussein plunged to his death. It was an ignoble end, three years and seventeen days after the dictator had emerged from an eight-foot hole in the ground outside Tikrit and told American soldiers, "I am the president of Iraq, and I want to negotiate."

Around the world, Iraq's diaspora community cheered the news. Iraqis living in the West were eager to talk to me about the execution. "I believe justice was served," said Ralph Ayar, a Chaldean Catholic Iraqi living in Detroit whose father had been killed by Saddam Hussein's henchmen for associating with Kurds.[7]

"Iraqis dreaded and feared Saddam," said Insaf, recalling her own flight, "or they believed he was the only solution. But no Iraqi was unaffected by his rule."

She believed Saddam's execution would be a turning point. "The people who have been feeding violence, thinking maybe one day Saddam can make peace in Iraq, he will be back—now that thought has to come to an end, and that's good."

But it had been an undignified end for Saddam, one that fed the sectarian divides instead of nourishing the new national unity yearned for by so many. The young government of Nouri al-Maliki had bypassed an opportunity to carry out Saddam's execution with sober dignity. Handed a turning point toward a new day under a new government, Saddam's henchmen instead served up the kind of hatred Saddam had visited on so many others, feeding the appetite for vengeance.

PLACES OF EXILE

Nineveh Plains, 2007

....

*They left the presence of the council, rejoicing that they were
counted worthy to suffer dishonor for the name.*

ACTS 5:41

....

Even as Saddam Hussein was going to his death at the gallows, a hit
list was circulating in Baghdad under his name. It contained sixty of
his enemies, all top political, military, and religious leaders, including
newly elected Prime Minister Nouri al-Maliki. The document instructed
Saddam loyalists to execute the listed "criminals, agents, apostates," in
addition to "their first, second, and third degree relatives."[1] The targets
were mostly Shiites, as each election had more firmly entrenched Shia
political control of a country that had been ruled by Sunnis since 1299.

In the modern era, from King Faisal I in 1921 through the Saddam
Hussein regime, Sunni heads of state led diverse governments. Yet in
some way the quarter of the country's population who were not Arab
or Muslim had representation among prominent officials. Saddam, for
all his faults, was an equal-opportunity oppressor.

Despite what Muthafar Yacoub had suffered at Saddam's hands, he
said, "Saddam was useful for Christians. He did not give freedom or
power to the Shiites over anyone." Church leaders had worked fiercely

since 2003 to broaden the work of their communities, opening new churches, schools, bookstores, and radio and television broadcasting. They feared Shia domination under the new government, where they could be forced to live in an Islamic republic like Iran, with ayatollahs holding sway over elected officials.

Muthafar and his family were living the nightmare of sectarian war, but in his own way he was soldiering on. By phone and e-mail he would tell me about the Baptist church he was helping to construct in Baghdad, even as mounting dangers surrounded his family. One morning his daughter Lydia stood waiting for her ride to school when a roadside bomb went off. She narrowly escaped being maimed or killed.

Prime Minister Nouri al-Maliki was surrounding himself with a hard-line Shia contingent determined to make the Sunni minority pay for its decades of rule. Maliki gave way to Shia militias who roamed the streets murdering Sunnis. The hit list was payback from Saddam's associates. The more Sunnis felt locked out of power, the more they turned to insurgency, hooking up with outside forces like al-Qaeda and sowing chaos in an effort to bring down the government.

Gertrude Bell—a British diplomat who traveled Iraq, mapped it, wrote about it, and became a kind of patron saint for women travelers like me—wrote to her father in 1920: "The Shia problem is probably the most formidable in this country." What will you do, an Iraqi minister asked her, if the chief *mujtahid*, whose voice is the voice of God, issues a *fatwa* to change the course of governance? "Imagine the Pope exercising real temporal authority in Italy and obstructing the Govt at every turn, and you have the position," she continued. "I don't for a moment doubt that the final authority must be in the hands of the Sunnis, in spite of their numerical inferiority; otherwise you will have a mujtahid-run, theocratic state, which is the very devil."[2]

As battle lines were drawn, both sides demanded the support of the Christian minority—and the Christian minority had plenty to fear whichever way it turned. In May 2007 a Sunni militant group killed two Assyrian Christians, husband and wife, who worked for the U.S.

embassy in Baghdad. The terrorists stopped the couple's car and abducted the husband while yelling, "You filthy Christian traitor!" The wife was killed when she attempted to deliver ransom to the kidnappers.

In a statement released under the name "Islamic State of Iraq," the killers said, "God's ruling has been implemented against two of the most prominent agents and spies of the worshipers of the Cross . . . a man and woman who occupy an important position at the U.S. Embassy. . . . The swords of the security personnel of the Islamic State of Iraq . . . are with God's grace slitting the throats of crusaders and their aides and lackeys."[3]

The U.S. State Department didn't acknowledge the killings. Spokesman Tom Casey said only that two local Baghdad embassy employees were missing. "Their whereabouts, at this point, are unknown," he told reporters in Washington. "We do have concerns about their welfare."[4]

The United States was trying to exit the war, and drawing attention to a group that called itself "the Islamic State of Iraq" and killed Iraqi U.S. embassy workers in the name of religion didn't aid that agenda. The troop surge announced by President George W. Bush in January put twenty thousand additional military personnel on the ground in Baghdad and Anbar Province. The surge in those areas was successful, but it left seventeen provinces—places where al-Qaeda militants could take cover—unaccounted for and to differing degrees unaffected.

As quickly as the surge began to succeed, support in Washington waned: In April both houses of Congress passed legislation calling for the withdrawal of U.S. troops from Iraq by the fall. Gen. David Petraeus, the commander of forces in Iraq at the time, pleaded for patience, telling lawmakers that the effort "may get harder before it gets easier."[5] But by then Americans and lawmakers were gearing up for the 2008 presidential election. The surge made good headlines back home, but 2007 would prove to be the worst year of the war for Iraqis: More than 17,000 civilians were killed.

The high death toll masked the direct targeting of Christians. In Baghdad, bombings and kidnappings had overtaken the Christian neighborhood of Dora. Its streets were barricaded; its shops shuttered.

Over 1,400 families fled the area, taking refuge in churches.[6] They tried to carry on by day with their normal lives, but at night they retreated to church sanctuaries, sleeping inside the churches and laying out mats for their children beneath pews.

Others fled north to Iraq's Christian heartland—Nineveh Province. Violence and deprivation sometimes followed them there. In under a year, church leaders said, about forty thousand Christians had left Baghdad and Mosul for safety in the wide expanse of Nineveh Plains.[7]

The region was a homeland for Christian groups with deep roots—Assyrians, Chaldeans, and even Armenians who had fled the Ottoman-era genocide in Turkey nearly one hundred years earlier. With its links to multiple ancient Mesopotamian religious traditions, it was also home to Turkmen, Kurds, and the world's only indigenous Yazidi community.

Violence directed at the minorities was already decimating their communities. Yet few media outlets seemed to notice; their annihilation didn't fit the Shia-Sunni sectarian-war narrative or take place in the Sunni Triangle that newscasters liked to report on from the safety of the Green Zone.

For example, in March 2007 a truck bomb in Tel Afar—a city of about 200,000, mostly Iraqi Turkmen—killed 152 civilians, making it the highest death toll yet from a single bomb in the four-year war. Tel Afar was west of Mosul in Nineveh Plains.

Five months later, on August 14, four coordinated bomb attacks hit a cluster of Yazidi towns west of Mosul toward the Sinjar Mountains, killing more than 500 people. The simultaneous bombings were among the largest terrorist attacks in history—second only to the 9/11 attacks in the United States—yet they received little attention in the American press.

+   +   +

In August, two weeks after the Yazidi bombings, I made my way through Queen Alia airport in Jordan once again, this time waiting for a commercial flight to Erbil, the capital of Iraqi Kurdistan. Flying into Baghdad was out of the question because the roads from the airport were being bombed, and anyway, it was so dangerous that no one I knew in Baghdad felt safe enough to risk the drive with an American from the airport into the city. Even Insaf chose to fly into the much safer northern region rather than Baghdad, giving me the opportunity to travel with her once again.

While Iraq and its predicaments were a puzzle to most Americans, Insaf was not an enigma to me. She was a mom, leaving behind two children and a husband to make a long trip overseas. She would do it over and over again. As we headed off in 2007, I had two children in college, one in high school, and one in middle school. We worried together over what our kids were having for dinner and whether they had clean shirts to put on in the morning. But we did not fret about our decisions to go. Insaf's love for her homeland, her hope for what it could be in the middle of war and devastation, were compelling. Because she was able to go, she went. I had come to track the flip side of the American surge, scouting the ignored reaches of Nineveh where Christians and others were holing up. I wanted again and again to see this changing, chaotic war zone through Insaf's maternal eyes. That way, it became somehow knowable.

When I wrote about Iraq, I received some letters thanking me for the reporting, but often my in-box swelled with reader mail asking why I risked going there. Some quoted passages from the Bible, mostly Titus 2:5, about women working at home. The readers, men as well as women, asked what right I had as a mother and a Christian to do dangerous work outside the home. I was thankful to have a husband and editors who supported these travels and held me accountable, both to continue the journey and to not take outsized risks. But I did ask Insaf what she thought: Were we reckless and out of step with Jesus' teaching?

She was thoughtful for a moment, then replied, "I only hear Jesus saying, 'Feed my sheep.'"

+ + +

The war years gifted Iraq's neighbor Jordan with plentiful international traffic, and Amman's airport had received a face-lift. Duty-free shops and Starbucks wannabes all vied for my attention. At the same time, more women than ever walked through the terminal in full-length black burqas. They moved across the tiled floors like small domes of darkness, only their eyes visible. Insaf and I were an unlikely pair, especially in the middle of this scene, chatting and catching up in our jeans and Western haircuts. She had become like a sister to me.

That didn't mean we didn't have our differences. In the airport she trolled the duty-free aisles, knowing exactly what she wanted and moving with purpose. I hung back, an observer, uncertain what to buy, skeptical of the importance of perfume in a war zone. Insaf got carried away speaking Arabic, even when she knew it left me out of the conversation. I would elbow her for a translation, and she would say, sometimes with irritation, "I will explain later."

Seven years' exile in Turkey had taught Insaf how to hold on to her resolve and also how to wait. I lacked her patience. Once in the northern city of Dohuk, I ran to an Internet café to check e-mail and got locked out of the apartment where Insaf and I were staying. When I banged on the gate, Insaf didn't appear, so I ducked into a shop to borrow a cell phone to call her. She didn't answer.

Foolishly, I was wearing only jeans and a T-shirt, standing in the street in bright sunshine while men lurked in nearby doorways, staring. Only minutes earlier I had been focused on my work and unbothered by the surroundings, but now I felt myself a potential target. I continued walking the street, outwardly purposeful but inwardly frantic—a lone American on the street, clearly exposed. Shoppers tried to help me, but none spoke English.

Finally, as the men looked on and the women on rooftops paused from hanging laundry to watch me, I again took to banging on the gate. Insaf calmly answered. "You don't understand the risks to an American like me!" I said, fuming.

She said, "I am sorry; I was only taking a shower."

The whole episode probably lasted twenty minutes, nothing compared to the years and years of danger for Iraqis. And I was the one who'd forgotten my key anyway.

Insaf disliked talking about the politics of war. She embraced setting her feet on Iraqi soil. She made plans to see as many people as possible and to go everywhere. During our 2007 trip, she made several excursions to Baghdad, including Christian neighborhoods like Dora, without me. She wanted to help the families there, and an American tagging along added risk.

She wasn't in danger of losing hope. She had traveled to Iraq at least once a year since 2003. This time she brought one whole suitcase full of fabric and samples, her sights set on training women, even women forced from their homes, to sew and set up small businesses.

"I cleaned, I sewed," she said of her own time as an exile, living in borrowed lodging in Istanbul. "I worked to keep my dignity and feed my children. Because I have all that experience, I can understand these women. They need to build their dignity as much as feed their families. Small projects will help them do that. And small projects will grow."

Insaf would continue to help me stay grounded amid the ambiguity of life in a war zone. Somehow the survivors got on with starting sewing businesses, opening bakeshops, and going to school every day, knowing that car bombs, street battles, and kidnappings were part of the day-to-day reality.

The courage of the American soldiers and Marines facing IED explosions or fighting door-to-door was readily apparent on nightly newscasts. Few saw the heroism it took for a mother to take a child's hand and walk her to school each morning, a shopkeeper to insert a key in a lock and open his jewelry store, or a businessperson to step up to a bank counter and make a deposit at the end of the day.

+ + +

Insaf and I traveled, sometimes together and sometimes separately, across Kurdistan and the Nineveh Plains. Many Iraqis had fled to these areas to escape the violence elsewhere. Like traumatized earthquake victims who felt safer outdoors than in their own beds, the Christians found refuge in a strange desert landscape away from familiar city neighborhoods. Nineveh was vast and vacant. The midday sun bounced off the dust in the air, creating a blue-green haze.

In spring the flatlands were lush with grass to the horizons and with swaths of yellow where field mustard bloomed. When we arrived at summer's end, the landscape was brown: a scorched earth after weeks of 120-degree days. Shepherds sat beneath sheets set on poles to escape the sun, and the sheep somehow managed to graze on the burnt grass. They'd pour over the hillsides like rice spilled from a canister, and the shepherds came following, their heads wrapped in scarves against the daytime blaze.

The ancient villages where Assyrians settled many millennia ago had gradually emptied of Jews, then of Christians. By the late twentieth century, the old limestone churches in Nineveh Plains had roving priests who read Mass first at one village and then at another, the bells tolling for the villagers to come when a priest arrived.

Villagers left for bigger cities and for jobs, though the land was arable, thanks to the Mosul Dam. In season it grew wheat, cotton, and barley. The Nineveh economy had faltered seemingly for good after the first Gulf War, when the United Nations began sending food rations to Iraq to counter its own sanctions. The UN brought in wheat from Russia and other foodstuffs, choking the livelihood of local farmers.

Now that Christians were under siege elsewhere, Nineveh was not a difficult place to settle. It was close to Mosul yet spacious, wide open, crisscrossed by paved roads, and dotted with towns. Frightened families spied out water or some patch of green and headed toward it.

Compared to what they'd left behind, families reported that making do in an arid plain seemed like luxury. Back home, black-masked militants entered their homes or slipped printed letters in Arabic under their doors, demanding that they convert to Islam, pay some exorbitant fee, or be killed. The letters characteristically ended, "To be safe, be Muslim."

I made a side trip without Insaf to meet Odisho Yousif and talk with him about his kidnapping and his continuing efforts to raise money to help Iraqi Christians whose lives had been upended by violence. An Assyrian priest introduced us, wanting me to learn about the dangers for Christians and about the network of exiles and others helping them to survive. I myself had to travel with bodyguards to our prearranged meeting spot.

After surviving his own kidnapping, Odisho divided his time between Dohuk and an old Assyrian town outside Mosul where he was reunited with his wife and two sons. He had round-the-clock armed bodyguards who took posts outside an open doorway.

As we talked, Odisho puffed on one cigarette after another. At certain moments in the story his hand trembled, sending ash to the floor. When he recalled how he had thought of his sons during captivity, and of the prospect of not seeing them again, his voice broke.

Upon his release, he had returned to making trips to Baghdad and delivering money, though he became more guarded about his whereabouts. I was instructed not to say where we met as it was on the front line of the Islamic onslaught against Christians. I asked him if he had to pay protection money now to stay alive, and he said no. Would he, if forced to? "You have to pay money," he said. "It is life or money, so you pay money."

I joined Insaf to continue the Nineveh journey to Telskuf, where we entered a convent and met Sister Mary Dominic. Like other Iraqi Christians, she too had journeyed north from Basra, where she taught in a Catholic school. Insaf recognized her: Twenty years earlier, they had known each other in Basra, where Insaf had married, but Insaf had left her Catholic roots.

"I gave my heart to my Lord and Savior Jesus Christ," she said to Sister Mary, who warmed to Insaf as they talked.

Telskuf is an ancient Assyrian town of about 11,000, mostly Christians. A busy market center once in the heart of croplands and melon farms, it sits about twenty miles outside Mosul at the northeastern edge of the vast Mosul Dam spanning the Tigris. We arrived in the morning, but already a corner bakeshop was displaying platters of fresh baklava, the baker stacking them like bricks, one large round platter supported by two beneath it. Sheep and goats wandered freely in the street, in and out of the high mudded walls of the old city. Already it was hot enough that sweat glued my cotton blouse to my back and ran wet down my legs, dampening my jeans so that they itched.

As we sat together in the convent's kitchen, Sister Mary told us about a much milder spring day, a Monday in April, when she had darted about the convent as she usually did, here and then there like a butterfly. She checked on the kitchen, where lunch preparations were already under way though it was just past nine in the morning, and gave instructions to a worker mopping the front hallway. The convent ran a kindergarten and primary school, and the sounds of children's voices bounced from classrooms into the bare hallway. Outside more students played in the courtyard, their screeches flowing through the open front door. Suddenly the force of an explosion snuffed out all other sound, and a rush of glass knocked Sister Mary to the floor.

Just beyond the convent's small courtyard, a car bomb had gone off in the street. As flames leapt into the air and a ball of smoke and ash rose from the car, the force of the detonation shattered windows in the convent, even though it was surrounded by a high wall. Neighboring shops, too, were blasted, and walkways leading in both directions were strewn with debris and blood.

Sister Mary told us how she noticed she was bleeding as she rose from the floor in a deafened haze. She recalled a threat from al-Qaeda posted days before on the Internet, warning it would kill Kurdish forces in Nineveh. Only a few doors down the street were the offices of the Kurdistan Democratic Party, or KDP, and a checkpoint manned by the peshmerga soldiers stood nearby.

The car bomb killed ten Iraqis that day, including two children at the convent and two adult workers. It injured about 140 Telskuf residents, including Sister Mary and another nun. Sister Mary's white habit was smeared in blood from shards of glass that had pierced her head and face and raked her neck and arms. Plus, the force of the blast knocked her down, breaking her arm. Her head remained wrapped in bandages for a week and her arm in a sling for much longer.

Now as we met four months later, she dismissed her injuries. "I am sixty years new," she said with a smile. "And I am very strong."

The hardest part of that day, she said, was not her injuries. It was the terror of "the little ones," who had until then never witnessed such violence. "It is a miracle all the sisters are okay and the injured students recovered."

In a few days a new school year would begin, and Sister Mary was ready to welcome new students, along with some of the little ones she had nursed along after the bombing. She lived in a whirl of coming and going as she kept pace with newly displaced Christian families arriving in Telskuf.

At the moment, fifteen Muslims and one Christian had just taken refuge in the convent. She discussed their plight as she darted in and out of the kitchen, putting away shopping bags and showing me the stores she kept on hand for those who showed up in need: three freezers full of beans, grain, and other foodstuffs. She served Insaf and me a quick lunch, barely sitting to eat herself, and asked us to accompany her on her afternoon rounds in Telskuf's old city.

We set off during the hottest part of the day, winding through narrow old streets, the sour smell of trash and the stench of donkey dung around us. The first man we came to stood at the door of a dim house carved into the old city walls. He sat down on a dirty crate pallet, smoking, surrounded by spit-out watermelon seeds. His clothes were filthy, and he was barefoot. I noticed that all the toes on his left foot were missing.

"I am your mother," Sister Mary told him, pressing a few Iraqi dinars into his hand and asking about his wife (who was a Muslim, Sister Mary later told us) and his son.

At other homes her routine was similar: Sister Mary asking after everyone in the family and seeking out the children, giving them hugs, and allowing them to kiss the cross hanging around her neck or the rosary beads dangling from her fingers. She usually gave money to the families, bills she pulled from a small, black crocheted bag. Sometimes she turned to Insaf, asking, "Can you give too?" A few times she asked Insaf to give a specific amount.

I grew uncomfortable with Sister Mary's entreaties. Other Christians I'd observed helping the poor or homeless were nowhere near so bold in demanding cash from Westerners. I stood apart, as I often did, taking notes and photos. Insaf wanted to help the displaced people, especially those without other resources. She asked her own questions about where they had come from and what they had endured, and she handed some of them American bills folded up. It was part of her stash of envelopes she kept at the ready for just that purpose.

It was hard to second-guess Sister Mary's obvious attachment to this itinerant community, her compassion for both the resident poor of Telskuf and the newly arrived, her smiles and attention freely given to everyone. We wound through the streets for hours, and she knocked on nearly every door in the oldest parts of the city. She called each resident by name, even those who'd just arrived. They in turn called to her: "Mother Mary, Mother Mary." She gave special attention to the many disabled people and to Muslims, more than a few of whom had found refuge in Telskuf. "Muslim people like me very much," she said matter-of-factly.

I wasn't at all surprised that Insaf ran into people she knew among those recently displaced from Mosul and Baghdad. One was a new mother whose husband had been killed by a roadside bomb. She spoke rapidly to Insaf in Arabic.

"Ah," Insaf said, turning to me to explain that the woman's brother was "a very important person with Saddam. She has been to his palaces."

As we headed back to the convent, we paused at the spot where the bombing happened. Now the market there was busy again with vendors selling onions and crates full of grapes. A hardware store hummed with shoppers, and on the street there was a kind of taxi stand where drivers could be hired for a ride to Baghdad. It was easy to forget that many who arrived here had left businesses and homes behind. The taxi service was helpful for those who tried to go back to check on their property or an aging relative, or to do their banking or other business.

As we said good-bye to Sister Mary Dominic and the other nuns later that day, Insaf promised to come back and help her again with the many poor. Sister Mary Dominic hugged us tightly, clasping her hands over my ears and pulling my face to her, kissing my cheeks. "*Inshallah*," she said—as God wills, we will see you again.

+ + +

Late that afternoon, we wound through a world of yellows, a bleached landscape along a road carrying us to Mar Matti. The monastery's pale stone walls hugged the mountain face, halfway up the 3,500-foot peak of Mount Al-Faf. This refuge, established in the fourth century, towered over the plains of Nineveh. From its terrace the plains could be seen stretching in every direction, and the monastery seemed suspended from the sky.

According to tradition, an elderly hermit named Matti (or Mattai, for Matthew) lived in a cave inside Mount Al-Faf. He was discovered on a hunting expedition by Behnam and Sarah, children of the Sassanid king Sinharib. Sarah had leprosy. Matti healed her, and the king's children plus the hunting party converted to Christianity. Learning of their conversion, King Sinharib ordered Behnam and Sarah to be put to death. Then the king himself became afflicted with leprosy, found Matti, was cured, and converted to Christianity, mourning the senseless loss of his children. Where a tomb was constructed in their honor, the early Christians later built Mar Behnam monastery. And at Matti the hermit's cave in Mount Al-Faf, monastics founded Mar Matti. It is one of the oldest monasteries in the world.

In 1845 the Syriac Orthodox monks turned Mar Matti into the fifty-room edifice it is today, the older caves connected by tunnels to the newer halls. As we turned up the long drive to Mar Matti, our driver warned us ominously, "There are terrorists, and the road isn't always clear."

Saddam Hussein decided to visit Mar Matti in the 1980s—but discovered it had no paved road. So he had one built. Until that time, visitors had regularly hiked a winding cinder path or ridden donkeys to the cloister. Insaf said her family often came in the spring with other families to picnic on the hillside and then wander inside the cool stone halls. When we arrived, we saw several families who had spread blankets and brought snacks to eat in the sunshine on the terrace.

At its peak in the ninth century, Mar Matti was home to seven thousand monks. The population had dwindled to two resident monks by the time of the U.S. invasion of Iraq in 2003, but now ten monks were in residence, and the halls echoed with visitors and activity, including transactions in a well-stocked gift store.

Six monks were from Turkey, along with a Greek, an Italian, and a Brit. Brother Yousif Fahmi, a man in his thirties, was the lone Iraqi from Mosul. He showed us the small church upstairs and a smaller chapel one floor below, its walls and floor all marble. It was under renovation, and construction workers were sanding the floors. We made tracks through the marble dust as we crossed the floor to an office where we had tea before making our way to the library.

Brother Yousif pointed us to Scriptures in Syriac, copied by hand in large calligraphy using red and black ink. The bound volumes were spread casually over dusty tables or stacked on the *ambo*, a reading desk where one of the monks could stand in the small chapel to recite the text during morning and evening prayers. We picked through some of them gingerly, as it seemed they should be preserved in a sealed vault instead of lying scattered in the open air.

The Mar Matti library at one time contained six hundred such Scriptures, including separate bound volumes for each book of the Bible. We saw one Syriac volume dated 1678, and Brother Yousif said the library contained liturgies that were 250 years old. One copy of the letters of St. Paul dated back 1,100 years. More recent volumes bore the stamp "St. Matthews Library." All were clearly in use.

Christianity has had an ascetic element from the start. Jesus withdrew to rest and to pray in private. He warned his disciples not to be weighed down by the cares of this life. The apostle Paul retreated into the deserts of Arabia after his conversion and later added his own counsel in favor of a solitary life. From their earliest days, some among the followers of Christ became solitaries, or *monachos* in the Greek.

In the upper reaches of Mesopotamia, from Tur Abdin ("mountain of the servants of God") seemingly spontaneous monastic enclaves formed, from Asia Minor through Mesopotamia and Egypt. The deserts and barren mountains surrounding the Tigris and Euphrates were natural environments in which to seek the solitary life, and by the end of the fourth century, monasteries dotted modern-day Turkey, Syria, and Iraq.

A lay movement, monasticism was built as much or more on study, prayer, and work as on the traditional vows of poverty, chastity, and obedience. It also gave women lay roles and at that time unheard-of vocations in learning, service, and work. Matti the hermit wasn't so unusual, gathering a reputation for healing the sick among the growing villages of Nineveh.

Besides their devotion to prayer and manual labor, the monks' focus on study meant that their libraries became vast repositories. Some of the earliest Syriac manuscripts turned up in Rome and Florence, their illustrations closely resembling the great illuminated Celtic Gospel books, which in turn became the first figurative paintings in British art. Timothy I, patriarch of the Church of the East from 780 to 823, sent an emissary to Mar Matti to borrow texts from its library. He used them to prepare what became a catechism of sorts for the Syriac-speaking Christians living among Arabic-speaking Muslims. It circulated widely throughout Mesopotamia, drawing the attention of the caliph Al-Mahdi. He summoned Timothy to the Islamic courts of Baghdad, and for two days Timothy debated the merits of Christianity versus Islam with the court scholars.

Timothy's work was translated from Syriac into Arabic, spreading the teaching of Christianity in the language of Islam. Similarly, with

Timothy's translations, the idioms of the Scriptures found their way into Islamic texts translated into Arabic.

Monasteries like Mar Matti provided a refuge for both the biblical texts and the People of the Book, as the Jews and Christians were known under Islam. These sanctuaries offered a place of exile from a world of war.

Our driver hurried us down Mount Al-Faf and out across the plains again, where the heat hovered so close it made you want to sleep. Over the next days we crisscrossed Nineveh and made our way into the hills of Kurdistan. Traveling sometimes with Insaf and sometimes with Assyrian relief workers and a pair of American Mennonites, I visited fourteen villages—Assyrian, Yazidi, and Kurdish—tracking down war victims who'd been kidnapped or forced from their homes, interviewing survivors of bombings and those who'd escaped terrorist threats.

At the beginning I simply wanted to see how displaced families were living, what life they had found in the rekindled towns and villages of ancient Assyria, what the future looked like to them. "You'll drink more caffeine in one day than in a normal week," a friend in Jordan had advised me when I told her my itinerary. "Bring Tylenol."

I ended up listening to the past, to what they'd had and what they'd lost. Exile was a story as old as Tur Abdin or Mount Al-Faf, each time presenting for those who endured it a future staring back, blank.

Finishing tea with Insaf after visiting with an Assyrian priest in the city of Dohuk, we headed out in search of Insaf's cousin. Najib owned a grocery store in Baghdad. He and his wife, Ban, had moved to Dohuk a year earlier after he received anonymous threats from Muslim militants for selling alcohol. Each week he traveled back to Baghdad to check on his property and his business. On one journey he was kidnapped.

His abductors demanded half a million dollars in ransom, using the contact list from Najib's cell phone to threaten Ban and other family members. It took three days for Najib's brother to negotiate the ransom down to thirty thousand dollars. All the while Ban and her family frantically raised the money through extended family spread from Canada to Australia to Russia.

Four days after the kidnapping, Najib's brother waited for hours to deliver the ransom payment—hours that were like years, Ban said.

We heard the story over bottles of water, with Najib's whole family gathered around to hear it again. After we finished the water, his sister served us Turkish coffee in small glass cups, thick and sweet with cardamom. Next came trays of baklava and other pistachio-laced pastries. And then a young man, a cousin, served us Pepsi in bottles. Ban helped finish the story before the expected tray of tea arrived.

"Will they take the money, or will they also take our brother? Will they kill them both?" she had wondered. But the kidnappers took the ransom payment and delivered Najib a free man.

"Now they know our family is rich," Ban said, "and they know the people to go to, the numbers to call to get the money."

Ban wanted to emigrate, to settle somewhere like Canada. She told me she would never feel safe again. Insaf tried to explain to her that the process takes a long time.

"How can I do things illegally, then, and it is okay?" Ban asked.

+ + +

Fadi Benosh, a thirty-year-old youth pastor, was kidnapped on his way home from Kirkuk, where he'd been helping another church plan afterschool activities. At an intersection where he stopped to buy food at a fruit stand, six armed men wearing masks suddenly attacked him and shoved him into the trunk of a car.

"I feel my life stop in that moment," Fadi later told me. "'Jesus Christ, Jesus Christ!' I called from the trunk. I could not think of anything else."

Fadi managed to wrench his cell phone from his pocket and call the Christian and Missionary Alliance Church in Baghdad, where he had worked since 2004. Quickly the church organized prayer vigils for Fadi's safety and release, and word traveled to Alliance World Fellowship headquarters in the Netherlands.

The kidnappers called themselves *mujahideen*, or Islam's fighters for God. They abducted six men that day, transporting them to a cave in a nearby mountain. Fadi told me that he was the only Christian and was quickly singled out to die. "We have to kill the Christian one, the one who doesn't believe in God, who is *kafir* [Arabic for unbeliever]," one of the gunmen declared over and over. "We have to kill him."

Inside the cave, Fadi believed that the prayers of his church were his only hope. "I sensed that God was with me," he said.

After six days, he was let go. Fadi had no explanation for his sudden release other than the prayers raised on his behalf. But he was traumatized for months. He couldn't eat or sleep, and he went into hiding. A tall and burly man, Fadi wore his black hair close-cropped and well trimmed, like most Iraqi men. He had a round face and a broad smile. It was hard to picture him living in fear.

✦ ✦ ✦

Riding south of Dohuk to cross Mosul Dam, we found small villages full of displaced Iraqis. Many had fled Baghdad or Mosul. All were Christians. All had their own stories of trauma.

Boutros Simon, a Baghdad resident, told us a story we would hear again and again. In May he found an envelope on his doorstep. Opening it, he discovered a bullet inside and a note scrawled in simple Arabic: "You are Christians and you have to leave."

"The Islamists forced us to leave the house," Boutros told us. "They promised to kill us. And they killed my brother."

Boutros stood outside one of many new cement-block homes built for displaced Iraqis on the edge of ancient Nineveh towns. From a distance, the homes stood out bright against the beige, treeless landscape, their roofs flat, a generator and a water tank mounted atop each. Few of these towns had reliable electricity, and water was scarce. Inside, the homes were plain, with poured-concrete floors and a thin coat of plaster smoothed over the cement-block walls.

Boutros wouldn't talk about his brother's death, but he showed me his car, a beat-up wagon with Baghdad tags and bullet holes where the family was shot at as they fled the city. Still tied atop the car were bedrolls and blankets wound up with cookware inside.

Most of the forty thousand Christians who took refuge in northern Iraq in 2007 were from Mosul or Baghdad, places where the U.S. troop surge was attempting to restore order. Yet violence against Christians continued.

+ + +

Given the unremitting heat, Insaf and I began to plan our days around moments of air-conditioning. We'd find a city or town with an Internet café where we would linger for the coolness as much as to check in. At one café, we met Ayman Dwardin, a mechanical engineer from Baghdad. After taking our coffee order, Ayman turned to me to ask, "Small cup or mug?" It was the first time I'd been offered a mug of anything in Iraq.

Ayman said Islamic militants had blackmailed him out of Baghdad once they learned he was a Christian and spoke good English. They entered his home one evening, demanding American-made weapons. They assumed he could acquire them as an engineer who had once worked for the government.

When Ayman told them he could not, they demanded he pay a fine for refusing to support the Islamic cause. He said he paid. The demands, however, only increased, as he was accosted at any hour, sometimes for days on end. Finally he fled north. Now he worked fixing cars and helping a cousin who ran the coffee shop. As he talked, he swept the floor, then stepped outside to shoo away a boy of about ten who was begging at the front door. Ayman paused, asked the boy something in Arabic, then came in, retrieved an orange Fanta from the cooler, and handed it to the boy. Not leaving, the boy fixed his eyes on me, plainly looking for an American handout. Ayman yelled at him, and the boy ran off.

Leaving Ayman, we headed to the town of Karanja, where we met eight-year-old Danny. He had a sister named Dalia in high school.

The children had lived with their parents in Mosul. One afternoon on their way home from school, Islamic militants stepped out of a car and grabbed Danny. He wrestled the gunmen long enough for his sister to run at the car to try to rescue him. One of the masked militants shot at Dalia but missed. She ran home to tell her parents what was happening. But she was too late. The gunmen whisked Danny away and soon sent a ransom demand to his house.

Danny's father, who asked me not to quote him by name, negotiated the ransom amount down to $750. "Can you imagine putting such a low value on your own son?" he said, shaking his head. Even with so small a sum, he had to borrow the money.

But the captors did release Danny, who stumbled his way back home. For many days afterward, he didn't speak, his father said. When I met him four months after the kidnapping, he could only mumble to his father, unable to speak to strangers.

Danny might have been freed, but his family was not released from the militants' grip. The kidnappers returned to the area, letting the family's neighbors know they planned to come after Dalia. As soon as they could, the family made their way out, settling in the town of Karanja and hoping the terrorists could not find Dalia in the vastness of Nineveh Plains. Like so many, they gave up everything to come, trading meager wages and property for the security of the unknown.

That evening as we headed back to Erbil, all I wanted to do was sleep off the heat and hardships of the day in the backseat beside Insaf. But she kept up steady chatter with Fadhil, who was driving, and our friend Kilim, who was along for extra protection and for company. Many American news organizations were paying tens of thousands of dollars to hire beefy drivers and bodyguards out of Baghdad for this kind of excursion. I was learning to trust the network of Christians I had come to know. They arranged transportation using people they could rely on who knew the local, always-changing security situation. Often these were strangers to me, but by putting my life in their hands, I was building goodwill in the Christian community (not to mention my own faith).

Fadhil wanted to practice his English. He kept reciting a poem he was trying to write for his wife's birthday. He wanted us to help him complete the last lines. When he broke off, it was to sing or pray aloud. He coaxed us to join him. We sang "Jesus Paid It All" and another song I didn't recognize, our words looping in and out, English and Arabic.

We passed the intersection where the road split to Mosul, and I watched how the lake of Mosul Dam shimmered under a rising moon. Evening deepened over us as we turned to head east toward Erbil. We kept the windows rolled down to feel the rush of air over our sweat-soaked bodies.

The car grew quiet. Fadhil looked to Kilim, motioning to Insaf and me seated in the backseat: "We have Canadian and American. Let's sell them for a million dollars."

Kilim smiled and shot back, "Yes! And with the money we will serve the Lord."

They laughed and drove on into the night.

10

THE KEEPER
OF NAHUM'S TOMB

Alqosh, 2008

....

My soul yearns for my temple courtyards with great longing.

"ABNEY EQDAH," A HYMN FOR THE FEAST OF TABERNACLES
SUNG BY IRAQI JEW SALIM DAOUD

....

In 1948, the last of the Jews in Alqosh handed Sami Jajouhana's family the keys to the synagogue in the center of town. Beneath a crypt inside the synagogue lay the tomb of the Old Testament prophet Nahum.

Since the time of the Assyrian and Babylonian captivity, Jews had inhabited Alqosh, a hillside enclave nestled in the Bayhidhra Mountains at the northern tip of Nineveh Plains. The town had been a haven first for Jews and later for Christians, a world away from Baghdad, Mosul, and Basra, the larger centers of religion and commerce along Iraq's great rivers.

Alqosh seemed far removed from those sprawling cities, where attacks against Christians continued unabated. That was the story I'd been following since my time in the Nineveh Plains the year before. Now that I was back in Iraq, I wanted to visit towns like Alqosh, places that had become de facto safe havens for Christians fleeing the violence.

Alqosh represented what the Hebrews called *avar ha-nahar*, the land "beyond the river," the region along the Euphrates. After the fall of Jerusalem's second Temple in AD 70, Babylon became the spiritual, religious, and cultural epicenter for Judaism for more than a thousand years.[1] The places that drew them, like Alqosh, now were drawing me.

"Jews and Christians used to live here together, without worry or trouble," said Sami, whose family was descended from a long line of Assyrian believers. It was no surprise to him when Jewish families entrusted the prophet Nahum's tomb to his family's care, starting with his father.

The gravesite lay under a sheltered area of a synagogue that was otherwise falling apart. Most of its roof and some of its stone walls had crumbled. On the interior walls and outside over its doorways were Hebrew Scriptures carved in stone. But no one was left in Alqosh to interpret them.

As we talked, Sami showed me the square surrounding the tomb and synagogue. "Moshe, Saidi, Sarah, Machea, Zacchaeus, Naji, Maurice," Sami recited as he shuffled from door to door in sandals, pants, and a long white T-shirt worn loosely over his stout, muscular five-foot-six frame. These were the names of his childhood friends, and he tapped on the doorways of their now abandoned family homes as he called each one. They wanted to leave, he said. And now they had all died in other, faraway lands. Sami, in his war-torn land, had survived.

Nahum means "comfort." His short book, part of the Nevi'im that includes the Old Testament Minor Prophets, is a harsh word forecasting destruction to Nineveh's Assyrians. But the Assyrians' destruction would bring comfort for the Jews, their promised return to Israel, and the coming of a Messiah. "Behold, upon the mountains, the feet of him who brings good news,"[2] spoke Nahum.

When the Jews left Alqosh in 1948, the last to go was the rabbi with his family. He handed Sami's father the heavy skeleton keys to the synagogue's large iron doors, set in a stone archway leading through thick walls to the tomb. The rabbi, who lived directly across the narrow street from the entrance to the synagogue and tomb, also entrusted to Sami's family a leather ledger, an outsized book with old pages of names that Sami clutched under his arm as we talked. They were the names of the Jewish families who lived in Alqosh, including many who had lived there until recently, when they had been forced to leave a homeland that had been theirs for thousands of years. As I turned to survey the rocky ruins of the synagogue's wall from the town square, I realized that their expulsion didn't look so different from the experience of the Christians I was meeting in the twenty-first century.

+ + +

During the past five years, as I covered the wars in Iraq, Afghanistan, and elsewhere, I had learned many survival lessons—what food to eat, when to get in a car with a stranger and when not to, that sort of thing. But the most important lesson, I was discovering, was a lesson of the heart: how to be at home in a foreign land, at rest far from any comfort zone. Forging friendships with Insaf, Odisho Yousif, and others made that possible. Preparing for this trip to Iraq, I realized I was visiting friends along the way, not just covering a war.

That's how I came to bring along my twenty-year-old son on my 2008 trip. Drew had just begun his junior year of college, and he had accompanied me on reporting trips before. In northern Israel when he was ten years old, we found time to explore the old quarters of Jerusalem—but also got caught close to Hezbollah artillery fire at the Israeli border with Lebanon. Drew was a great traveling companion no matter the circumstances, learning Hebrew numbers from children his age while I interviewed their parents.

We had always wanted to return to the Middle East together, though most everyone told me I was crazy to take him away from college studies and into a war zone. But I knew my son. He was fearless and fiercely devoted to the stories that came from my work. Plus his love of antiquities and just about anything smelling of adventure made Iraq a must-see. After I'd visited Nahum's tomb with Insaf in 2007, I sent Drew a description. He wrote,

Isn't it just a great exercise in faith to see the physical dirt near his tomb, the mountains of which he spoke? We've been talking in our cultural heritage class about the *irrelevance* of historical accuracy when it comes to the "myths" of the Old Testament. Jesus said people would never believe, even if they were given signs, even after hearing Moses and the prophets. But how reassuring—on the other end—to behold with our own eyes a physical reality that matches the stories that otherwise live only in our heads. It's a reminder that one day we shall see in full.

As another reporting trip came together, I asked Drew to think about joining me. With the 2007 American surge widely deemed a success, I considered northern Iraq relatively safe. Contacts there said it would be okay to bring my son, and my husband agreed. Drew would miss a week of classes, not easy for a double major with an overloaded schedule. One day near the end of the summer while I was on the phone with an Assyrian priest, Drew showed up at my desk to press a note under my nose: "I can come."

When we reached Alqosh, our scheduled guide failed to show, but we found a young man from the town to take his place. Eder was an Assyrian Christian, a student at the University of Mosul. He spoke decent English, and before I could finish asking about his name, he interrupted me and said, "It means 'God's watchfulness over his people.'"

He and Drew talked over the area's archaeology and discussed classes they were taking in college. Eder led us on a brief tour of the city, and when I told him I wanted to know whether any Jews remained in Alqosh, he found Sami to explain the history of their disappearance. Sami was at home, directly across from the old synagogue—whose crumbling walls and Hebrew inscriptions stood as a testimony to the Jews' centuries-long presence in northern Iraq.

+ + +

The Torah recounts how "all Israel were reckoned by genealogies"[3] and how they were written in the Book of the Kings and carried away to

Babylon. In Alqosh the Jews came first under Assyrian and later Persian domination.

Sami stood in a long line of keepers who had guarded the treasures of Jewish faith and worship under endless conquerors, from the Assyrians, to the Persians, down to the Muslims. Through the time of the Abbasid caliphate—which flourished between about 750 and 1250—and beyond, the Jews in the Eastern Dispersion kept books of pedigrees, tracing their lineage back to King David in Israel, in accordance with custom and Jewish law. From Jerusalem, Ezra depended on this lineage when he sent for Levitical priests from Babylon. And as the Jewish people lived on in the east, *ever ha navar*, long after the Assyrian, Babylonian, and Persian empires fell, even Muslim caliphates revered the keeper of the book.

When Benjamin of Tudela, a famous Jewish traveler, visited Baghdad in the twelfth century, he found forty thousand Jews in the city of Baghdad and reported seven thousand living in the city of Mosul, among them appointed officials who served in the Abbasid caliphate. Benjamin met the head of one Jewish academy, a Levite, who traced his pedigree back to Moses. Amid the ruins of ancient Nineveh, which at that time stretched nearly fifty miles from outside Mosul to Erbil, he found "villages and hamlets" of many Jews. He visited the synagogues dedicated to the Old Testament figures known to both Jews and Christians: Ezra, Obadiah, Jonah, and Nahum.[4]

Benjamin also encountered Daniel, the son of Hisdai, who was venerated by Jews and Muslim rulers alike. His fellow Jews called Daniel "Our Lord, the Head of the Captivity of All Israel." The Muslims addressed him as *Saidna ben Daoud*, "Lord, son of David," and gave him a seal of office signifying that all of Mesopotamia was to salute him and obey his word.[5] Daniel had possession of the book of pedigrees going back as far as David, king of Israel.

Sami, in his day-old tee and his slouchy pants, was a different sort of keeper. He had his own pedigree. He always carried the leather binder, which displayed, in a way, the diminished fortunes for Christians and Jews.

I could not tell how old the book was. And since the Jews' departure, it had become more of a guest book. Sami wanted me to sign my name, and as I paged through it, I could see that nearly all of the recent visitors were American soldiers, most with Jewish names, all based at one time or another at Camp Freedom outside Mosul. Several, including an army chaplain, tried to raise funds to repair the synagogue. A U.S. construction contractor carried out a structural survey of the site, and Iraq's Department of Antiquities agreed to fund the $600,000 project—but nothing happened. The contractor was dispatched to Afghanistan, and the funds likely ended up lining someone's pocket in Baghdad.

+ + +

After the creation of the modern state of Israel, Sami Jajouhana's Jewish neighbors were forced out, along with nearly all the Jews in Arab lands. Many people saw this expulsion as ethnic cleansing that would veer toward genocidal violence before it was over.

Starting from captivity, the Arab Jews learned to hold their own in Mesopotamia. Throughout the centuries the Jews grew into prominent forces in finance, textiles, and culture. By the early twentieth century they made up one-third of Iraq's population. With independence from Great Britain in 1932, Iraq chose Yehezkel Sasson, a Jew, as its first minister of finance. "Hezkel," the popular nickname for the finance minister, became common slang: In the markets, Iraqi merchants called buyers and sellers who haggled too much over prices "hezkel."

The Jews by then were the largest and most prosperous ethnic group in Baghdad. Hebrew was one of Iraq's official languages, and the "Israelite community" was listed alongside other formally recognized communities of Arabs, Kurds, Turkmen, Muslims, Christians, Yazidis, and Sabaeans.

My older Iraqi friends, whether Muslim, Jewish, or Christian like Sami, remember those days. The Muslims and Jews, along with Armenians, Assyrians, and Europeans, would sit together at riverside cafés while waiters brought to the table salad and grilled *masgouf* fresh from the Tigris. Afterward the patrons paid for the meal in Indian rupees.

Nightlife in those days was rich and varied. The Iraqi National Symphony Orchestra performed classical European music as well as Arab folk pieces to sold-out audiences. The musicians' early instructors were Russian Jews, and the musicians were either Jewish or Christian.

Islamic teaching in the day prohibited playing instruments. That didn't stop Muslims from visiting nightclubs or secreting the new gramophones in their home parlors. Hdhairy Abou Aziz was a singer so famous that he had a one-hour radio program on Fridays from noon till one o'clock. "For this hour, all movement in Iraq stops," recalled Yeheskel Kojaman, a Jewish musician from Baghdad. "Everybody is in the coffee shop or the house, listening to Abou Aziz."[6]

With the arrival of Fritz Grobba, Hitler's new ambassador to Iraq, in 1932, Jewish life began to change. Grobba stoked pan-Arab nationalism and bought one of Baghdad's daily newspapers, which serialized *Mein Kampf* in Arabic.

Unlike European Jews, the Jews in Iraq had been considered fellow Semites to the Muslims who ruled in the Ottoman period. But by the late 1930s, Jews found themselves written out of Iraqi textbooks, sidelined in public affairs, and blamed for the Zionism taking root in Palestine. Anti-Jewish feeling spilled into the streets, where armed mobs targeted Jews, killing some and destroying their businesses.

World War II divided Iraq between pro-British Iraqi leaders and a pro-German army, which had both spiritual and political backing from the Mufti of Jerusalem, Haj Amin al-Husseini. In 1941 the Mufti relocated to Baghdad, where he declared jihad against British sympathizers and Jews. The Kurdish army in the north, along with a few Shia tribes in the south, refused to join in.

Iraqi soldiers and paramilitaries launched attacks on Baghdad's Jewish Quarter, starting on the eve of the feast of Pentecost. They pulled Jews off buses and beat them to death while Jewish families hid in their homes in Bataween, the Ottoman-era quarter inhabited by Jews and

Christians along the Tigris. Gunfire and sounds of slaughter breached their walls—the cries of women screaming as they were raped, babies crushed and children mutilated, stabbings and gunfire as old and young were killed. Two hundred Jews were killed in Bataween in one night, and no army, police, or British guards came to their aid.

The Jews suddenly found themselves living outside the protection of the law, fearful. Muslim overlords discriminated against them in business, marginalized them in public life, blocked them from politics, and threatened them with death. Any book of pedigrees no longer held sway in an Arab Muslim court. And like the Christians I'd met who were trying to elude the jihadists, Jews took the way of escape handed to them, quitting a homeland that had been theirs for thousands of years, even back to the time of Abraham.

With the creation of the modern state of Israel, Iraqi officials arranged for Jews to depart by planeloads, a vast displacement called Operation Ali Baba. By 1951 an estimated 110,000 Iraqi Jews, or about 80 percent of all the Jews living in Iraq, had left.[7] For thousands who could trace their lineage back millennia in Iraq, there would be no right of return.

At the time of the U.S. invasion in 2003, handfuls of Jews still lived in various parts of Iraq, including the north. But the last ordained rabbi in the country had died in 1996, and the only remaining synagogue in Baghdad closed just weeks before the U.S. invasion.[8] No official clergy remained, even to lead in reciting kaddish over their losses.

Saddam Hussein had renovated some of the oldest Jewish shrines, including the tomb of Jonah in Mosul. He posted guards to protect them, arguing they were revered also by Muslims. The support he gave Jewish sites was a way to stave off retaliatory strikes from Israel following the Gulf War. His Republican Guards looted the one remaining synagogue in Baghdad, confiscating at gunpoint its ancient prayer books and Torah parchments. In 2003 Americans found them in the basement of the Baghdad Intelligence Agency.

Sami confirmed there were no longer any Jews living in Alqosh, or anywhere in Nineveh Plains or Mosul. That left eight Jews in all of Iraq, as best I could tell. They resided in Baghdad, and most of them were elderly. They lived in hiding, and some of them claimed to be Christians, hanging crosses in their homes to conceal their Jewish identity. The Iraqi Jews living in London or in the United States could only sigh at this news and offer resigned caution: "First Saturday, then Sunday," they said, meaning first the Jews will disappear, then the Christians.

All that history made Sami important and emblematic to me. He stood grasping at the doorway to Nahum's synagogue, fingering its lock, bearing the remnants of both Jewish and Christian heritage in Mesopotamia. He was quite possibly the only person left in Iraq with a Jewish book of pedigrees and memories of life in the shadow of both synagogue and church, where Jews and Christians lived side by side, their children playing together and the church bells mingling with Sabbath rituals.

✦ ✦ ✦

After we visited with Sami and saw Nahum's tomb, Eder led us on foot down the hilly, narrow streets of Alqosh's old city to one of the churches, where doors were open and we heard singing. As we crossed the threshold into St. George's Chaldean Church, we saw the worshipers gathered around a baptismal font, singing in Aramaic. A priest in a white cassock chanted vows, and the worshipers chanted back. Then he lifted high from the water a dripping, naked infant. The priest held the crying infant boy above the crowd and turned in a circle for all to see. A few cameras flashed, but the gathering paused only to hear the priest chant, then joined him again in song. Women trilled, and the priest handed the boy to his father as his mother reached out to enfold him in a blanket.

The church moved as one to pews, and the chants resumed. The young men sat jammed into rows at the back of the sanctuary, their hair slicked down and their pressed white shirts tucked into black pants, spiffed up just as young men might be at a church in America. The older worshipers, mostly women, filled pews in the front. Everyone sang out a cappella chants sung in the Syriac dialect of Aramaic. The Iraqi church was scattered everywhere, and those in the pews had migrated from many other towns. But everyone knew the Chaldean chants. Their ancient words held these worshipers together.

We lingered, then made our way back out into the street. An old woman in a simple printed dress leaned against a doorway and watched us, and young boys laughed as they raced under an archway, then moved on.

"Many people here now are coming from Mosul and Baghdad because they feel they can be safe here from the kidnappings," Eder explained. "This is our village, and we know everyone. Here there are no strangers."

Drew interrupted him, "We're strangers."

"No," Eder laughed. "You're friends. That's truth."

+ + +

Eder suggested we visit Rabban Hormizd Monastery, two miles outside of town and up a mountain of hairpin turns. We hiked Alqosh's narrow roads, the doorsteps of houses coming right down to the street, and passed hills of cemeteries topped with crosses to find our driver and make our way there.

The air cooled as we reached the old monastery and headed into its stone entrance. Rabban Hormizd is a series of caves carved into a solid-rock mountain, in recent years home to more hikers than hermits. Eder knew the way through the caves and urged us into the darkness. He held a small penlight, and Drew dug into his backpack and pulled out a reading headlamp, which he fastened on before following Eder. I walked closely behind them, clutching my notebook and trying to take it all in by staying near their small circles of light.

We descended rough, uneven steps to a room of walls washed in some pale and peeling pigment, visible through holes in the walls that let in daylight. High up on the walls were faded ancient frescoes and a framed portrait we assumed was Rabban Hormizd himself. From there we descended into darker and darker rooms, a narrow hallway with chambers—dank cells of dirt and stone where the ascetics of old had lived and died—hewn from the rock on either side. Eder told us that many patriarchs of the ancient Assyrian church had been interred in some of the chambers.

In 1890, an Englishman working for the British Museum named Sir E. A. Thompson Wallis Budge visited Hormizd. He reported that the monastery housed ten monks who lived without doors to block the elements or fire to create heat and light. The monks ate meat only on Easter and Christmas Day. On other days the usual fare was lentils and dark bread. Budge said the monks seldom if ever took wine, drinking instead rainwater collected in rock cisterns.

Historians say the monastery, founded in AD 640, flourished until the tenth century, and again from 1551 on, when it became an official residence for the patriarchs of the Church of the East. At one time in the mid-1800s, as many as eighty monks made their home there, some of them living in niches carved into the face of the rock, reached by small terraces and without doorways or other protection.

Like Mar Matti, Rabban Hormizd at one time had a library rich in manuscripts, where the monks studied the letters written by the apostles of Jesus and recorded them in Syriac. The Ottomans had looted the library, but as recently as 1966 a church scribe was still at work copying the Syriac manuscripts archived at the monastery.

Inside Rabban Hormizd, we continued down dark passages until we met a wall. Eder confessed he didn't know the way beyond it. So we backtracked and emerged into fading afternoon light, the sun dipping behind the mountain and casting shadows beneath the clouds over Nineveh Plains.

Down the mountain at the crossroads leading back to Alqosh, Drew and I said good-bye to Eder. He stuck out his hand to shake Drew's hand first—a gesture he'd learned from American soldiers—then mine, then Drew's again.

"We will meet again," he said. "And you will be back." We agreed hopefully and made a quick exchange of e-mail addresses. But I never heard from Eder again, though I e-mailed him more than once and thought often of his young exuberance and ready smile for strangers. I thought of his solidarity with the Jewish and Christian history in Alqosh, and of his sturdy resolve to go against the dangers lurking each time he made his way to class at the University of Mosul.

Over the next several days in September, the month of Ramadan, Drew and I made our way to other ancient shrines and found them abuzz with the needs of newly displaced Iraqi Christians. When we turned into the road leading up to Mar Matti, the monastery, the wind kicked up, and we walked up the hill pushing against it.

The number of families on hand surprised us. Usually they came only for an afternoon in the cooler air, enjoying a place to picnic away from the fasting of Ramadan. But in recent months many Christian families had fled to Mar Matti. Many more would do so over the next year, escaping terror and violence.

We found Brother Yousif Fahmi there, still superintending the monks as well as the new arrivals. "Now we are five monks, and our bishop is here. And we have students who come for training," he said.

Since I had last seen Brother Yousif, his own brother had been killed. Insurgents had gunned him down in the street near the family's home in Mosul, and his parents had to run away to one of the Nineveh villages. Brother Yousif wouldn't say where they were, and he was noticeably more cautious, nervous. Mar Matti may have been a refuge high above the Nineveh Plains, but he worried over the dangers to come.

11

A CHURCH OF MARTYRS

Mosul, 2008

....

The enemy has a say about when wars end.

LT. COL. JOHN NAGL (RETIRED)

....

Heading to work for Eveline Aoraha involved wrapping a handgun in a soft printed scarf and thrusting it into the bottom of her black leather purse. She always zipped the bag.

On a sunny Indian-summer morning in mid-September, Eveline and her driver picked me up in Dohuk on her commute to Mosul. Drew did not accompany me; it was too dangerous. Instead, an Iraqi friend of Odisho Yousif's had arranged for Drew to spend the day in the hills of Kurdistan near the safer Turkish border.

Eveline was one of three Christians on a governing council of forty-one in Nineveh Province. Since 2004, terrorist insurgents had killed twelve of her fellow council members. Mosul was the provincial capital, but persistent threats had forced her two years earlier to move from the city to a town fifty miles north with her husband and children.

Ten minutes south of Dohuk, we entered Nineveh Province. The driver guided the car west toward Mosul Dam and then south along its edge, where it dumped the Tigris River into an empty landscape dotted with sheep grazing on brown scrub. Trucks loaded with cement roared past, taking roads west across the mountains to Syria or east toward Qaraqosh, which was the largest city out in Nineveh Plains and mostly Christian.

Eveline wore a neatly pressed, moss-green skirt that ended just below the knee and a coordinating jacquard-patterned jacket. Over her black blouse hung a gold cross necklace. Her dark hair was cut neatly around her face, which was carefully made up, including mahogany-red lipstick that she checked in the rearview mirror. From the backseat she leaned forward every few minutes to speak to the driver, whose broad shoulders seemed to fill the front of the sedan. Eveline spoke Syriac to him until we approached a checkpoint, where she would switch to Arabic as we drew close to Iraqi police.

As we drove through villages, she kept a running commentary for me. When we passed one, she said, "They have a church, but nobody can go to pray there." As another approached, she pointed and said, "It used to be a Christian village, but it was Arabized by Saddam."

Power lines stretched into the distance, and Eveline noted that electricity was better here than it was in Baghdad—running ten and twelve hours a day in this part of Iraq, thanks to the proximity of Mosul Dam, one of the largest dams in the Middle East, located just upstream on the Tigris.

Overall, the year 2008 was better for staying alive in Iraq than 2007 had been. In a bad month a year earlier, three hundred Iraqis would die. This year Iraqi deaths from violence were averaging less than a hundred a month. But even though fewer killings were happening in Baghdad, more were taking place in Mosul.

Two days before we headed there, a suicide bomber had killed two policemen and wounded forty others. Insurgents had killed more than sixty residents of Mosul in the month of September by the time I arrived—and the month still had one week left in it. For a city that once had 1.7 million residents—Iraq's second-largest—it easily had the country's highest per capita rate of insurgency.

IN IRAQ IN 2007, Insaf Safou and I visited the Alqosh synagogue, which had been left in the hands of Christian caretakers when the Jewish community fled Iraq following World War II.

Danny, kidnapped in Mosul, was held until his father negotiated a ransom for his release—just $750.

Odisho Yousif raised money from a worldwide network of Assyrians to help oppressed Iraqi Christians—only to be kidnapped himself in 2006. Here, he describes his kidnapping and escape.

DISPLACED GIRLS leave for school from a bombed-out building in Baghdad.

The year after visiting the Alqosh synagogue with Insaf, I returned with my son, Drew, where we met Sami, the keeper of the synagogue housing the prophet Nahum's tomb.

An Iraqi army escort accompanied provincial council member Eveline Aoraha and me when we left Mosul on September 22, 2008. With two bombings and shootings in a main market that day, Iraqi authorities insisted on the military convoy protection and an armed soldier inside our car. Here he holds his AK-47 pointed out the window.

AMERICAN TEACHER Jeremiah Small with Kurdish friends in Sulaymaniyah (Iraqi Kurdistan), months before he was shot by a student in his classroom at Classical School of the Medes

Canon Andrew White with members of his congregation at St. George's Church in Baghdad

Women worshiping at the Christian and Missionary Alliance Church in Baghdad

Muthafar Yacoub—formerly an exile, now a pastor—pledged not to leave Baghdad, even after surviving bombings and terrorist threats.

ISIS FIGHTERS commandered an Iraqi armored vehicle after Iraq's army fled during the June 2014 takeover of Mosul, Iraq's second largest city.

ISIS leader Abu Bakr al-Baghdadi, in his first public appearance after the ISIS takeover of Mosul, delivers a sermon at Mosul's Grand Mosque, July 4, 2014.

A HOME IN MOSUL IS TAGGED

with graffiti—the Arabic letter *n*—used to identify Christians. This letter stands for *Nasara*, or Nazarene, the name Christians are known by in Arabic.

Insaf Safou holds the baby of a displaced family outside Erbil in June 2014. The necklace, with a gold pendant map of Iraq, is one she always wears.

A group of more than 150 Kurdish Yazidis set up camp in an unfinished building in northern Iraq. The Yazidis have been systematically driven from their homeland by ISIS militants.

Displaced Iraqi Christians line up for food in the parking lot of a school camp in northern Iraq.

SUNNI MUSLIMS FLEE RAMADI a few weeks before the capital of Anbar Province fell to ISIS in May 2015. More than five hundred Iraqis were killed during the takeover. Displaced Iraqis were forced to cross the Euphrates over pontoon bridges to escape.

ISIS DESTROYED the eighty-year-old Church of the Virgin Mary in Tal Nasri, one of dozens of churches in the Khabur River area of Syria destroyed by the terrorist group starting in February 2015. ISIS kidnapped more than two hundred Christians from the villages, later executing at least three men, with most of the remainder in captivity eight months later.

Members of the Assyrian Christian militia Dwekh Nawsha on patrol in Telskuf, a Nineveh Plains city captured by ISIS and then retaken by Kurdish peshmerga with U.S. air strikes in 2014.

Destruction in Telskuf reveals an upper-room sanctuary for Christians in a home overtaken by ISIS before U.S. air strikes routed the militants.

I spoke with Najeeb Daniel and his wife, Dalal, in the Erbil shopping mall where they lived after ISIS forced them from their home in Qaraqosh. The mall has been converted into a temporary residence for hundreds of displaced families.

DWEKH NAWSHA FIGHTERS, including this American who had joined the militia, face ISIS-controlled territory on the front line in Baqofa. In the distance, ISIS earthmovers can be seen digging trenches for the defense of nearby Mosul.

"The center of the Islamic State is in Mosul," said Eveline. "The terrorists want to stop life here, and to stop development."

Eveline called her slain colleagues on the provincial council "martyrs to democracy," and each time one was gunned down, the local parties put forward a substitute in his or her place. The council now included Arab Muslims, Assyrian Christians, and Kurds. The oldest was eighty and the youngest a thirty-four-year-old veterinarian who was a wife and a mother. I made the trip to Mosul with Eveline to try to understand what made them keep going in the face of so much violence.

Eveline preferred not to talk about the dangers she personally faced. She wanted to believe the experiment in Iraqi democracy could succeed; the militants could be tamed; and representative government, starting at the local level where she served, could survive. In conversation she swept aside questions about her own safety and the obvious fact that among all of Mosul's political, religious, and ethnic factions, Christians were its most vulnerable. Sectarian violence was killing Muslims, but it was wiping out the city's Christian community.

+ + +

It didn't start this way in Mosul. Unlike Anbar Province, where the insurgency began early on, Mosul had seemed to thrive at the beginning of the war. David Petraeus, who commanded the 101st Air Assault Division, took charge of Nineveh in 2003, and the locals soon adopted him as something of a governor. In 2004 Petraeus and his troops walked the streets of Mosul freely, even at night. And unlike U.S. commanders elsewhere, Petraeus welcomed former Baathists once they signed a pledge of good faith. This allowed the Nineveh government, unlike that in nearly every other province, to function.

With a trained local cadre, Petraeus established an Iraqi Civil Defense Corps, the first in the country: a homegrown security force of Kurds and Arabs who successfully trained and policed the city alongside the 101st. They patrolled Nineveh's rural areas, where brigade commanders served as wardens over swaths of desert and farmland, settling tribal feuds and land disputes while doling out money for local civil improvements. Using some of the funds confiscated from Saddam's coffers in the invasion, they began 4,500 reconstruction projects.

Petraeus understood the challenges ahead as few others did. "We're in a race with ourselves," he told Marine Corps veteran Bing West. "Now we're seen as liberators. Eventually we'll be seen as occupiers."[1]

Nineveh's deputy governor, Khasro Goran, told me nearly the same thing. "The first year with Petraeus in Mosul was good. All the people see Americans as liberators, not occupiers—visiting houses, waving to children, eating with them in their homes."

Mosul had all the flavors of Iraq. It had a historic mix of Sunnis, Kurds, Arabs, Jews, and Christians. It had a progressive business establishment. It had proximity to oil fields. Crime was low, and relations with occupying U.S. troops began well. In Mosul a military career could be made. And for Petraeus, at least initially, it was. The city was poised to model what the rest of a new Iraq could look like. The 101st had led the way on D-Day, turning the tide of World War II, and it looked as if the airborne division might also create its own beachhead in Iraq.

But the gains unraveled. Starting with Ambassador Paul Bremer, the Americans in Baghdad overruled Petraeus's efforts at a civilian-military partnership. They wanted everything run out of Baghdad. That meant rejecting a federalist approach, one that appeared better suited to Iraq, in favor of a centralized one.

Next, the Shiite-led government of Nouri al-Maliki in Baghdad installed a mostly Shiite police and army presence in Mosul, which is mostly Sunni, just as U.S. troops began pulling back from the city proper. The new Iraqi army sidelined the local forces trained under Petraeus, stirring resentment. The Sunni Arab soldiers and former Baathists reinstated under Petraeus had nowhere to turn.

By the time I made the commute to Mosul with Eveline, city officials said about 250,000 residents had left. Many, perhaps the majority, were Christians. Some found a way out of the country to Syria or beyond. Others moved north to safer areas, as Eveline and her family had done, making as-needed commutes into town for business. Like Eveline, they came in by day to work or to attend universities, then returned each afternoon, well before dusk, to the plains and cities farther north.

We were about twenty miles north of Mosul when our driver stopped in Telskuf, where I had visited Sister Mary Dominic a year earlier, to pick up another provincial council member, a Yazidi named Kassan. As Eveline and I continued to talk behind him, he avoided eye contact with me and stayed quiet, speaking up only when a Yazidi wedding party of about seven cars loomed ahead of us on the two-lane highway. Each car in the party seemed to have ten passengers or more, men dressed in suits and women in brightly colored dresses and head wraps, with tassels and ribbons seeming to flutter out the windows.

We passed turnoffs to other largely Christian towns—Baqofa, Batnaya, and Bartella—then came to Tel Kaif, eleven miles outside Mosul. "Muslims put marks on the houses of Christians here," said Eveline, as we drove slowly through the town of ten thousand. She said the men who spray-painted these symbols were caught by Iraqi soldiers and jailed in Mosul.

"It's a Christian town, but Christian families are threatened by terrorists," Eveline explained. Christians were fleeing Mosul *to* towns like Tel Kaif, "but it's getting dangerous," she said. "Wherever there are Christians, they come and chase them."

Eveline believed Nineveh Plains should be made into an autonomous region for Christians, with its own Christian council and Christian police force. "We cannot trust the Iraqi constitution," she said. "It's religious, not democratic, and it favors Islamic law. Now we want our own constitution and everything separated."

The hour was early, but Tel Kaif hummed with activity: women going to market and men trading stories before the sun got too hot. Sheep edged nimbly along the streets, kicking up dust clouds that settled on the stacks of watermelons and onions the vendors were selling by the roadside. A sign for Tuborg beer hung above a store with an elevated concrete-slab entryway. The doors of the store were flung open, and a man was arranging bags of pistachios on a table in the open doorway. Another shopkeeper carefully lined up the liter soda bottles still being reused for fuel ("benzine," the locals called it) that ran their generators and sometimes their cars.

The Chaldean Sacred Heart Church dominated the city center, and cemeteries with tombstones topped by stone crosses dotted the old hillsides. Historically one of the largest Assyrian towns in northern Iraq, Tel Kaif had swelled to about thirty thousand residents under Saddam's Arabization plans. Some reports said Tel Kaif was 90 percent Christian; others said it was now fifty-fifty. The numbers mattered, but no one had carried out a census in decades. With Christians from Baghdad, Basra, and Mosul filling the old villages of Nineveh Plains, Eveline and others contended that the Christians deserved more than three representatives on the provincial council.

By now the majority of Tel Kaif's residents had emigrated—mostly to Detroit. The Chaldean community in Michigan could rival Nineveh, initially drawn by jobs in the auto industry when Iraq was a U.S. ally, back in the fifties and sixties. The number leaving grew with each war—the Iran-Iraq War, the first Gulf War, and the current war—as life became more challenging for the Chaldean community. The older Chaldeans in Detroit remembered weddings that turned into village festivals and churches packed out with thousands for two Masses every day. Now church attendance could be measured in the hundreds, but the priests also taught daily classes of about a dozen to read and write in Aramaic.

"The church will be here. It's not going anywhere," said Asa'd Hannona, one of the priests. "There always will be some Chaldeans in Tel Kaif."[2]

As we drove out of town, we began to see more checkpoints manned by soldiers with tactical armored vests, hard helmets, and machine guns. A few miles from Mosul, Eveline unwrapped the gun from the bottom of her purse, handed it up to the driver over his shoulder, and smoothed the scarf over her head. I pulled a dull blue scarf from my bag and did likewise, twisting the ends several times around my neck and tucking them in.

It was only the second time I'd felt the need for a head covering in Iraq. I wore a long skirt and long sleeves, too, in obedience to the Muslim restrictions taking hold across the city. Only a few years before, women in Mosul wore Western clothes. Now even Christian women did not take to the streets without head coverings.

Our driver clenched the gun in his left hand and clutched the steering wheel with his right, and he accelerated without turning his head. Inside the car, conversation fell off and we grew quiet. I wrote in my notebook: "Go together. Go fast."

The landscape was changing as we neared the city. Trash littered both sides of the road, and as we came alongside the Tigris, we passed gravel berms topped by razor wire. These soon gave way to Hesco barriers about six feet tall, filled with sand and gravel. They formed a continuous wall along the waterway, protecting against IEDs but also blocking the view, giving us the sense that we were entering some kind of gauntlet instead of a once-beautiful city.

On the western bank of the river we could see the hulking ruins of Bashtabiya Castle, a twelfth-century edifice that formed the oldest surviving part of the city walls. In the 1740s, after invading Persians laid waste to villages in Nineveh Plains, the Christians hurried to Mosul to fight the Persians. They battled alongside Ottoman troops from the outcroppings, and at one point Christian masons built up the walls as quickly as they were bombed by Nadir Shah and his Persian Army. During a forty-day siege, they formed a line of defense on behalf of the Ottoman empire that even its Muslim pashas admitted was crucial to saving the city.[3]

Glancing at Eveline, I asked, "Is it okay to take a photo?"

"Taking photos is not a problem, but your skirt above the knee is," Eveline replied coolly. I smoothed down my skirt, suddenly aware of men walking beside us, glancing sideways into our car.

The ruins of Nimrud and remnants of ancient Nineveh lay on the eastern banks of the Tigris, rising like monuments of dust. Early excavators reported that the walls ran at one time from present-day Mosul to Erbil: fifty miles across flatlands.

The western banks of the Tigris coming into Mosul had once been lined with parks and picnic grounds. Now they were closed, broken down, or mostly empty. A Ferris wheel sat idle, and outdoor restaurants were boarded up. Traffic had slowed, with multiple lines of cars converging to jam into a single lane with checkpoints. These were manned by Iraqi and U.S. soldiers armed with M16s and handguns shoved slantwise into the front of their armored vests. The soldiers searched every car, demanding to see identification and to know the business of the drivers. Some intersections were blocked by American military personnel mounted in parked MRAPs, armored Mine Resistant Ambush Protected vehicles designed to withstand IEDs. The U.S. soldiers sat tall and broad shouldered, some wearing mirrored sunglasses; otherwise they were indistinguishable from the Iraqi soldiers, wearing the same desert camo and vests, their heads entirely covered in black knit masks. Only their eyes showed through small slits. Overhead, Black Hawk and Apache helicopters crawled across the sky.

We inched across Ninawa Bridge, an old span with single lanes of stalled traffic in each direction. Walkways on either side were full of men in a hurry, making better time across the bridge than the cars. In the center of Mosul all the hotels were closed, and many shops shut down by midday, Eveline explained. A man crossed the street in front of us carrying a mattress on his head, and women rushed along sidewalks to vegetable stands that sat dark beneath loose canopies stretched over a wide square. The only activity in Mosul was business, residents on necessary errands or unavoidable commerce. The lots for soccer and other games were vacant, and no one idled long enough for conversation.

It was the month of Ramadan, which normally meant everyone would stay indoors in the daytime and venture out to eat and celebrate an end to the fast at sundown. But Mosul was under a nightly curfew starting at 9 p.m., and few restaurants dared to open to serve the *iftar* meal, a large and lavish fast-breaking meal that in other parts of the country began after nine and sometimes lasted until two in the morning.

Once across the bridge, our driver raced us through the narrow streets of central Mosul, taking tight turns without braking and then swinging into a gated government office building just as electric gates yawned open to make way for the car. Even inside the locked-down compound, soldiers met us at the car doors with their weapons out. One pressed his hand onto my head and propelled me to the doorway and inside the building. We hurried down a hallway with windows all along one side. The windows were covered in black curtains that parted occasionally, the eerie midmorning darkness broken here and there by painfully bright shafts of rising sun. The soldiers' weapons jangled against their belts and against the carabiners they used to affix squawking walkie-talkies at their waists. Just as we turned into the provincial council chambers, the lights went out.

+ + +

In January a massive explosion detonated by insurgents in an abandoned building had killed sixty people—all civilians. It wounded 280 people and flattened several buildings in Mosul's Zinjeli neighborhood. Gunmen opened fire on police who arrived, and a suicide bomber targeted Mosul's police chief, who came to investigate. The bomber killed him and two other policemen.

The incident sparked a new phase of war with the insurgents, and Prime Minister Maliki ordered reinforcements to be sent to Mosul. Al-Qaeda responded with more attacks on military personnel. They killed five U.S. soldiers on patrol in the city before the month was out.

Roadside bombings increased, and once-docile neighborhoods of Mosul became war zones. West Mosul, where al-Qaeda appeared to be headquartered, became a warren of blasted-out buildings with glassless windows, bolted storefronts, and lifeless streets, apart from occasional bursts of gunfire. Streets fanning out from the area were cratered from

IED blasts, and broken water mains sent water bubbling into gray slurries that mixed with dust and gravel. Those streets abutted central Mosul and the Old City, with its iconic Clock Church and the twin domes of the Latin Church.

The Christian quarters were largely undefended and became easy targets for al-Qaeda and its local Sunni adherents. Kidnappings, killings, and bombings in broad daylight became commonplace. By targeting church leaders, al-Qaeda terrorized everyone else. In 2005 Chaldean Catholic archbishop George Yasilious was kidnapped and then released. A year later Orthodox priest Boulos Iskander was kidnapped and beheaded. On the first Sunday in January, insurgent groups attacked four churches at once. A car bomb near Maryam al-Adhra Church in northeastern Mosul exploded first, wounding four people and damaging the church building. Another bomb-rigged car parked near Mar Yousif Church detonated, damaging the church but leaving no casualties. In central Mosul explosions went off near a monastery, and a fourth bombing took place at Meskantah Church—also damaging buildings but leaving no dead or wounded.

Residents grew to fear the smell of cinnamon. Militants packed homemade explosives inside a sack of spices, their detonators connected to a cell phone to be triggered by a remote call. Steel balls and stray pieces of discarded iron, such as a fencepost ornament, were placed around the explosives to maximize shrapnel from the blast, killing and maiming as many as possible.

Assaults continued. In February armed gunmen ambushed Archbishop Paulos Faraj Rahho, the leader of the Chaldean Catholic church in northern Iraq. Rahho had just completed the Stations of the Cross procession at the Cathedral of the Holy Spirit in Mosul's Bakir neighborhood when kidnappers sprayed his car with bullets, wounding him in the leg, and pulled him from the car, killing his driver and two companions.

Rahho had survived previous threats. In 2004 insurgents marched him from his official residence and forced him to watch while they torched it. Later, gunmen on the street stopped him, but Rahho kept walking—daring them to shoot. In February, as kidnappers held him at gunpoint and then stuffed him into the trunk of a car, he managed to pull out his cell phone and call the church, instructing his colleagues not to pay ransom. "He believed that this money would not be paid for good works and would be used for killing and more evil actions," one of them said.[4] No ransom was paid, reportedly. A month later, his body turned up in a shallow grave on a side street at the edge of town.

Despite the danger, thousands turned out for the sixty-five-year-old's funeral, jamming the church sanctuary and spilling into an outside courtyard. Rahho was beloved even beyond his native Mosul. He was warm and compassionate, with a biting sense of humor.

Born in Mosul to a Chaldean Catholic family with roots in the ancient Church of the East, Rahho had traveled far and wide, studying in Baghdad and then in Rome. But he felt called to return to Mosul, content to be a local pastor to the city's estimated 20,000 to 30,000 Christians. In Tel Kaif he built the Chaldean Sacred Heart Church I'd passed on the way into the city with Eveline. He also opened an orphanage for children with disabilities.

Rahho was well regarded in the Muslim community, too. After Islamic militants burned down Rahho's home, a local imam offered him shelter at a mosque. But the archbishop could be outspoken on behalf of the Christian community. He opposed the draft constitution, uneasy about Article 2 (the so-called "time bomb," in the words of another clergyman), which made Islam the official religion of Iraq.

He could be outspoken, too, about the unjust pressures Muslims imposed on Christians. Asked by a reporter about the dilemma facing his fellow believers to leave, convert to Islam, or pay jizya, he said, "We, Christians of Mesopotamia, are used to religious persecution and pressures by those in power. After Constantine, persecution ended only for Western Christians, whereas in the East threats continued. Even today we continue to be a church of martyrs."[5]

For the Christians in Mosul and in all of Iraq, the death of Archbishop

Rahho was a point of no return, a point beyond which no one who claimed to be a Christian could feel safe. When I met Iraqi refugees later in Syria, they would cite his death and the date his body was found, March 13, as the moment when they decided to leave Iraq, when there was no longer any reason to stay.

"Be informed that we will cut your heads and leave your dead bodies with no organs and no heads in your stores and houses," read one threat letter I was shown by a family who'd fled Mosul for Syria. "We know your houses and we know your family. We will kill you one after the other. Depart the Muslim areas." Such letters would be printed in bulk; signed by "al-Mujahideen," "al-Jihad," "al-Tawheed company" or other militant groups; and shoved under a front doorway or left in a stairwell.

Women received threatening messages on their cell phones telling them to stop working. Kidnappings became so common in Mosul that their ransom notes simply demanded *daftar*, slang which everyone knew meant $10,000 in ransom. Some families, after leaving Iraq for Syria or Turkey, found that militants could still reach them by phone. But some believed their only option was to leave. As one dad told me, "To stay is to be killed."

The pace of fighting and terrorism continued in Mosul through the summer, slowing only when American soldiers shot and killed Abu Khalaf, al-Qaeda's leader in Mosul and an associate of Abu Musab al-Zarqawi, the leader of al-Qaeda in Iraq whom American forces had killed in 2006. Thanks to the success of the U.S.-led surge, al-Qaeda in Iraq had been reduced by most estimates from a terrorist army numbering 12,000 to just 1,200 fighters. It was a victory that went largely unreported and unnoticed in the United States, where a presidential campaign was under way and the withering collapse of housing and financial markets was upending the U.S. economy.

✛ ✛ ✛

The heavy military presence we observed on our drive through Mosul testified to the terror the remaining insurgents had unleashed on the city. Once we were inside the provincial chambers, Eveline and I made our way to the office of Khasro Goran, the Kurdish deputy governor of Nineveh Province. The power was out, so during our hour-long discussion, I never saw his face.

"Because of the success of the surge in Anbar, Diyala, and Baghdad, the insurgents come up to Mosul," Goran told me.

Goran was trying to forge the way for his fellow Kurds to recapture influence in Nineveh politics after they had been forced from the region by Saddam. Article 140 of the Iraqi constitution required a referendum on Kirkuk and other "disputed territories," which included Nineveh, Diyala, and Saladin Provinces, to determine whether they would become part of the Kurdistan region in the north. Saddam had forcibly removed Kurds and other minorities in favor of Arabs in all these disputed areas, which also contained the most extensive of Iraq's oil fields, adding to the financial stakes. Kurds like Goran needed support from Assyrian Christians like Eveline and other minorities—alliances that would work in their favor once the referendum, already twice delayed, was held. In return, Goran and other Kurds became strong advocates for protecting the Christian population. To hold the referendum required normalization and a census, Goran noted. "We don't have any of these."

When I spoke to Duraid Kashmoula, the governor of Nineveh Province (and a Sunni Muslim), he voiced support for Christians too. "We are protecting the churches when we learn of a threat to bomb them," he said, fingering prayer beads as we talked in the dark. Eveline said Christians were divided, with some supporting leading Sunni politicians while others sided with the Kurds. That left them vulnerable to intimidation and violence from all sides.

Militants also targeted elected officials like Kashmoula, along with their families. In his four years in office, Kashmoula's seventeen-year-old son and two brothers had been gunned down in Mosul. He himself had escaped three bombings—narrowly, he told me. A dozen of his bodyguards had been killed, and just weeks before we met, his administrative assistant had been killed.

Despite all the visible efforts at security, during the same week I arrived in Mosul, insurgents bombed the house of a member of parliament, wounding bystanders (the lawmaker himself was in Baghdad at the time); and they set off a bomb near a soccer field, killing five children. They injured a resident in a roadside bomb attack and detonated a vehicle near a police building, killing two and wounding about forty, including fifteen policemen. Before the week was out, gunmen killed an Assyrian Christian named Bashar al-Hazin as he walked from his church to his home.

"We are always adjusting," Eveline told me, "because life in Mosul now feels like life on another planet." Nearly all the Christian women now wore *abayas* in public, their heads and sometimes their faces covered to make them indistinguishable from Muslim women. Militants in the city insisted that even store-window mannequins wear head coverings. And they told restaurant owners to stop putting cucumbers and tomatoes beside one another on a plate. It was sexually suggestive.

It was a radical shift, indeed, for Christians like Eveline who'd grown up in the tightly knit community of central Mosul, where most neighbors were also Christians. Three or more churches were within a five-minute walk of nearly everyone. In one, Mass was said in an Eastern Syriac dialect; in another, in the Western Syriac dialect; and in later churches built by the Dominican missionaries, in Latin.

Suha Rassam, a Mosul native and Chaldean Catholic who taught medicine in Baghdad before emigrating to England, wrote about her childhood this way: "We found no difficulty in praying in any of the churches, partly because the readings were in Arabic, and partly because we had been instructed in the essential elements of the Mass, but mainly because that was the status quo. We prayed in Arabic with our parents, and grandmother told us different Bible stories before going to bed. Our picnicking was in ancient monasteries where we were introduced to the stories of the martyrdom of their founders or patron saints."[6]

Like many others, Rassam had attended a primary school run by Dominican nuns, but then she went to a state-run high school where she was educated alongside Muslims. "We received equal opportunities for secular education," she said.[7] Religious education was required for Muslims only, who attended a class on the Quran in the last hour of school, allowing Rassam and other Christian students to go home early. She went to college in Baghdad, studying medicine alongside Muslims while living with French and Iraqi nuns.

Iraqi schools taught the history of ancient Mesopotamia but seldom if ever mentioned the presence of Christians in Iraq before Islam. It just wasn't in the textbooks. Nor was the role Christians played in an emerging Arab Abbasid civilization mentioned, nor in modern times the background of the dominant Arab Baath Socialist Party, whose founder was a Christian. Suha Rassam said the lack of church history available in Iraq led her to do research elsewhere, eventually getting a postgraduate degree in Eastern Christianity while in London. For Iraqis without the opportunity to study abroad, the absence of a place in Iraq's formal history relegated them over time to second-class citizenship, and it left both Christians and Muslims ignorant of what had come before in their country's long history.

Against that backdrop, it was not so surprising that in the chaos of Mosul in 2008, terrorists had freedom to target Christians with impunity.

Leaving Mosul that day, we learned there had been more bombings and a shooting in the market. Smoke rose from West Mosul, where al-Qaeda had its headquarters. Our driver and his handgun weren't going to be enough.

The provincial officials wanted Eveline and me to have an army escort out of town. So two armed trucks, one behind us and one ahead, sped us past the clog of checkpoints and traffic jams. I kept my head down but could see the Iraqi army pickup in front of us, a machine gunner mounted in the back bed with four soldiers riding sidesaddle, all holding AKs and wearing balaclavas, jumping up in the truck bed to motion cars out of the way. Their sirens seemed to draw more attention than deflect it, but we were in a hurry to get out of the city. Knowing what has to be done puts away fear, and we knew we had to get out of town. Like so many other Christians from Mosul were doing, we held our breath and sped north to safety, out into the hot plains of Nineveh.

+ + +

Back in Dohuk, I appreciated more than ever the peace of the Kurdistan provinces and the sight of my son when we reconnected at our hotel. It was a different world from Mosul. The sun was going down, which meant Muslims would break the day's Ramadan fast with the traditional *iftar* meal. We headed to the lawn outside the hotel where long tables were set with white tablecloths. While we drank tea served in small pinched glasses and waited for platters of food, Drew told me about his day. Two trusted Assyrian acquaintances had driven him north, where he met village boys near Zakho, a city at the Turkish border. He had struck up a conversation, asking them to teach him numbers and words in Arabic and Kurdish. Then he persuaded them to go swimming with him in the Khabur River downstream from Dalal Bridge, a structure built of river stones that dated to Roman times.

Back in our hotel room, Drew showed me video clips he'd taken of the boys jumping from rock outcroppings into the lazy water, laughing and calling out, "Hi, buddy!" It was a rarefied afternoon for a young American, swimming in cold water flowing down from the mountains of Ararat, jumping off ancient rocks with seemingly carefree Iraqi boys.

The fact remained: I'd left my son so I could travel under armed guard into one of the most dangerous cities in the world. He had headed to the hills with strangers for a swim in unknown waters. Yet somehow it unfolded for him like a day not so different from any summer day at a swimming hole. And it ended with platters of biryani and kebab, recounting our day over dinner as we might have done at home, only we were surrounded by Iraqis as the evening air cooled.

Entrusting my son to Iraqi acquaintances had been a way of coming to appreciate them for what we had in common, not viewing them as foreigners I would never understand. Apart from Drew's coming and from having to trust my only son to Arabs, Kurds, and Assyrians, it's a lesson I might not have learned. So much about being a reporter depends on having one's act together, being self-sufficient, and keeping an observer's distance. Traveling in a place like Iraq with one of my children along, even a child of twenty, made me more vulnerable, more dependent on others, more aware of my dependence on God to see us through.

Relationships deepened as a result. For years afterward, I would meet up with someone from that time, and they would smile in recognition. "Om al Drew!" they'd say—Drew's mother.

After a week in Iraq, I headed with Drew to the airport in Erbil. He would board a midnight flight for Istanbul to begin his journey back to the United States and college life. I knew he'd spend his layover in Istanbul sleeping on the airport floor with his backpack for a pillow. Then he would board another flight for the final leg home.

As Drew reached home, I would be heading into Syria on my own, where I planned to meet up with Iraqi refugees and to entrust myself to a string of drivers, church leaders, and aid workers I'd never met. There, standing in the dark outside the Erbil terminal, I hugged my son good-bye one more time, not wanting to let go. In a short span of long days, we had seen so much together: monasteries, caves, archaeological sites, cities of refuge, and cities in peril. The Iraqis I'd come to know were now his friends too. We'd even found time to spend several days with Insaf and Shawki in the north, where some of Insaf's Baghdad relatives had moved for safety, our paths crossing at a family birthday party. Through it all, Drew's energy had buoyed me when my own enthusiasm flagged.

Iraq was not altogether improving as most Americans hoped, and we had skirted danger only because our Iraqi handlers had pledged to protect us. I was learning to lean into a land of persecution, learning with the dispossessed Iraqis to take joy, even picnics, smack in the middle of hardships and threats so close you could feel them waiting. But as Drew pulled away and I watched him hurry toward his flight, the loneliness of the days ahead loomed, and a land that was becoming familiar seemed suddenly strange again.

12

FASTING AND FLIGHT

Aleppo, Syria, 2008

....

The Iraqi voice is heard as an echo, not as a sound.

SYRIAN PHYSICIAN JANY HADDAD

....

In October I followed the Iraqi refugees to Syria. Driving across the border as they had done was suicidal, I was told, so I caught a flight from Erbil to Damascus. Along Straight Street in the old city, I had lunch with Syrian church leaders to learn how they were coping with the influx of Iraqis. Ramadan had just ended, bringing in Eid al-Fitr, the festival marking the breaking of the monthlong fast, and restaurants were jammed.

After lunch, a pastor named Rami drove me to a town on the outskirts of Damascus called Jaramana, an Assyrian enclave where so many Iraqi Christians had migrated they had revised the street names. On a corner called Fallujah Place, I changed money amid honking taxis and shouts of shoppers bartering in Arabic. Through an open doorway I could see Iraqi barbers cutting hair, and next to them Iraqi pizza makers shot circles of dough high into the air while bantering with men on the street. Mosul, where many of these Iraqis had come from, was a city on lockdown, even as many of its residents carried on their lives in the freewheeling frenzy of

Jaramana. In Syria's safer atmosphere, the Iraqi Christians were welcomed into old churches or started new ones of their own.

After spending a night in a downtown monastery, I boarded a bus to travel through the Syrian countryside several hours north to Aleppo. Once there, I spent a week climbing stairs and back alleys, helped sometimes by church leaders who arranged meetings with some of the refugees. I talked with many Iraqis in their temporary homes; I stood with others as they waited in line for food parcels and listened to their tragic stories of flight.

One of the refugees I met was Parsegh Setrak, a fifty-four-year-old engineer from Mosul who worked under contract with Bechtel, a large construction and civil-engineering company. Starting in 2005, militants threatened him on the way to work, and they bombed his office twice before it was closed. But what forced him to flee with his family were the threats to kidnap his seventeen-year-old daughter.

"They would follow her on foot, and then in a red car. This happened many times, and many girls were being kidnapped from school and killed because they are Christians," he said.

One day Parsegh's daughter emerged from school to see three men waiting in the red car. She ran down the street in the other direction, then made her way home. But rounding the corner, she saw the red car. The men were stalking her.

The next day Parsegh began selling everything the family owned. Then he, his wife, and their three children packed themselves into his car with some clothes and a few family photos, and they escaped to Syria. Because of checkpoints and questioning at the border, it took eighteen hours to make what should have been an eight-hour journey to Aleppo. They found a fourth-floor apartment to rent in a building where the elevator went only to the second floor. The apartment's main room was furnished with a bare wooden table and a secondhand sofa shoved against an empty wall. As Parsegh spoke to me, his daughter, gangly and almost twenty years old now, drew near. He wrapped his arm over her shoulder and pulled her close.

The Syrian border was only eighty miles from Mosul, and the neighboring country was a natural place for Iraqis to flee. By 2008, two million Iraqis had left their war-torn country, and 1.2 million of them had ended up in Syria. An estimated 350,000 of those were Christians. In other words, Christians at the time made up about 3 percent of Iraq's general population but composed 30 percent of its refugees—a fair picture of the inordinate fear, discrimination, and persecution they experienced throughout the war.

Aleppo, Syria's largest city, was a logical draw. It was somewhat larger than Mosul, but both cities had a historic mix of Muslims and Christians. Aleppo had long ago earned a reputation for sheltering the oppressed, becoming a sanctuary for Armenians and Assyrians escaping genocide at the hands of Ottoman Turks a century ago. The Armenians arrived from the mountains naked and penniless, but between the two world wars, the Armenian population swelled rapidly in the city from about three hundred families to over 400,000 people.

Aleppo was a gateway to Syria's northern regions and the upper reaches of ancient Mesopotamia. Both the Euphrates and the Tigris rivers crossed the country to the east. Two ancient Silk Road routes were modern highways passing through the city, one leading to Ramadi in Iraq's Anbar Province and the other to Mosul.

During one week in October, six thousand Christians fled Mosul following a string of attacks. Gunmen entered Christian businesses and shot their owners dead—a grocer, a butcher, a pharmacist, and others—fourteen slain in two weeks. On the second Sunday of the month, Christians across Iraq began a three-day fast to focus attention on the killings in Mosul. "These are like the days when the people of Nineveh fasted at the time of Jonah," said Iraqi pastor Haitham Jazrawi.

Churches in Mosul had ceased holding services. Too many Christians were killed or kidnapped coming from or going to them. In Baghdad, Canon Andrew White, the British vicar who had taken up pastoring St. George's Church full time after Maher Dakhil's death, met with General Ray Odierno, commander of U.S. forces in Iraq. White asked for additional military protection for Mosul's Christians and for churches generally. Odierno listened with concern and said he would do what he could.

In Aleppo the Christians were arriving from Mosul—nearly 150 families in about ten days' time that October. "Most of these families arrived with their handbags and nothing else. It is a pitiful situation, and we feel handicapped and paralyzed and not able to help them," a church worker told me. For more than a year, the churches in Aleppo had been feeding hundreds of Iraqi families on a regular basis, assisted by a few nongovernmental aid groups. Church members donated items to furnish their apartments and made regular visits to check on them and assist with errands. But there was no existing system to help the Iraqis find housing, schooling, or medical care. And by law the refugees, even once they'd registered with the UN and were awaiting asylum in another country, could not hold jobs in Syria.

Aleppo's churches had started schools for the Iraqi refugee children, helped adults begin small businesses and barter with one another, and welcomed them to attend worship services in their own congregations. "We are the sons of martyrs,"[1] a clergyman told me as he handed out food parcels—each a plastic bag loaded with rice, flour, oil, canned tomatoes, and other foodstuffs, all drawn from a back room stacked with grain and shelves of oil provided by overseas relief organizations. "We understand what others are going through because we have been there. Our parents did not teach us to hate, and so we help other refugees."

I found the Iraqi families in fourth- and fifth-floor apartments, up stone steps and in buildings with broken elevators, behind pizza parlors, and tucked into small hovels in the thick walls of the Old City. They had kidnapping stories, stories of their homes and businesses bombed. They had lost brothers, sons, and daughters. Some had urgent medical conditions or persistent tremors and other signs of trauma. Almost all spoke of the financial pressures that came with being jobless in a country that would not allow them to work.

Raad Ghanem Youssef had the kind of story I would hear over and over. Insurgents had killed his son and his brother in 2004. After militants kidnapped another son and a daughter and released them, he fled with his family to Aleppo.

"We are looking to leave Iraq and Syria for good, and go to Europe or America," he said. "We have applied to the UN and have had two interviews, but we count only on God."

Raad Youssef was trying to get medical treatment for his son, who was having memory lapses and showed signs of post-traumatic stress disorder. At all times Raad kept copies of the family's UN refugee documents in a clear plastic bag tucked inside his buttoned shirt, in case someone came along who could help his case. He showed them to me and asked if I would help. I took photos of them but told him I doubted an American journalist could sway the UN. Sitting in the Iraqis' temporary homes, hearing how much they'd lost and seeing how little they had, I found it hard to keep the journalist's distance, the emotional disconnect needed to do the job.

Nisreen Herma was another of Mosul's bereaved. Her husband had died of injuries he had received in the Iran-Iraq War. Her twenty-four-year-old son, Besman Yousef, was single and a deacon in Mosul's Church of the Holy Spirit. He lived with and supported his widowed mother. In 2007 Besman and two other deacons were leaving the church with Father Ragheed Ganni around 7:30 in the evening when gunmen came toward the men and shot them in a hail of bullets. The insurgents then parked cars laden with explosives next to the bodies, leaving the Christians to die and preventing police or anyone else from approaching the scene for hours.

For Ganni and the deacons, their deaths on the Sunday after Pentecost ended a season of harassment that had begun on Palm Sunday when militants fired into the church during the service. More shootings and grenade-throwing attacks followed, along with nearby bombings. After the initial shooting, Father Ganni had written an e-mail to his friends: "We empathize with Christ, who entered Jerusalem in full knowledge that the consequence of His love for mankind was the cross. Thus while bullets smashed our church windows, we offered up our suffering as a sign of love for Christ."

Ganni then wrote, "This is war, real war, but we hope to carry our cross to the very end with the help of Divine Grace." And in a final e-mail before the gunmen attacked, he wrote, "We are on the verge of collapse."[2]

More than a year later, Nisreen was still distraught as she talked about her son Besman. She wore black and clutched a tissue, her face drained of color, ready to give way to tears at any moment. "We lost everything, we lost everything, we lost everything," she murmured.

Nisreen had no one left. She stayed in Mosul forty days to grieve for Besman, she said, then left for Aleppo, where her life was on hold. Living in an upper flat among borrowed chairs, a table, and a sofa, the only personal things Nisreen still had were her memories, the most inescapable being her son's violent death. She had relatives in Sweden and hoped to move there, but she wasn't at all certain she could satisfy the UN officers who had to certify her refugee status. "You look in their faces and see that you are not acceptable," she told me.

For Iraqis like Insaf Safou or Eveline Aoraha, life involved a circle of exile and homecoming. For Insaf, it was out to Canada then back again to Iraq. For Eveline, it was out to Dohuk then back to Mosul. Each felt restless, longing to be in her homeland, yet not at rest with the danger and violence. Coming and going was the only way—exile at intervals.

For others, like Nisreen Herma or Raad Youssef, there was no circle, only a straight line. They left Iraq planning never to return. What they had suffered was too much.

And then there were a few, like Bishop Rahho in Mosul or Bishop Antoine Audo in Aleppo, who counted the costs but simply decided to stay. Despite the desperate circumstances, they found exile a choice they could not make.

In many ways, Bishop Audo was representative of the Christian's journey in the Middle East. His father had migrated to Aleppo from

Alqosh, where I'd visited Nahum's tomb. Bishop Audo's father found work and married in Aleppo. His son, the future bishop, studied outside Syria, including at the Sorbonne in Paris, before returning to Aleppo after training as a priest. Now he presided over the Chaldean Church in Syria and served as Syria's national director for the Catholic relief organization Caritas, which supervised food distribution for thousands of Iraqis.

There were forty-five churches in Aleppo. When Audo was young, Christians made up a fourth of the city's population. Now they hovered at about 10 percent. A widely recognized church leader, Bishop Audo constantly had to ask himself whether to stay in Syria or to go. But at sixty-two, he moved comfortably about the streets of his neighborhood near St. Joseph's Cathedral, the church where he presided over a Eucharist service every day.

He was well known among Chaldeans in Iraq, too. When Bishop Rahho was killed in Mosul, Audo was asked to take charge of the Chaldean church there. With thousands of new refugees under his care in Syria, he declined.

As a balmy evening fell after a long day of climbing stairs to visit with refugees, I sat down with Bishop Audo on a bench beside a basketball court, watching children play games under the flickering shadows of olive trees. In the approaching darkness, the Muslim call to prayer began around us, and we listened as hundreds began filing into the expansive mosque built between the old Chaldean and Greek Catholic churches, the mosque's minaret aglow in bright green light. From across the street, drivers honked persistently—the sign of a wedding procession headed to one of the churches, with cars polished and bedecked in flowers.

The bishop had sad blue eyes that tilted down at the corners, but his mouth pulled against them in a sympathetic smile. He spoke English with a French accent from years studying at the Sorbonne. For a decade after that, he had worked in Beirut as part of a translation team producing what's now called the New Arabic Version, an Arabic-language Bible similar to the New International Version in English. If Bishop Audo spoke haltingly in English, it was only because it was low on his list of languages. He spoke Arabic first, then Syriac and Hebrew, along with French, Italian, and English.

Having talked with so many Iraqi Christians over the past several days, I wanted Bishop Audo to help me understand their plight.

"What does their future look like?" I asked. Would the church in the Middle East survive?

"It is very important for us as Eastern churches to have this presence here in the Middle East," he began, "and at the same time we have the experience of living with Islam. It will be very negative if we go abroad, if we don't have the presence of Christians with Muslim people. It is important to give Islam the opportunity to live with another religion.

"Even the Muslims need historical references, even if they are in opposition. Christians represent something that comes before them. In Syria we have a tradition of living together. There is respect for us here, even though we have this fanaticism growing."

"Syria is changing," I told him. I described how, a few days earlier, young men had pelted me with rocks and spit in my direction as I climbed along a busy walkway leading to the city's medieval citadel. I'd noticed more and more women wearing hijab—in some cases floor-length black burqas with faces covered—than during my previous visit six years earlier. In the streets where Western dress was once common, I saw veiled women moving in tow with their husbands, their eyes and skin visibly smooth, young. They were the teenage wives of older Muslim men, walking three steps behind them with the children, their lengthy veils casting long shadows under a heavy sun.

"It is a sign," Bishop Audo said. "Unfortunately the Muslims feel themselves very strong. They want to have opposition, and they want to have war, even if they say they want peace and reconciliation."

I felt the foreboding in his voice, the weight of caring for so many and seeing so many leave, of knowing so many in Iraq who had been killed.

"How do you keep going when you, too, could be somewhere else?" I asked.

"Day by day," he said. "It is a stress every day. But this is the church of Mesopotamia now for two thousand years. The call is to continue with a presence to give a taste of faith to Kurdish and Arabic peoples, and others. So I am doing my duty as a witness—praying, attending to the Eucharist, showing the presence of the Lord, and serving him with joy."

+ + +

As I spoke with Bishop Audo, Americans were preparing to head to the polls, consumed with a financial crisis spiraling the country into what became known as the Great Recession. By the end of the year, America would have a new president. On the campaign trail, Barack Obama pledged to focus on the domestic economy and to withdraw U.S. troops from Iraq within sixteen months of taking office. Casualty figures for U.S. military personnel were the lowest since the war began in 2003— 314 deaths in 2008 compared to 904 in 2007. American and Iraqi leaders assumed that the war was turning for the better and that it was safe to bring the troops home, or at least most of them. Once Obama took office, a new timetable for ending combat operations in Iraq took hold.

But as the saying goes, politicians campaign in poetry and govern in prose. The 2007 troop surge appeared to be successful, but was it a lasting success? And could it be sustained once American soldiers went home? By 2008, the wars following 9/11 had lasted longer than America's combat operations in World War II. But at the end of that war, the United States left nearly half a million soldiers in the European and Pacific theaters. Seventy years later, it had fifty thousand in Japan. What would it take to secure and build on the gains made? How many soldiers were needed to police Iraq? That was a question no one seemed ready to answer.

And the people I talked with in the Middle East had another pressing question for the new president: Should U.S. troops go home while so many Iraqis could not?

+ + +

One evening several hundred Iraqi Christians showed up for a meeting in the basement of one of the Armenian churches in Aleppo. The Armenian Orthodox priest, Dativ Michaelian, normally met with the refugees once a week so they could swap stories and tips and also have time for Bible study and prayer. He set up this particular week's meeting for my benefit, offering to have refugees come so I could hear their stories all together. Instead of the few dozen I expected, the hall was full.

Armenians lived all over Iraq, and these had come to Syria from Mosul, Kirkuk, and Zakho in the north; Baghdad in central Iraq; and Basra in the south. Some were newly arrived, while others had been living in temporary quarters for many months.

I sat at the front, facing men and women of all ages in rows upon rows of chairs. I had jotted questions in my notebook, but as I looked over the crowd in the dim light, I was overwhelmed. Where to begin? Father Dativ introduced me in Arabic, explaining I was a journalist from America interested especially in the plight of Iraq's Christians. I greeted them in return, explaining that I was also a wife and mother and that I wanted to understand what they were going through—what were the challenges for their families and their hopes for the future?

Hands shot up, and it quickly became clear I wouldn't be the one asking questions. As far as I could tell, no Americans were working among these refugees in Syria, so this was perhaps their first opportunity since quitting Iraq that the Armenian Christians could ask an American directly about U.S. actions and plans.

"Will I get special treatment for being injured in the war?" one asked.

Before I could explain that I couldn't answer that sort of question, another stood to speak.

"There's the United States' cost to the war, the casualties counted by your Defense Department," he said. "And there are other casualties—the casualties counted in Iraq, and the living casualties, like us here. What will the United States do about these casualties?"

"You try to talk about this as a subject, but when your life is the subject, it's very scary," another added.

"Why is America standing up for the rights of Muslims and not for Christians?" a young father asked.

As I listened helplessly, another stood simply to say, "America has destroyed our country."

The distance that evening seemed impossible to bridge. At home I knew Americans thought they had sacrificed enough in Iraq. In the Aleppo church basement, all the Iraqi refugees could see was what America was *not* doing. Jihadist groups had killed and mistreated them in the wake of a U.S.-led war, forcing them out of their towns and their countries. The jihadists had targeted Christians for being on America's side. That made being ignored by the United States harder to bear.

Congress had passed a law loosening the restrictions for some targeted Iraqis to gain asylum in the United States. A Department of Homeland Security fact sheet said they could apply for asylum—protected residency in the United States—without going through the UN interview and referral process, which could take years. But in the past year the United States had granted asylum to a total of 1,600 Iraqis. By contrast, even a decade after the Vietnam War ended, the United States was accepting about 14,000 refugees from Indochina per month. Yet only the Iraqis who'd worked with U.S. government contractors or the military received preferential status. In fact, the Iraqi Christians in Aleppo complained to me they felt discriminated against in the process because UN personnel who decided their refugee status were usually Muslims. Often, Syrian church leaders told me, Iraqi Christians were placed at the end of the waiting list for interviews and processing, their applications in some cases delayed for years.

Once I was back in the States, I contacted Roger Winter, who had been director of the U.S. Committee for Refugees for twenty years and had served in the State Department. Roger had helped me after I covered refugee situations following wars in Sudan and Bosnia, but this situation was different.

"The bad guys are directly stalking Christians and other targeted groups in order to kill some and get their community out. The organized stalking to drive them out makes them so vulnerable," Roger explained. Yet the policies of the United States and its coalition allies toward those being stalked for religious reasons made resettling them in other countries their last possible option, he said. To admit the Christian refugees, in essence, would be to acknowledge the political failure of the Iraq War and the United States' failed policy in Iraq.

"In other words, it is supposed to not happen," said Roger.

Berty Abdelsimah, a Christian aid worker trying to help the refugees, said, "President Bush hung his hat on freedom and democracy. The decimation of the Christian population is a result not factored in."

Though most of the displaced Iraqis I met in Aleppo wanted out, I met some Christians who were determined to maintain a presence in the Middle East. To them, the immigration hurdles were a godsend.

Dr. Jany Haddad was part of an evangelical church in Aleppo, but he worked with all the churches to set up medical care and other services for the Iraqi refugees. Every day he saw the hardships facing Iraq's growing numbers of homeless, and the tension for the region's believers between staying and going. He wanted them to stay.

"Don't evacuate the Middle East of Christians," an Armenian physician living in Aleppo agreed. "Let them stay, but help us take care of them."

Where, I wondered, would that help come from? America's newly elected president, Barack Obama, had promised voters to get our military out of Iraq as quickly as possible. American citizens had come through the war years very differently from the Iraqis. In the United States, "Never Forget" bumper stickers with the silhouette of the Twin Towers were still on display, along with flags in yards of families whose sons and daughters were serving in Iraq or Afghanistan. For most Americans, the war was about defending the homeland or the American way of life. Iraq's Christians and other minorities who'd long considered themselves allies of the United States didn't seem to enter into the equation.

PART 3

INSIDE
THE HOUSE
OF WAR

13

THE COMING OF
A NEW CALIPHATE

Baghdad, 2011

....

*Being killed, according to their account, is a victory. This is where
the secret lies. You fight a people who can never be defeated.*

ISLAMIC STATE SPOKESMAN ABU MUHAMMAD AL-ADNANI

....

On August 18, 2011, U.S. Secretary of State Hillary Clinton designated
as a terrorist a man known variously as Ibrahim Awwad Ibrahim, Ali
al-Badri, Awad Ibrahim al-Badri al-Samarrai, Abu Dua, al-Husseini al-
Qurashi, or Abu Bakr al-Baghdadi. In October the State Department
announced a $10 million bounty for information leading to his capture
after a string of attacks in Baghdad were blamed on his organization.

In 2010 a mujahideen council had named Abu Bakr al-Baghdadi the
emir of al-Qaeda in Iraq's militant offshoot, the Islamic State of Iraq.
He rose in the ranks of Islamic jihadists after two leaders of al-Qaeda
in Iraq were killed during a firefight with American and Iraqi soldiers.

Baghdadi, the world would learn, was different. He was an Iraqi
national, the first to lead any branch of al-Qaeda. He professed "noble
lineage"—he claimed to be a descendant of the Quraysh tribe, the
Prophet Muhammad's own. His status promised to attract new followers, and his leadership signaled "the opening of a new chapter for the
al-Qaeda organization in Iraq, a chapter that might be more sanguinary

than previous ones," reported one Arabic-language paper.[1] In other words, more bloodthirsty.

Iraqi defense minister Abdul Qader Obeidi called this "the third generation of al-Qaeda."[2] The first al-Qaeda fighters had erupted from Afghanistan, and the second wave had taken hold in Iraq's Anbar Province before the U.S. surge shut them down. Now the third wave was emerging under Baghdadi's new leadership, showing "definite signs of regeneration"[3] in areas where U.S. forces had defeated it, such as Anbar Province west of Baghdad and Diyala Province northeast of the capital. Rumors suggested that members of Saddam Hussein's Baath Party, including the fugitive commander Douri (the King of Clubs), were part of the regeneration. They had infiltrated the police force and had sleeper cells in command positions, particularly in Anbar. In Diyala, car bombings and several beheadings took place. The fighters killed eight Sunni clerics and then planted a black flag in the Diyala town of Sharaban.

In the midst of ominous signs of a terrorist revival, and four months after adding Baghdadi to its terrorist watch list, the United States brought its last soldiers and marines home from Iraq. If Secretary of State Clinton saw the new terrorist leader as a threat, she took little action against Baghdadi after the designation.

Meanwhile, Vice President Joe Biden declared himself "very optimistic"[4] about Iraq's future. The killing of Osama bin Laden in Pakistan in May and his burial at sea signaled that it was time to bury the war on al-Qaeda, whether it was over or not.

The Obama administration seemed unwilling or unready to deal with the political realities in Iraq, including the collapse of allies in Baghdad following Iraq's 2010 election. Iraqis had dwindling interest in a second Maliki administration. Ayad Allawi, a candidate who ran under the largely secular Iraqiya coalition, won more popular votes in the election than Maliki. But Maliki wouldn't give up his seat. With Iraq's parliamentary system and political parties organized in blocs, months of negotiations over forming a government ensued. Maliki claimed voter fraud and demanded recounts. Grasping, he said opposition groups had used satellites to alter computer-generated vote tallies.[5]

It was an important moment for the democratic process. Representatives from Iraq's Sunni Arabs, Shia Arabs, Turkmen, and Kurds, along with at least one Christian, came together to meet in Baghdad with Vice President Biden. The diversity in the room demonstrated the kind of Iraq they yearned to live in, and they pressed Biden to accept the Iraqiya winner, Allawi. Later, just as the country's leaders, including Maliki's own deputies, agreed Maliki should be pressured to step down in favor of Allawi, Biden phoned Maliki to offer his support.[6]

No one claimed Maliki had won the election. In fact, Biden cited as precedent Al Gore winning a popular election in 2000 only to lose under America's electoral system. Despite the meeting with leaders of multiple Iraqi groups, Biden continued to signal that the United States needed a Shia strongman in charge, a message echoed by the U.S. ambassador Christopher Hill.

Only General Raymond Odierno, commanding general of U.S. forces in Iraq, warned against backing Maliki. He said the United States in effect was stabilizing Iraq only to hand it over to Iran. As if on cue, Moqtada al-Sadr, the Shia cleric who for years had directed the insurgency against Sunni provinces, returned from self-imposed exile in Iran to Najaf, his home city in central Iraq. His return signaled the ayatollahs' hand on Baghdad. The Sunnis in restive centers like Anbar and Mosul felt cheated, excluded from Baghdad deal making.

As in earlier years when the Bush administration had rushed a vote on the constitution to pave the way for Maliki's first election, the Obama administration now tried to strong-arm the parliamentary system. Both actions had disastrous consequences. Biden was a nice man who had the wrong instincts on Iraq, said Odierno's political advisor Emma Sky. Obama's only interest in Iraq, she concluded, "was in ending the war."[7]

Like all Americans, I was war weary. As U.S. combat operations in Iraq wound down, I spent more time in Afghanistan, where President Obama dispatched additional troops to fight al-Qaeda. A day after I ended a reporting trip there in 2010, gunmen brutally attacked and killed a medical missions team whose work I'd been following. The Taliban claimed responsibility for the attack, saying the aid workers were foreign spies spreading Christianity. In the city of Kabul I'd had breakfast with the wife of one of the team's leaders the morning before the assault.

President Obama perhaps was ready to end these wars, but the jihadists showed no signs they were ready to give up. And as I had learned in Iraq, paying attention to what happened to the Christians was an important way to understand the war the Islamic militants were prepared to fight.

+ + +

The Prophet Muhammad had divided the world into two spheres— *Dar al-Islam* (House of Islam) and *Dar al-Harb* (House of War). On his deathbed in AD 632, Muhammad ordered that "all the infidels be driven from the Arabian Peninsula."[8]

Christianity spread from the northern reaches of Mesopotamia; Islam entered from Arabia to the south. In the seventh century, it never occurred to the Byzantines who controlled Syria and Palestine, or to the Persians who controlled Mesopotamia, to fear what might come from the hot wastes of the Arabian Peninsula.

But Muhammad's army went to war to bring all that was once under the domain of Judaism and Christianity into the House of Islam, mustering armed forces from the clans of Arabia united under the banner of *Islam*, meaning "submission." Within five years, they unleashed their armies across the ancient empires of what is today the Middle East, from Palestine to Syria, then to Mesopotamia, sweeping across the Persian empire.

Because Abraham had dwelled in Greater Syria after leaving the land of Ur, the Muslim armies set their sights not only on the lands of ancient Israel but also on Mesopotamia, believing they had a claim on all the Abrahamic lands of the Bible.[9] They captured Damascus in 634, and in 636 they met a Persian army that was exhausted from losing to the Roman army outside the ancient walls of Nineveh. Muslims and Persians met well south of Nineveh, facing off on a wide plain rich in silt and black earth where the Tigris and Euphrates met.

The Arabs called it *Sawad*, Black Land, encompassing most of modern-day Iraq south of Kurdistan. The two great rivers flowed close together, the Euphrates higher than the Tigris, allowing for a system of canals between them. Irrigation fed sugar cane, flax, fields of grain, and groves of date palms, along with two yearly harvests of wheat and barley. The Muslims eyed the Sawad's abundance jealously, a lush land that fed, watered, and cultivated the world's two earliest civilizations, first the Sumerians at Ur and then the Babylonians.

At the time of the invasion, the southern delta region was rich also in Christians. At least thirty-three churches and an array of monasteries spread over Najaf and its surrounding area, about one hundred miles south of Baghdad. At Hirah, a town on the Euphrates, the Syriac Church of the East diocese was founded in the fifth century. Najaf contained perhaps the largest Christian cemetery in Iraq, covering an area of more than one thousand acres.

Persia's general took months to position his army on the eastern bank of the Euphrates on the open plain near Qadisiyah facing the Arab army, which was commanded by a forty-year-old cousin of Muhammad. About 30,000 soldiers of Islam prepared to battle about 50,000 Persian "polytheists," plus a large contingent of elephants. They confronted one another between marshlands and a channel of the Euphrates near Najaf.

The Persians mocked the Arab archers, until Arab arrows began piercing their coats of mail. In three days' pitched battle, the Persian archers, mounted on elephants, bested the Muslim army at first. But the Muslim commander ordered his men to destroy the elephant corps. In the stampede, many Persians were killed, including their general. The Persian army surrendered.

The Battle of Qadisiyah brought Muslim rule to Mesopotamia and led to the Muslim conquest of the whole Persian empire. The armies of

Muhammad called for a universal caliphate, a religion-state that would become the brand for future Islamic purists all the way down to jihadi movements like al-Qaeda and Baghdadi's Islamic State of Iraq.

Within a decade of Muhammad's death, the caliphate spanned three continents. Arabic replaced Greek and Aramaic as the language of the day, and religious conversion was expected. The conquering Arabians ordered the mostly Christian Sawad tribes, "Accept the faith and you are safe; otherwise pay tribute. If you refuse to do either, you have only yourself to blame. A people is already upon you, loving death as you love life."[10]

Much of the Christian populace paid the jizya, or tribute, the tax required to live in Muslim-ruled areas. Muslim clerics designated church clergy to collect taxes, promising kickbacks, fostering church corruption and sowing seeds for further subjugation. For a time the Christians survived, though the payment proved to be no guarantee of holding on to property or legal status. Taxes for the "protected" Christians mounted, and for those who couldn't pay, the price was higher still—their children were taken from them and sold as slaves. The higher the taxes, the greater the pressure to convert to Islam.

Within the House of Islam sprang a House of War, and in 750 the Umayyad caliphate of Damascus went down to defeat against the Abbasids of Babylon. Mansur was the most powerful leader of the Abbasid caliphate, and he ruled from 754 to 775. He was the son of a Berber slave woman, making him half-Arab. His successors, too, were nearly all sons of eminent Arab fathers and foreign slave mothers. The early Muslim world and its people would be called Arabs, yet in reality many were Persians, Kurds, Berbers, Assyrians, or Christians from the Sawad tribes.

Mansur moved the royal courts of the Muslim world from Damascus to Iraq, where he built his fortified capital city on the western bank of the Tigris. Soon palaces and mosques stretched to both sides of the Tigris, with bridges made of boats connecting them. Baghdad would become the center of the Near East and western Asia from the eighth through thirteenth centuries. Commerce and culture from all over the world moved in and out of its doors.

The Abbasids would be credited with the Islamic Golden Age—a time when overland and maritime trade linked Mesopotamia to India, China, and Indonesia, spreading Islam along the route. Medicine, science, and technology flourished as Mansur and the other early caliphs dined with and courted Christian leaders, often claiming these leaders' scientific and mathematical advances as their own.[11] The era would be remembered as unique, one where, in the words of Muhammad, "The ink of the scholar is more holy than the blood of a martyr."

The Islamic rulers who launched out under Muhammad in the 600s cemented so comprehensive a religion-state through the Umayyads and then the Abbasids that it lasted to the rule of the Ottoman Turks. What began in 632 continued until 1922.

Mansur would confirm the breadth of his dynasty with official visits to Syria and Jerusalem in 771. Holding court in Baghdad, he went on to construct another conclave near the ancient city of Raqqa on the Euphrates, built on the same plan as Baghdad. Mansur intended Raqqa as a forward base from which to initiate military campaigns at the Byzantine Empire and invade the Roman world.

In the twenty-first century as Abu Bakr al-Baghdadi laid plans for his militant fighters to usher in a new caliphate, he would look not only to Baghdad, but also up the Euphrates to Raqqa in Syria, for his headquarters, a place to reestablish the grandeur of Mansur, and to once again launch a forward base aimed toward "Rome" and the West.

+ + +

Baghdadi wasted no time taking advantage of Iraq's political unraveling. An October 2010 attack on Baghdad's Our Lady of Salvation church had all the markings of a "more sanguinary" version of al-Qaeda under his Islamic State of Iraq. In a hail of grenades and bullets, bombers wearing suicide vests stormed the church during the main weekly service one Sunday evening. They gunned down two priests and took scores of worshipers hostage. In the fusillade, gunmen shot the priests at point-blank range, pushing one, Father Wassim Sabih, to the ground as he grasped a crucifix and pleaded for the lives of his congregants.

The attackers left fifty-eight people dead and seventy-five wounded. After a four-hour siege, suicide bombers blew themselves up inside the church along with their hostages. Churchgoers had witnessed terror strikes in Baghdad before, but these attackers "seemed insane," said fifty-year-old survivor Ban Abdullah.[12]

"Blood, flesh, and bones," said one Iraqi policeman guarding the aftermath. "You can't bear the smell."[13]

The massacre marked a moment of reckoning for Iraq's Christians: At least fifty-four churches had been bombed and a thousand or more Christians killed in directed acts of violence since the U.S. invasion. The latest report showed Iraq's Christian population at 500,000, down from its estimated 1.2 million in 2003.

"It's a hemorrhage," warned Chaldean archbishop Louis Sako. "Iraq could be emptied of Christians."

Within months of the attack, an estimated 45,000 to 95,000 Christians had left Iraq,[14] and Sako and other church leaders worried to me over the phone about the church in Iraq becoming so decimated that it would become unsustainable. Christians were a pawn in a political process they had no control of, Sako told me, with militant groups striking at them to prove they held the upper hand. "Christians are an easy target," he said.

I asked, "What will you do then? Is it time for Christians to set up their own protective forces?"

Sako dismissed my question before I finished asking it. Taking up arms was out of the question, he sighed, but then he seemed to recover his confidence. "Christian presence and Christian works continue to be more appreciated in Iraq than not," he said, "even though sometimes it is like a fragile light."

The increasing violence did not prevent Insaf from returning regularly to Iraq. Her work among women had grown and now went by the name Impact Iraq. For years a Canadian-American organization called International Teams had provided oversight and bookkeeping know-how for her ministry, but in many ways Insaf remained a one-woman organizer. She connected personally with pastors and women in the churches and listened to their needs, always finding new ways to help them. She spoke at conferences and Arab churches in Canada and the United States to raise awareness and money. She networked everywhere. Then she returned to Iraq with whatever she had or could organize—a six-thousand-mile commute spanning two worlds, but for Insaf constituting one job.

In 2009, when Insaf began organizing conferences for women from churches all over the country, she traveled to Iraq with her daughter, Nour, who was in college in Toronto. This was Nour's first trip back since leaving Iraq as a young girl. When it came time to return home, Nour left behind a beau, and two years later she married Malath Baythoon, a young assistant at the Evangelical Alliance church in Baghdad. Insaf and her family hosted parties and showers for the couple in Toronto, but the marriage took place in Erbil. There were hundreds of guests and long tables of food and presents. After the celebrations, Nour joined Malath to live in Iraq. She took a job with a British bank, and Malath became pastor of a young Evangelical Alliance church in Erbil.

Insaf had returned to Iraq dreaming she and her family would one day live there again. She longed for her children reared in the West to know the land of their birth, to have their hearts knit, she said, to Iraq. Now her daughter was the one to move back. She would be knit there, as it turned out, giving Insaf a home in Iraq after all.

The sadness of Baghdad, as Shawki put it after one visit, plus the dangers everywhere, slowly pressured Insaf to give up her dream of moving back herself. Increasingly Insaf's family and friends lived in the West. Her sister Angham had moved to Detroit after the death of their grandmother. Her brothers all lived in Canada, and her youngest sister was in Sweden.

As the months passed and the world moved on, clergymen I'd come to think of as fixtures in Iraq also began to leave. Ghassan Thomas, who pastored the Evangelical Alliance Church—the first church I visited in 2003 and once the largest Protestant church in Baghdad—survived the city's worst war years before finally making the decision to emigrate. He had kept his young children in school, housed Christians inside the church when the streets grew too dangerous, and continued holding church services, coffeehouses, and youth activities despite personal threats and explosions near his church in the Karada district. He was a popular preacher and increasingly took his sermons on the road. He made trips to Iraqi Kurdistan and to the United States, in part to fundraise and in part to escape threats to his own life. Finally in 2012 he left for good, pastoring a church of Iraqi refugees in Turkey until he could emigrate with his family to Australia.

Younan Shiba, the Assyrian evangelical who had started a church in Baghdad in 2003, departed for Chicago. By 2005 he had been facing so many threats from Islamic extremists over his work with Muslim converts that he sent his family away before leaving Iraq himself.

Young churches that were launched in the hopeful days of 2003 and 2004 now were closing their doors. Some closures weren't unexpected. Anyone who had started a church to earn a name for himself—or money—found it hard to stay, in the face of targeted attacks. Insaf and I visited churches bankrolled by outsiders, including Americans. At one church, the latest sound equipment and large-screen televisions dominated the room. At another, a pastor showed up in a new white Mercedes. When we spoke, he wanted to talk about American movies. The arrival of Americans and other Westerners had brought out sharks, sometimes even among the priests and nuns of the old churches. They convinced churches in the United States to support them and then grew their own fortunes alongside their congregations. Insaf had learned to be wary: "They know you have the money, and they love you because of what's in your pocket."

I was learning about perseverance by watching those who remained. Muthafar Yacoub saw his small church in Baghdad close its doors, but he moved to the Alliance Church alongside new senior pastor Joseph

Francis. Following Maher Dakhil's death, St. George's landed dynamic leadership in Canon Andrew White, a Brit who became its vicar in 2005. When he moved to Baghdad, Canon White lived for a time in a Green Zone trailer until he moved to the church grounds. Despite seemingly endless energy and a high profile, White led a congregation in continual decline under a relentless barrage of terrorist attacks.

For St. George's and many others, support from abroad was essential to keep church doors open. Canon White raised funds more easily than most, drawing financial support in England, the United States, and elsewhere and with it launching outreach ministries to poor Christians and to Muslims.

At the Evangelical Church in Kirkuk, pastor Haitham Jazrawi's wife, Mayada, looked for some way to minister to Muslim women. She found it by starting a prison ministry. Nearly all the female inmates were Muslims, some of them mothers, and no programs existed to help them. Mayada and other women from her church delivered soap, toothpaste, and other items to the inmates. Many could not read or write, so Mayada and others tutored and read to them.

Insaf became one of Mayada's chief suppliers, sending packages or showing up herself to deliver wrapped gifts for the women and clothing for their children. On one visit Mayada discovered that the inmates had removed stickers from the wrapping paper that read, "God loves you," and placed them on their cell walls, some forming the shape of a cross.

"No one these days takes a care about us," one of the prisoners told Mayada.

"All we are doing is making them feel alive again," Mayada said.

+ + +

Arab uprisings around the region peaked in 2012. By midyear the United Nations declared Syria to be in a state of civil war. Baghdadi seized on the opportunity to establish a base of operations in Syria, and in July the Islamic State of Iraq released an audio recording of Baghdadi announcing a plan named "Breaking the Walls."[15] His priority, he said, was to free Muslim prisoners and eliminate judges. Al-Qaeda was returning to its strongholds in Iraq, he announced, and he called on Sunni tribesmen to send their sons to "join the mujahideen." He ended his recording with a threat for the United States: "You will see [Islamic warriors] at the heart of your country with God's willing, since our war against you has just started."[16]

The following summer, Baghdadi's jihadists launched jailbreaks in Iraq, freeing more than five hundred prisoners from Abu Ghraib prison near Baghdad. Abu Omar was typical of those released, an Iraqi national quickly recruited to fight in Syria. ISIS commanders gave him a cell phone and $10,000. He made his way north, crossing the border to Turkey, where he linked up with Baghdadi's militant commanders. Then he crossed into Syria, where he joined the mujahideen to fight the government forces of President Bashar al-Assad.[17]

The al-Qaeda that carried out attacks on the United States in 2001 had transitioned to al-Qaeda in Iraq with the American war and morphed quietly, menacingly, into a new cross-border, transnational army. Now calling itself the Islamic State of Iraq and al-Sham (or Syria), or ISIS, the group plastered billboards in Aleppo with statements reading, "Together we cultivate the tree of the Caliphate" and "A Caliphate pleasing to Allah is better than democracy pleasing to the West." The militants moved readily on Christian areas in Syria's north, primarily Raqqa and Hasakah Provinces—both of them rich in oil, agriculture, and centuries of Christian heritage.

Aleppo was becoming like Mosul in Iraq, Bishop Antoine Audo told me. The Chaldean bishop's family was originally from Iraq's Nineveh Plains, and he had for years supervised relief and aid for hundreds of thousands of Iraqis who had fled to Syria, mostly from Mosul. Now that Syria had its own civil war, the Iraqi refugees were finding their way to Turkey or Europe, or returning home. Syrians, on the other hand, were turning into refugees inside their own country. Commerce came to a standstill and breadlines grew as the jihadists used cover of a popular revolution to impose an Islamic state.

Jany Haddad, the Armenian evangelical and physician I'd met during my 2008 visit to Aleppo, grew frustrated with the lack of outside aid and international attention in the developing crisis. The city's hospitals were filling with children maimed by explosions. Doctors and medicine to treat them were running short. Soon, he told me, it would be too late for more powerful nations to roll back ISIS and its affiliates.

Syrian Christians and others believed that Saudi Arabia, Turkey, and Qatar offered ISIS tacit support. For those nations, the Sunni militants formed a bulwark against rising Shia power in Baghdad and Tehran. Western nations, meanwhile, were engaged in nuclear diplomacy with Iran. To the Syrians, that explained the U.S. and British reluctance to impose a no-fly zone or to offer humanitarian aid in the Syrian crisis.

The pastor at Dr. Jany's church announced suddenly that he and other families were leaving to move abroad. Dr. Jany e-mailed to tell me that he would remain in Aleppo "serving the One who is in control of everything, even our single hairs as counted by Him."

+ + +

In 2010 and 2011, the Obama administration found itself caught up in Arab Spring tumult, supporting democracy movements from Algeria to Yemen. President Obama and Secretary of State Clinton called publicly for the ouster of sitting heads of state in Syria, Egypt, Libya, and Yemen. They seemed oblivious to the reality that those calls were leading to bloodshed and anarchy. The initial uprisings by secular freedom fighters were hijacked by Muslim extremists leading armed revolutions. In the one place where the United States had spent its own blood and treasure to promote democracy—Iraq—U.S. leaders had stepped in to keep a strongman in power.

By ignoring the rise of Islamic militants under the Arab Spring mantle, the United States was headed for a train wreck with its own foreign policy, which for the past decade had made fighting terror the priority. Soon the United States would find itself opposing Syria's president Assad—and at the same time opposing the terrorist groups also fighting for his ouster. The flow of weapons and new jihadists paved the way for genocide in Christian and other non-Muslim communities.

The American leaders could not say they did not know. They had labeled Baghdadi a terrorist threat, and he had answered in agreement.

14

THE DEATH OF
ONE AMERICAN

Sulaymaniyah, 2012

....

They shall not return to us, the resolute, the young,
The eager and whole-hearted whom we gave.

RUDYARD KIPLING, "MESOPOTAMIA"

....

"I have a student who wants to kill me," Jeremiah Small told his friend Amir on a Friday afternoon.

The thirty-three-year-old American teacher had been working in Iraq for six years, teaching high school English to mostly Kurdish students at a private school in Sulaymaniyah, a mountain city in Iraqi Kurdistan.

Pastor Yousif Matty had opened the Classical School of the Medes in 2001. It received support from several American nonprofit organizations but was run by Iraqis. In all, Matty had started three schools in Iraqi Kurdistan; together they had more than two thousand students in kindergarten through twelfth grade. Classes were taught in English, often by Christians. The curriculum was built on an international track designed to help graduates get into universities overseas.

Every year a small number of American teachers came to teach alongside Iraqi teachers. Most Americans stayed for one school year; Jeremiah Small came to teach high school English for a year in 2005 and never left.

By nearly every account, he was the favorite teacher at the Medes school in Sulaymaniyah. He ate local dishes and learned the local Kurdish dialect well enough to barter in street markets. He found a tailor willing to fit him in the traditional *shalwar*, the baggy khaki trousers worn by Iraqi men. With his shalwar held by a crimson cummerbund at his slim waist, Jeremiah would join in Kurdish folk dances with the elementary students, even though he towered over them. He and several other teachers shared a home, its doors almost always open to students. At the end of a day, he would prepare food for high schoolers who wanted to pull a study session late into the night.

I met Jeremiah in 2008, after the school got in touch with me to ask if I would give a training session to high school students starting their own school newspaper. I'd already visited the Medes school in Sulaymaniyah twice: once before the war when it had about seventy-five students, and again during the war years as it outgrew one building and moved into another. I said I'd love to meet with the students. Jeremiah was the teacher helping with the newspaper, and that was when our friendship began.

He sent me student essays so I could get a feel for his pupils, along with several videos they had made. One showed the important role of the *chaikhana*, or tea house, in Kurdish life. Another described *seropay*, or sheep-brain soup, and explained why Kurds like it so much. It featured a lively exchange, filmed in black and white, between the men of Kurdistan seated at long tables to eat seropay and the students who tried to convince Jeremiah to try it. After a few spoonfuls, he appeared to devour it and then asked for more.

The day I planned to meet with Jeremiah and his students was a school holiday, so the whole class—about fifteen young men and women dressed in nice jeans and flannel shirts—arrived at Jeremiah's home. He set up a projector for my notes and photos; I lectured and the students responded for most of the day. They spoke English well and asked good questions. When we broke for tea, they wanted to know about my favorite movies and where I lived in the United States. Then they talked about where they wanted to go to college.

Mr. Jer, as they called him, joked easily with his students, but he kept our discussions moving. I could see how he pushed and prodded them, repeating what one would say and then asking questions of others. He listened carefully but was always ready with one more thought or question, drawing even casual illustrations from literature they'd read.

My son, Drew—who was with me on that excursion—had joined me for the day. Sulaymaniyah proved a welcome respite for us from places like Mosul. We could walk its streets freely, taking in bakeries overflowing with baklava, fresh cookies, and other pastries. We joined shoppers at downtown markets where conversation and bartering came easily, and we Westerners felt welcomed. After our session with Mr. Jer's class, we returned to our hotel, which was within walking distance of his home. I had to work on a magazine deadline, so Drew headed back to Jeremiah's house to meet more students and teachers. At some point Jeremiah pulled out his Kurdish outfits for Drew to try on. After he'd helped Drew with the shalwar and the wide sashes, Jeremiah joked about what bad Kurds the two tall American men made.

During our time in Sulaymaniyah, Drew and I watched a movie or two at Jeremiah's home. We ate together and talked about all the promise of Iraq. Jeremiah had unbridled ambitions for his students' futures.

Along with teaching his students to love Shakespeare and John Bunyan, and working through a class on world religions, Jeremiah chaperoned high school camping trips and taught students to rock climb. "He knew the mountains surrounding the city better than we did," said Amed Omar, a 2010 Medes school graduate. Amed said Mr. Jer was "very Kurdish, very hospitable, very connected to all our lives."[1]

Jeremiah's friend Amir was an Iraqi who had once worked as a translator for U.S. military personnel at a base outside Mosul. He lived with his family in Erbil, about 100 miles west of Sulaymaniyah. Every Friday he and Jeremiah talked by phone. They shared news of their families and their jobs. Then they prayed for each other. After Jeremiah mentioned the threat, Amir asked him more about the student, but Jeremiah laughed it off. "It's okay. He just doesn't like me. He says I pray all the time and talk about Jesus."

Amir, a Muslim who had converted to Christianity, couldn't laugh it off. He was nervous every time he thought about what Jeremiah had said. So he called Jeremiah a few days later, on Wednesday, not wanting to wait until their next Friday phone call.

He asked Jeremiah about the student. "Everything is well," Jeremiah told him. In fact, he and the young man, along with other students, had been out together earlier that evening. "Don't worry; just pray," Jeremiah told Amir.

The next morning Jeremiah sat grading papers in the living room as his roommate Erik, a fellow teacher, headed out the door around eight o'clock. Jeremiah warned Erik against inhaling too much dust. A cloud of hazy orange grit had settled over the city, not unusual with the dry air and high mountains in early spring. Jeremiah didn't teach until second period, so he finished his papers and left a little later.

At the start of his eleventh-grade English class, an eighteen-year-old Iraqi student named Bayar Sarwar stood at the back of the room. He took a handgun from his pocket and fired at Jeremiah, shooting him multiple times in the chest and head. With the class looking on in horror and teachers rushing to the scene, Bayar turned the gun and shot himself.

At the time of the shooting, a team of college students from America, all education majors, were about to depart the States for Iraq. They were making the journey largely to work alongside Jeremiah at the Sulaymaniyah school, all risking a trip to Iraq over spring break to vie for the privilege of shadowing him in the classroom. On the day of the shooting, Jeremiah's photograph appeared on the home page of Servant Group International, the Nashville-based Christian organization that supported Jeremiah and other Americans to teach at the school. His face was a recruitment bid for a new team of teachers to join the faculty that fall.

That Thursday morning—March 1, 2012—Jeremiah Small died in a wash of blood on the classroom floor. Students streamed from the two-story school building and filled the courtyard outside, waiting for parents and authorities to arrive. The high school students staggered into the dull light of the dust-filled air to stand in a collective dazed shock. They held on to one another as they made calls on their cell phones. Younger students, too, emerged from the building in tears. Everyone knew Mr. Jer. Some students thought they were under a terrorist attack and waited for more gunfire. But Sulaymaniyah, a university town surrounded by high mountains, had been far removed from terrorism and most war violence.

As news of the shooting spread, parents, along with police and paramedics, flooded the campus. Inside, the medics could do nothing for Jeremiah; he was already dead. They loaded his body onto a stretcher, swathed it in a blanket, hastily carried it outside, and drove away. A separate ambulance carried Bayar to Sulaymaniyah Emergency Hospital, where he survived for several hours before he died.

I was sitting at my desk back home in America that Thursday morning, seven time zones away, when an e-mail flashed across my computer screen. A friend of Jeremiah's whose wife had also taught in Iraq wrote to tell me that Jeremiah had been shot and killed in Sulaymaniyah. I couldn't breathe.

Could he really be dead? Dazed, I got up to find my husband. When he saw my face, he thought something had happened to one of our own children. I choked on my tears trying to tell him the news.

Jeremiah felt like family to me. The physical and emotional shock I felt was multiplied across the country for my son, Drew, and for hundreds of others. Jeremiah's devotion to his students and to Iraqi Kurdistan was evident to everyone who knew him, even an outsider like me. After the newspaper training session in 2008, Jeremiah had sent me articles and essays his students wrote, along with the regular e-mail updates he sent to family and friends.

"Confounded and amazed," he wrote in one e-mail, just a few weeks before the shooting, "I discover myself repeating over and over, 'I have the best job in the world.'"

Some of his students had lived abroad, their Kurdish families forced to flee Saddam Hussein during or after the first Gulf War. They were multilingual and savvy about the world. I never met Bayar, but his story was similar. His father had been a member of the Kurdish pesh-merga and had gone on to become a dentist. During the first Gulf War, the family moved to Iran, where Bayar was born. They lived there until 2003, when they moved to Australia. Bayar completed elementary school in Australia before the family decided it was time to move back to Iraqi Kurdistan.

From the moment Bayar fired what reportedly was his father's pistol, questions and controversy surrounded the shooting. Bayar's family were well-known Kurds. His mother was a niece of Jalal Talabani, the president of Iraq. The seventy-eight-year-old Talabani had helped found the Patriotic Union of Kurdistan, one of two key Kurdish political parties, and was arguably one of the United States' closest allies in Iraq. Obviously the shooting had the potential to put Kurdish leadership in a bad light, while at the same time raising questions about what, before the shooting, had been low-profile private schools with Christian educators.

Some called Jeremiah a martyr, and Kurdish leaders, including Bayar's father, understandably reacted to the characterization. Rumors began circulating that Bayar belonged to an antiterrorism squad headed by an uncle, and that rather than using his father's gun, he'd come by a weapon through this group. Some said he had accused Jeremiah of trying to evangelize him. Others said Bayar had actually converted to Christianity. Some at the school said Bayar shot Jeremiah as he bowed his head to pray for the class, something he did routinely. Others said the two had argued, and Bayar pulled the gun as Jeremiah turned from him. It was hard to believe Jeremiah would argue with a student in front of the class. This much seemed consistent as I talked to students and others after the shooting: Bayar was described as troubled and difficult to get along with, and Jeremiah was described as bold and unrelenting. "Surely more than almost anybody I know, he lived on the edge of his faith and was completely unafraid," one of Jeremiah's friends told me.

Of all the many conflicts and tensions in Iraq, the shooting brought heightened tension to a place where there had seemingly been little. Kurdistan's leaders took a hard line against Islamic-led militant groups, with better security than the rest of the country as a result. They also valued the schools, many sending their own children there. Everyone knew Yousif Matty was a Christian, yet he had a reputation for working alongside Muslims going back to before the war years. His schools were recognized and approved by the Kurdish ministry of education.

Yousif wasn't interested in a safe haven or special enclave for Christians. He said he often told authorities, "As Christians, we want to cooperate with Muslims. We want to live with you, not at the edge of life. We want to be at the heart of Kurdistan. We don't want to be lazy; we want to work for the good of the community." The bold approach worked, he said: "What I am doing is not something that is secret. They appreciate it."

An unspoken, uneasy backdrop to the shooting was that Kurds and many other Iraqis felt abandoned by the departure of all U.S. troops at the end of 2011. Iraqis had believed a contingency force would remain for security. The departure left the Kurds vulnerable and seemingly forgotten, although they had begun the war as the strongest American allies in the region. The departure also left American workers in Iraq more open to attack.

I noticed the shift. After the shooting, students and leaders of all kinds were skittish, suddenly reluctant to talk with a reporter. In an undistinguished place where Christians and Muslims had worked side by side, tragedy suddenly surfaced, and an era of goodwill seemed to end.

The families hoped it could be otherwise. Jeremiah's parents, along with their children (Jeremiah was the oldest of seven), decided Jeremiah would be buried in Iraq. His father, Dan, made his way to Sulaymaniyah, where he met with American diplomats to make arrangements for the funeral and burial. The rest of the Small family followed, and together they attended the traditional Muslim burial services for Bayar, which became a joint service where the community also honored Jeremiah. It was held in a mosque, where the men gathered, while women congregated in a nearby funeral hall.

At the service for Jeremiah, held in a local community hall, the two fathers stood and embraced. Bayar's father offered an apology, which Dan Small accepted, offering the family's forgiveness in return. The Small family came to demonstrate forgiveness and reconciliation, they said in a statement for the press, and "to make sure Jeremiah's work is blessed to continue in the lives of those he loved."

Afterward, Bayar's father suggested in press interviews that Jeremiah had forced his son to convert to Christianity, something students and fellow teachers denied. Dr. Sarwar told a reporter, "Christians are our brothers, but the Christians I have known are very different from those who work at that school. The latter bring danger. They are more dangerous than al-Qaeda. Therefore, I warn the parents, if the school system remains as it was, they should not send their kids to that school."[2]

Already the school had responded to increasing tension in the community. Administrators had decided to close the school for a few weeks. They sent the remaining American teachers abroad to grieve and recuperate in safety. Some later had trouble reentering.

But the schools continued and enrollment held steady—even grew. Others in the mostly Muslim community, including Jeremiah Small's former students, published tributes to his engagement with the city. Jeremiah had worked to raise money for ambulances and paramedic training at a time when the city had none, never imagining his own body would be carried away in one. At the time of his death, he and his students were raising funds to build Sulaymaniyah's first public library.

His students, including Muslims, rushed to his defense. Meer Ako Ali, a Medes school graduate who was in Lebanon attending a university, wrote a touching tribute to Jeremiah in the *Kurdistan Tribune*:

> God knows I would not be who I am today if it was not for
> [Jeremiah Small] and what he presented to me. I am sure
> hundreds of his other students feel the same way. . . .

Our community has grown so vile that we kill the people who come to serve us, the people who dedicate their lives to us. Killing a teacher (especially over a slight disagreement) not only means that we despise education and are closed up, it also points out . . . the fact that we do not take disagreements well: we kill whoever has different opinions in the most brutal ways. . . .

I condemn the rule of totalitarians that is looming over us, killing whoever disagrees. I join the thousands of affected students and families in demanding justice for the murder of Jeremiah Small and an end to the use of force in silencing differences.[3]

Although I had maintained regular contact with Iraqis like Yousif Matty, I had not visited Iraq in nearly four years at the time when Jeremiah died. Like many Americans, my work had moved on with the end of combat operations and U.S. withdrawal. I was between trips to Afghanistan and had just returned from northern Nigeria, where I saw the burned churches and heard the horror stories of attacks on Christians by a new Islamic militant group called Boko Haram. Americans were keeping their fingers crossed, hoping Iraq could outrun the resurgence of Islamic militancy spreading under the guise of the Arab Spring in the Middle East. Iraq had oil, it had amassed wealth, and it had high rates of literacy with many professional workers. Furthermore, it had young people like Jeremiah's students with personal ambition and high hopes for their future. It seemed impossible that Iraq could devolve into a failed state, like Somalia, Sudan, or the parts of Nigeria where I had just been.

In championing close to a thousand students in his classroom during the time he taught in Sulaymaniyah, Jeremiah Small embraced Iraq's future. His ambition was energetic and relentless in the face of war and turmoil. Seeing the Iraqis through his eyes and letters, I adopted his outlook, hoping another generation could bind and mend what the present generation had torn asunder, and that minds were being shaped in this old land to think in new ways.

+ + +

Insaf traveled to Iraq in March 2012, the same month Jeremiah was killed. She came to lead a women's conference in Erbil.

Seventy women registered for the conference, but one hundred showed up. They came from Baghdad, Mosul, Sulaymaniyah, and Kirkuk. Forty-five women traveled by bus from Baghdad, enduring hours of road travel and multiple checkpoints to get there. Since the U.S. pullout, Iraqi civilian deaths had averaged about five hundred per month. Even as the women in Erbil met to talk about suffering, the persecution would continue.

Insaf had invited three speakers to present Bible teaching and counseling on suffering and abuse. One of them, Sahar Sarsam, was a psychologist and Insaf's longtime friend from Kirkuk. Sahar's daughter had been one of Jeremiah's students and was in the classroom when Jeremiah was killed. Her daughter was grieving, but Sahar came to speak to the women anyway, her messages amplified by such a close tragedy.

Other women had relatives in Syria facing the horror there. Word kept arriving of the slaughter of hundreds of Christians—including entire families with their children—in the city of Homs. For years Iraqis had fled to Syria during similar killings and kidnappings, but now the Syrians were coming across the border to Iraq.

As the women met, word came that a church leader from Mosul had gone missing. Everyone thought he had been kidnapped, but he was found killed. Such abductions were becoming more common. After a twenty-nine-year-old man from Kirkuk had been kidnapped and decapitated in May 2011 because his family couldn't pay a $100,000 ransom, the Chaldean Catholic archbishop in Erbil, Bashar Warda, had spoken out: "The murder was meant to intimidate Christians so that in the future they will more readily pay ransom demands."[4]

At that time, Archbishop Warda counted 573 Christians killed in religiously motivated attacks. Others said the number was closer to a thousand, while thousands had been killed in the course of war and tens of thousands had been forced to flee that sort of violence in order to stay alive and protect their families.

The head of Mosul's police force said he had records for sixty-nine assassinations of Christians from 2005 to 2011. Terrorists went to great lengths to capitalize on Christians who were leaving the city: They visited real estate agents to demand the names of Christians who had recently sold their homes. They would then target those Christians for kidnapping, knowing they would have money. One real estate agent who refused to cooperate was killed.

Such brutal intimidation did not stop the women from gathering. "Our sisterhood is bonded by both the fellowship of suffering and the triumphant truth of who we are in Christ," Insaf wrote to me in an e-mail.

By this time, the violence in Iraq should have seemed commonplace. But Jeremiah Small's death undid me for weeks, I think because it undid so many hopes. Killings, kidnappings, disappearances—nothing seemed to stop them, and no place seemed safe any longer. Every Iraqi awoke knowing that the violence might hit close to home that day.

Jeremiah's killing seemed to target the future. It represented the suppression of young, energetic voices. It signified the silencing of one who had tried to cross cultural and religious divides. It was one more thread pulled from the fabric of civilization that so many wanted to see made new.

After more than 4,400 American combat deaths in Iraq over the course of the eight-year war, Jeremiah Small was the first American casualty in the postwar era. The English teacher from Washington State would be the only American killed in Iraq in 2012. His death, far from bringing closure to an era, seemed to open a fresh wound.

15

THE NEW JIHAD

Aleppo, 2013

....

Open these doors, these doors of mercy for us.

ARMENIAN LITURGY FOR PALM SUNDAY

....

Christians in the Syrian city of Homs were paying $600 for a cab ride to Lebanon—about an eighty-five-mile journey. The exorbitant sum was their ticket to safety and sanity following a two-year siege of the city in central Syria.

Homs fell to rebels early in the civil war that began in 2011. Since then, it had been relentlessly fought over, with mortars and rocket fire targeting the city's Christian Quarter. Every church and school in the area had been destroyed, said survivors. They described months of living in apartment buildings crumpled by shelling and barrel bombs. The damage left so much rubble and destitution that many found it hard to escape. Residents shredded pillows to burn for fuel. When the foam and feathers were gone, they burned their clothes, needing the fires to boil weeds to eat.

Syrians who had hung on for years into the war, trying to salvage their homes and their businesses, were now giving up, fleeing. On a blustery day in early spring I would meet up with some of them in Lebanon's Bekaa Valley, where they were living in tents set up next to fields of strawberries and red cabbage. In the shadow of snowcapped Mount Hermon, hundreds of Christians were arriving every day at a border crossing barely ten miles away. The families who made it out arrived without shoes, some with only the clothes on their backs. "I can't go to bed and not worry I will wake up with the wall on my head," one mother from Homs told me.

I first visited Homs in 2002 while reporting on a delegation of Christians meeting with Muslim clergy. At St. Mary's, a Syriac Orthodox church built over an underground church dating back to AD 50, the group had tea together. A British businessman, one of the Christians in the delegation, spoke movingly of his brother's death in the Twin Towers, his desire for an end to jihadi bloodshed.

In 2013 a pastor from Homs sent me photos of the city's destroyed churches, and I recognized the room where we had met: Plaster from bombed-out walls covered the velvet couches where we had sat, and glass from exploded windows spilled over everything. By that time nearly 400,000 Syrian Christians had been forced from their homes, and nearly forty churches had been destroyed. "If this continues the way it is, there will come a time when there will be no more Christians in Syria," Riad Jarjour, a Presbyterian pastor from Homs, told me.

ISIS gathered strength in the crumbling chaos, amassing fighters and smuggling weapons in the north, near Syria's border with Turkey. As the terrorist organization fought to gain control over other militant groups, street chants by masked fighters—"Christians to Beirut, Alawites to their graves!" —gave way to all-out attacks. In March 2013 the Islamist militant group al-Nusra Front seized the northern city of Raqqa, with a population of about 200,000. The next month the Islamic State of Iraq (ISI) announced that it had absorbed al-Nusra Front and now should be known as ISIS.

Raqqa had once been the northern post of Baghdad's Abbasid caliphate. Caliph Mansur built a walled city on the same plan as Baghdad, with gates and towers by the Euphrates, which flowed from Raqqa down to Anbar Province and to Baghdad. Mansur intended Raqqa as a forward base to launch attacks on the Byzantine frontier. Abu Bakr al-Baghdadi named Raqqa the ISIS capital.

Anyone who studied the history and geography could see the ISIS strategy: Raqqa faced the western frontier toward "Rome," the ISIS metaphor for the decadent, *kafir* ("infidel") West. Eastward, the Islamic fighters would follow the Euphrates to Fallujah and Ramadi in Anbar Province, and on to Baghdad itself.

At the time ISIS took control, Raqqa's Christian population numbered about three thousand. The Islamic fighters took captive those Christians who didn't flee, turning their churches into mosques and holding cells, forbidding crosses, Bible reading, and prayer in public, and demanding the Christians pay in gold a jizya in exchange for "protection."[1]

Christians suspected of siding with the Syrian government were executed, along with Alawites from Assad's minority Muslim sect. Over the next months, increasing reports of brutality emerged, as Christian areas were left wholly unprotected. One young man testified that he was hung by his arms, robbed, and beaten by rebels "just for being a Christian."[2] ISIS henchmen constructed crosses in a central square by attaching two-by-fours to light poles, and there they hung their victims crucifixion-style. They appeared to be already dead, said eyewitnesses, but the public display sent a message: Christians were no longer tolerated, and ISIS planned to rule by fear.[3] The holding cells in Raqqa and Aleppo housed American hostages, too, including journalist James Foley, who would be beheaded in public videos designed to taunt the United States.

Children, according to a UN fact-finding mission, were "killed or publicly executed, crucified, beheaded, and stoned to death." The team also reported "the capture of young girls by [ISIS] for sexual purposes. Girls as young as twelve."[4]

As the findings surfaced, the United States focused on the Syrian government's use of chemical weapons. President Barack Obama's declared "red line" over the weapons' deployment was clearly crossed in August. When he was briefed on a chemical weapons attack that had killed 1,400 Syrians, American air strikes seemed unavoidable and imminent.

On the night four U.S. Navy destroyers were poised to launch Tomahawk missiles in the eastern Mediterranean, the warring sides took cover. Syrian commanders ordered their forces back to barracks. ISIS dispersed its fighters to remote reaches of Syria, including the area around Homs, where some ISIS fighters holed up in a historic Crusader castle. Then they waited.

Abruptly, President Obama changed course. He ordered the destroyers and missile launchers to stand down, saying he would seek congressional approval before moving forward.

When the congressional effort failed, as it was certain to in a Democratic-led Senate and Republican-led House, the White House deferred to the UN to account for Syria's chemical weapons stockpile, a process that would take months. By failing to act once the red line was crossed, the president saved the United States from involvement in a civil war. But his decision not to act sent a profound message across the Middle East: The United States had no stake in the widening war with terrorists. This message served to disperse ISIS throughout the country and at the same time embolden jihadists to act with impunity.

As the ISIS shadow spread from Raqqa, life became more hellish than ever for Christians in Homs, Aleppo, Raqqa, and elsewhere. "Massacres are taking place for no reason and without any justification against Christians," said former Lebanese president Amin Gemayel. "What is happening to Christians is a genocide."[5]

In Aleppo, Bishop Antoine Audo said, "People are terrified." With explosions and gunfire sounding in the distance, Bishop Audo told me by telephone, "They fear a situation that is becoming more and more violent and uncertain."

I spoke to Bishop Audo several times in November and December 2013, as the cold crept into his upstairs apartment and there was no heat to ward it off, no electricity for a light to see by. I had visited his home during my 2008 visit to Aleppo, joining him one evening for creamy vegetable soup prepared by a housekeeper earlier in the day. We sat at a small table. Books dominated the larger table in his lamp-lit sitting room, stacks arranged carefully according to his reading of the moment, Bibles on one side, history and geography on another. Bishop Audo had often traveled overseas before the war. His table revealed an eclectic reading habit in multiple languages to bolster his skills.

As we spoke, I thought of the dark apartment and Audo's diminished day-to-day existence. He had no power and was lighting a candle when I reached him, he said, to prepare the coming week's sermons.

The phone went dead. I redialed. I would be cut off again and again or interrupted by sudden, deafening static during our conversation. Each time I would redial to begin again, staring as I did so into the hollowed eyes of Syrian children on my computer screen. This was a war most Syrians didn't want, and they were the ones paying the heaviest price. Children suffered from malnutrition, from shrapnel wounds; some had limbs blown off, and some had the pallid death mask of nerve-gas asphyxiation.

The day we spoke, a government rocket killed six civilians at a traffic circle near St. Joseph's, the Chaldean cathedral not far from Bishop Audo's residence. ISIS fighters killed and beheaded a man that day, too, raising his decapitated head for onlookers just outside the city. Audo confirmed these details and said there were reports in the villages of Christians, even young children, being beheaded and dismembered.

Not giving in to the devastation, the sixty-seven-year-old bishop told me he had just returned from officiating at a wedding. His route took him through areas of rubble and cratered buildings. After two years of civil war, the debris was so pervasive that even when the bombs weren't falling, the limestone and concrete dust was rising. Aleppo was one of the largest cities in the Middle East, its old center with its ancient souk and citadel among the best preserved anywhere, until the war. Day or night, the air now hung thick with war debris, the crumbled buildings exhaling their losses so unceasingly that satellite imagery captured the haze from space, thick like a cloud covering.

Militants kidnapped two prominent clergymen in Aleppo, but Bishop Audo wasn't changing his routines, except to wear regular clothes rather than vestments in the streets. He refused to hire his own security, even though he was a well-known church leader throughout the country, with a distinctive crop of white hair. As rector at St. Joseph's, he continued to hold a daily Eucharist service, earlier than usual so that parishioners wouldn't have to walk home in the dark. Twenty to thirty people were coming. Every day on his way to and from the church and on visits, he saw dead bodies in the streets.

"I am not afraid. It's a question of confidence. I am confident of God's provision as I am doing my job, and I like to go in the streets to feel the situation and the suffering of the people," he said.

During the Iraq War, Audo had helped thousands of Iraqi refugees find food and housing. Now he was doing the same for his own city—in some cases, for his own parishioners. Everything was in short supply, particularly fuel and medicine. Snipers were picking off shoppers as they stood in line to buy bread. Audo and the Chaldeans (with support from the Catholic relief agency Caritas) were distributing food baskets to three thousand families every month. They had arranged drivers to deliver the foodstuffs, to ferry victims in the area to hospitals, and to provide some medicines that were scarce. They had found housing and had given rent support and blankets to hundreds of families who'd lost their homes in bombs and rocket attacks. They were helping Christians and Muslims alike, he pointed out.

"It's very bad in Aleppo," he said. "We go four or five days without electricity, and sometimes without water. Imagine, in such a big city."

For all he endured, Audo believed Christians in the Middle East had a responsibility to continue living alongside Muslim people. But most Syrians, he said, had come to fear the extremists. They were not used to living in an Islamic theocracy. "We are not Saudi Arabia."

Audo didn't waver over the significance of Christians remaining in Syria and the region, despite its horrors. "It's important for us as Christians to be alive in the original lands of our fathers in the Middle East. Not only for us but for the church in the world," he said. "We have a long history of living together with Muslim people. It is Christianity who has the Arab culture, and it is very important to have Christian-Arab presence. If we lose it, I am convinced it will be a big loss for Islam, too."

+ + +

In early spring 2014 I flew to Baghdad. This time I traveled without Insaf. Unlike our first flight together in 2003, my 767 from Beirut took a direct-line approach to landing at Baghdad International, setting down on the runway, pulling into a Jetway, and discharging us into a well-lit, bustling terminal.

Inside the terminal, the gift shop and striped carpet were the same as before, but unlike on my last visit, I appeared to be the only American anywhere. An Iranian businessman helped me find my way to a taxi that delivered me to a checkpoint, where I had to wait what seemed like an eternity for my driver. The hot sun baked my bare head; women were few, and they all wore head coverings. This was my first trip to Baghdad since the U.S. withdrawal, and the streets felt strange, hostile. An Iraqi soldier approached me. "You should not be waiting here," he said.

I glanced around the dusty lot designated for arrivals, surrounded by military. I told him my driver was on his way. "Isn't it safe here?" I asked.

"Come this way," he motioned, and I joined him at a covered check-point stall where there was shade.

Once the driver arrived, we sped into the city along a newly paved, eight-lane boulevard divided by freshly planted palms. It was mostly deserted. At intersections Iraqi army convoys stood guard in armored vehicles, their uniforms and trucks covered in the black-blue-gray camouflage pattern, in contrast to the desert colors of the Americans.

I made my way to the west bank of the Tigris, a secluded section of Baghdad just off main thoroughfares where residential streets and government ministries mingled, and where the al-Mansour Hotel with its aqua swimming pool towered over the lazy river. I wouldn't be staying there or in any hotel but inside the compound of St. George's Church, just a few blocks away. It sat just outside what had been the Green Zone, now called the International Zone, on Haifa Street. A leafy hedge sur-rounding the church compound concealed thick concrete blast walls.

St. George's had survived the disappearance of Maher Dakhil, his wife, his son, and two lay pastors, plus explosions in 2004, 2005, and 2007. In 2009, the church had recovered after a bomb detonated nearby—but the explosion killed a hundred people and injured hun-dreds more. It damaged every building on the church's property.

My driver had to navigate two checkpoints manned by swarms of Iraqi soldiers to reach the church's iron entrance gate. The gate could be opened only from the inside. The church had expanded its familiar rose garden from when it reopened under Maher in 2003, and bloom-ing bushes of every color greeted me.

Canon Andrew White, "the vicar of Baghdad," had presided over ser-vices since Maher's disappearance. He was popular, and the St. George's sanctuary was often full. About three hundred parishioners gathered for a Sunday afternoon worship service—a far cry from the eight hundred who had come a decade earlier, but significant by Baghdad standards in 2014. A faithful few dozen came for Bible studies, a youth service, and a prayer meeting during the week. I would spend the week before Easter living inside the compound in a roomy but sparsely furnished guesthouse, seeing Baghdad once again at ground level, through the Iraqis' eyes. Every morning I fixed tea or Nescafé by a window in the guesthouse kitchen.

When someone heard me stirring, one of the women working at the church would knock on the door to offer me warm flatbread as big as a platter and fresh *gaymer*, the white cheese I'd learned to love while living with Muthafar and Ghada years ago.

The church had been repaired and refurbished many times, its walls evolving from beige to a chalky pink with successive coats of paint. It had plush crimson carpeting in the center aisle and new wooden pews instead of the plastic chairs of earlier years. In a bit of poetic justice, the church hired a carpenter who had once worked for Saddam Hussein, who had closed the church in 1991. A banner at the front was a gift from Americans at Wheaton College in Illinois, where Canon White sometimes lectured, and the original British dedication plaques honoring war veterans hung on side pillars.

Canon White's persona was as outsized as he was. At six feet three, he towered over most Iraqis, standing in size-sixteen shoes. Yet he approached parishioners, especially children, like a teddy bear. He had boisterous hugs for women and men, including a red-headed church gardener with autism, and he stood before services to greet everyone at the church doorway. His rapport with Iraqis was surprising, considering that Canon White didn't speak Arabic. He knew enough Aramaic to recite prayers and catechisms along with the congregation, and he kept a translator at the ready—when I visited, a young assistant from Jordan with a Muslim background.

Canon White maintained a steady schedule of long days in Baghdad and travel throughout the Middle East. He made frequent trips home to England, where his wife and two sons still lived. Faiz Jerjees, an ordained Iraqi Anglican priest at St. George's, supervised the church in his absence.

St. George's also ran a medical clinic and kindergarten on the church grounds and managed relief work through a foundation. It fed five hundred poor families—mostly Shia Muslims—twice a month out of a storehouse next to the church building, and it supported other churches and charities in the city.

All these activities happened while the vicar, who would turn fifty in 2014, managed a seventeen-year battle with multiple sclerosis. Asked about his condition, he liked to tell visitors, "The Church of England doctors said I was not well enough to be a clergyman in the Church of England—so I went to Baghdad."

Multiple sclerosis slowed Canon White's speech and made it hard for him to stand very long without assistance. Outside the church compound he walked with a cane. Inside the church offices he often welcomed parishioners while reclining on a bed too small for his frame. Even so, it took four cell phones to keep his life in order—two for calls inside Iraq (one for each cell network, in case the other wasn't working), one for daily calls to his wife, and an international Truphone for everything else.

Returning from overseas travel in time for Holy Week, Canon White greeted the congregation with loud enthusiasm: "You are my people, in my beloved Iraq, and I am so glad to be back with you." It was a warm, sunny afternoon in early April, and I had watched the worshipers arrive by the busload to greet the vicar and one another, seemingly unconcerned about the rising dangers in Baghdad.

ISIS fighters were pressing toward the city from Anbar Province about fifty miles away, where they had taken the city of Fallujah in January. Violence was definitely rising. Canon White had been sounding alarms about the ISIS threat to Baghdad for months. When I spoke to him by phone after Christmas 2013, I resolved to make the trip to Baghdad to see firsthand the sturdy resolve of the tall vicar and his congregation in the face of rising threats of which few in the United States were aware.

So I shadowed Canon White as he went about his business in the city, riding in the backseat while he took the front passenger seat. His driver had survived being stuffed in a trunk by kidnappers and several shootings—"You'd see five bodies lying on the street outside the Green Zone any morning," he said as he navigated the chaos of Baghdad's traffic unfazed. We skirted several bombings in the city during the week I was there, hearing the thuds not far away. My departure was delayed when the U.S. Embassy, citing "credible threats" against Americans, warned against any U.S. citizens passing through the airport, a heavily fortified enclosure.

The danger had touched St. George's directly. On Christmas Day three months earlier, ISIS-linked terrorists had targeted Christian neighborhoods and a church in Baghdad, killing thirty-seven and wounding sixty. In February a car bomb near St. George's killed two close associates of the church, shopkeepers who helped with supplies. Later a car bombing along a main thoroughfare in central Baghdad's Karada district killed a man who had attended the church, along with three others. In the first three months of 2014, more than two thousand Iraqis had been killed nationwide in terrorist-related violence.

Canon White kept to his schedule anyway, which included presiding over two chapel services at the U.S. Embassy and visiting the shut-ins of his congregation. "We are all in such a desperate situation, and all we have is our Lord and each other," he said, stepping into his SUV. He kept his own driver and usually an Iraqi army escort. Armed soldiers would hop into the car or onto the back bumper as we set off down Haifa Street. A truck with a gun mount and more soldiers would fall in behind us.

In Baghdad al-Jadidah one Friday afternoon, Canon White planned to visit five Christian families, including one with two grown, severely disabled men. The vicar wore his collar and dark clergy jacket, and groceries filled the back of the SUV as we set off. We passed the district's market, which teemed with shoppers and vendors beneath heavy canvas tarps held up by poles. Flocks of fattened sheep grazed on garbage, picking their way around concrete blast walls. Car bombings had returned to Baghdad al-Jadida ("New Baghdad"), so barricades blocked traffic to side streets. Residents would park their cars at the top of their own street to walk home.

At the first home, police appeared in the doorway, saying we had to leave. Five kidnappings had taken place in the district that morning, and officers feared we would be targeted. The soldier who allowed us through the last checkpoint already had been reprimanded, punished, and docked five days' pay, we were told. Still, Canon White negotiated. He persuaded the security detail to permit one more visit. "Yallah," said his driver. *Let's go.*

Two men who looked like victims of palsy jumped up and down on the flat terrace roof of their home when the SUV rounded the corner. Canon White waved. Inside the house, our driver hauled groceries to the kitchen as the disfigured brothers, both in their thirties, tumbled into the main room, one limping and the other crawling across the floor. Spit oozed from the corners of their mouths, which their mother (who looked about my age) wiped with a single cloth. Both men wore pants soaked in urine. Canon White embraced them, and we prayed.

When the vicar pulled a small wooden traveling communion box from his jacket, it was clear he had celebrated the Lord's Supper with them this way before. Their eyes widened, and the men raised themselves, stiffening like sentries to stand straight on crooked legs before the vicar. I held the box while he poured wine to serve them. They closed their eyes, their hands cupped and extended to receive the communion wafers. Their mouths parted at the same time to drink from the common cup as Canon White recited from the Gospel of John.

Later, as the security details sped us through dusty streets dodging barricades, I asked Canon White what he hoped to see from his ministry in five years. He answered simply: "I hope that we are serving the churches in the community and the community itself, and that we are seeing faith deepen in our own congregation."

On Saturday we made our way to the U.S. embassy, where White regularly conducted chapel services. It took an hour to get through security. After passing through Iraqi army checkpoints, we had to surrender our own driver and car and allow someone with proper credentials to take us to the entrance. We were searched by heavily armed guards, then passed through metal detectors, where I gave up my passport, camera, and phone. We weren't done yet. Even inside the 104-acre fortified compound—nearly the size of Vatican City and ten times the size of any other U.S. embassy—diplomats escorted us to an armored white Suburban and drove us to the meeting hall.

An expansive lawn lined with date palms stretched the length of the compound, and a groundskeeper was mowing what already looked like a golf course. On a patio, embassy personnel sipped lattes and chatted in the cool, bright morning sun. Just as I began to feel like Alice in Wonderland, up ahead on the patio expanse appeared a life-size chess set.

The fortified complex was about all that was left of the American presence in Baghdad, and Canon White was used to the alternate universe. He greeted a smattering of Americans, Brits, South Africans, and a few others who worked in the International Zone. He conducted services as he always did, sitting at a lectern and quoting Scripture, on this day from the story of Jesus raising Lazarus in the Gospel of John. He talked of miraculous healings among Iraqis and waved in the general direction of Haifa Street as he told stories about "my people, out there."

Later I asked one of the attendees, "What's your impression of St. George's and Iraqi churches in general?"

He looked at me blankly. "I've never been to St. George's or any-where out there."

"Really?" I said.

"Our rules of engagement are clear. We stay in the zone and transact our business from here. Iraqis come here to meet us."

A physician who had worked at the embassy for three years asked me about the city, then said, "You know, I read in my Bible about Ur and Babylon, places just there across the river, and I can't go to see them."

I was stunned. But I shouldn't have been. Americans at home and in Baghdad wanted no more casualties in Iraq. The cost of safety, though, was the loss of connection with Iraqi lives, with the people who made being in Iraq meaningful at all. From where they sat, the city was as abstract as Kansas or the moon. The way ISIS lurked, not only at the city's edges but in the minds of Baghdad residents, seemed abstract too.

+ + +

Back out in the city's streets that week, I visited a number of churches, as many as security would allow, all of them operating at half their size from the start of the war. Christians who had financial means or family already living abroad had emigrated. Many more had moved to northern Iraq, to Qaraqosh and the villages of Nineveh Plains or to Iraqi Kurdistan, where churches operated more freely and bombings rarely if ever occurred.

At the Armenian church in Baghdad's Karada district, Archbishop Avak Asadourian told me, "It's only a matter of time—thirty years, and no Christians will remain in the whole region." He had been primate over the Armenian Church in Iraq since 1982, when it numbered about 40,000. At the start of the Iraq War, the numbers had fallen to 18,000, he said, and now fewer than 10,000 Armenian adherents remained. The hopes and dreams of the Christians in Baghdad from the early days of U.S. occupation, when they anticipated new freedom and opportunity, had vanished.

"I used to say to parishioners, 'Don't leave.' But I can't say that anymore," Asadourian said. "It would be on my conscience if something happened to them."

It was the start of Holy Week, and the archbishop, despite his bleak outlook, looked forward to the traditional Turun-Patzek, or "Opening of the Doors" service. On Palm Sunday congregants would gather outside the massive fifteen-foot-high wooden doors of the church, chanting a liturgy that processed them across the threshold into the sanctuary. The ceremony symbolized a procession from a season of Lent to the passion of Christ, from sacrifice to abundance, as they celebrated Jesus' triumphal entry to Jerusalem, his death, and his resurrection:

Open to us, O Lord, the door of your mercy, and make us worthy of your dwellings of light, together with your saints. Receive us also, O Savior, into your mansions prepared for your saints, and inscribe our names in the Book of Life.

The archbishop, as he had done for thirty years, would lead the clergy in swinging wide the doors to usher them in. The rite was a welcome symbol of the original Palm Sunday: Jesus' entry into Jerusalem, where worshipers from around the world had gathered for the Passover feast—an entrance marking Jesus as the Passover lamb, a sacrifice for all people everywhere. "I am the door," I would hear Canon White recite all week, quoting Jesus as he taught from the Gospel of John. "If any man enters in by me, he shall be saved."

Yet these Easter celebrations were a shadow of what they'd once been in Iraq. In years past, church courtyards in Baghdad, Mosul, and Qaraqosh teemed with throngs of worshipers: a pageant of palm branches, singing, and walking in procession. In one old photo an Iraqi showed me, worshipers stood on the church rooftop waiting for the procession. An elderly Iraqi Christian who lived in the United States boasted, "In Iraq when we have Easter, we go to all the churches. Here there is no Easter; here we have egg and bunny."

Most Americans, including American Christians, weren't aware of Baghdad's sudden uptick in terror activity, or the ongoing threats to Iraq's Christian community as Easter celebrations commenced. Yet in the minds of many Iraqis, the U.S. government was to blame, explained Canon White: "The Americans came and they liberated them but didn't see through any of the change. The country fell into chaos, violence, and poverty, and then the Americans left."[6]

At the Alliance Church, I met with Muthafar Yacoub, now one of the church's pastors. A decade earlier the church had grown to more than 1,000 members, but now about 250 people attended. Like St. George's, it sat behind tall blast walls, but inside were new classrooms and a coffee shop that overlooked a courtyard with date palms, their trunks wrapped in twinkling lights.

Muthafar and his family had moved several times since I stayed in their Rasafah home in 2003, but he had no plans to leave Baghdad again. "I want to stay all my life," he said. "I love my country, and I covenant with the Lord to serve Iraq. I love Baghdad, and I am sure if he wants me here, he will keep me safe."

Muthafar worked with the Alliance church full-time. His wife, Ghada, who never returned to dentistry, helped lead the women's ministry but was currently away in another part of the city caring for her parents. I had seen Muthafar and his family in 2008 at a conference for evangelicals on Lake Dokan in Iraqi Kurdistan. The hilly lakeside resort had drawn about eight hundred evangelical believers, who came for days of singing, teaching, and testimonies about the growth of the church in Iraq. Many, maybe most, of those believers had left in the intervening years, escaping to Jordan or Germany, Detroit or Chicago.

In 2014 Muthafar moved with Ghada and their two daughters to the home of his cousin, who had left for Canada. His daughter Lydia was about to finish her university degree in pharmacology, never wavering from the time I first knew her when she had vowed to go into medicine. Roda was in tenth grade, but besides school, she rarely left the house unless she was with her father. "She has a lot of fear," Muthafar said.

The girls had narrowly escaped bombings over the years and knew too many friends who had been killed. The four family members stayed in contact now wherever they went, Muthafar explained. Rarely fifteen minutes went by without them texting one another to check in. Some years had been better than others, but now with ISIS rumored to be at Baghdad's doorstep, the girls and their parents were cautious once again.

Muthafar and his family grounded me in the reality of life in Baghdad, as they had done at the beginning of the war. He had a sister whose family had moved many times for safety reasons, and they now lived in Qaraqosh in Nineveh Plains. He had no plans for his family to join them.

"Everyone tells me life is easier in the north," he said, "but the only safe place is the place where God wants me to be." He recognized that threats in Baghdad once again were rising, but he was convinced his family should remain in the city. As we spoke, Roda texted her father, worried, wanting to know when he'd be home.

16

EMPTYING MOSUL

Mosul, June 2014

....

Ask Mosul, city of Islam, about the lions—how their fierce struggle
brought liberation.
The land of glory has shed its humiliation
and defeat—and put on the raiment of splendor.

AHLAM AL-NASR, POETESS OF THE ISLAMIC STATE

....

The Islamic State of Iraq and Syria moved on Mosul overnight in June—lightning fast, but in some quarters long awaited.

Samah Anwar was afraid of going to school in Mosul every day, especially that spring term. Islamic militants with their tattered beards and foreign accents had once again infiltrated the city's western neighborhoods. Iraqi soldiers lined the streets, while explosions and gunfire could be heard at any hour.

War had prolonged the time it took to finish school, and Samah, a Yazidi woman from an outlying village, was in her last term at the University of Mosul medical college. "Each day when I was going to Mosul, I was thinking, *It's the last time I'll see my parents, my family, my village.*"

For months, residents witnessed the rise of street violence. Bombings and killings became everyday occurrences, and Samah said she grew used to seeing the dead or wounded on the street on her way to class.

Samah was a slight woman with the build of a girl, though at twenty-three she was old (by Yazidi standards) to be single. Her family came from the Nineveh village of Bashiqa, where Christians and Yazidis lived alongside one another but in mostly segregated communities. Samah left her tight-knit family each day, determined to complete her education. Her wide, dark-brown eyes flashed as she spoke, but she was matter-of-fact, having spent most of her lifetime living in war and fear. One minute we were talking about her family; the next she was asking me about Westlife and other boy bands. When I said I didn't know anything about them, her jaw dropped. "How can you speak such good English and not know these bands?" she exclaimed.

In the last term of her five years' university-level training, Samah was preparing for final exams in medicine when ISIS invaded on the morning of June 10. She had stayed home in Bashiqa, ten miles northeast of Mosul, to study. "It happened suddenly," she said. "We awakened in the morning to see our village filled with immigrants. They were hungry, thirsty, dirty." Some wore only the loose gowns they'd slept in.

Startled by their appearance, Samah's mother invited the Mosul evacuees off the street and spread out flatbread and cheese. Samah began pulling shoes and clothes from a closet for them. "We helped them with whatever we had," said Samah. "They arrived with nothing."

ISIS had swept into Mosul during the darkness of the early morning hours, brandishing automatic rifles atop convoys of Toyota Hilux pickups. The fighters erupted across the city with purpose and strategy, many dressed head to toe in black and wearing black balaclavas or scarves tied across their faces. The commotion in the darkness achieved precisely the terror they desired. In Christian neighborhoods, drowsy residents emerged from sleep to face life-or-death demands. Without protection from Iraqi police and army forces, they were at the militants' mercy. Those who chose to stay without meeting the fighters' demands were discovered shot dead in their homes, slumped over sofas and armchairs. From fellow students, Samah learned that ISIS had taken seventy women hostage at her university.

Sinan Almeerak, another student at the University of Mosul, was a twenty-six-year-old Christian. He lived with his parents and other siblings on the east bank of the Tigris in a house fronting the main road leading south to Kirkuk. At about 1 a.m., noises awakened the family.

"We saw many people fleeing, and many army cars departing too. Then my uncle called to tell us that Daesh had come," Sinan later told me.

In the darkness, the militants of ISIS (*Daesh* in Arabic) first took control of the commercial and historic heart of Mosul on the western bank of the Tigris. They captured Nineveh's provincial government headquarters, the seemingly impenetrable compound I had visited with Eveline Aoraha in 2008.

Iraqi army regulars simply abandoned their posts. Against advice, Nouri al-Maliki had installed second-rate Shia commanders in mostly Sunni Mosul. They had little stomach for protecting the city, and ISIS swiftly routed Iraq's security forces. One Iraqi army explosives specialist said that seeing a commander run away in the midst of a firefight "is like being shot in the head."

News reports showed the highways out of Mosul littered with the soldiers' uniforms. The near-instant retreat seemed preplanned, and residents wondered if it had been orchestrated by former cadres of Saddam Hussein. Izzat Ibrahim al-Douri, the King of Clubs, remained a fugitive, rumored to be conspiring with Sunni militants. As the ISIS command structure became more clear, twenty-five of its top forty leaders would turn out to be former Iraqi military leaders.

With little opposition, ISIS militants penetrated the city systematically, overtaking two prisons, two television stations, police stations, the central bank, the airport, and the military base outside of town that once served as the hub of U.S. military operations in northern Iraq. They captured Humvees and weapons, dispatching some of the booty back to Syria and using the rest to further attacks in Mosul and the surrounding Nineveh Province. In one overnight lightning strike, American armaments designed to fight terror had become the weapons of terror.

ISIS fighters had strewn tires from captured military vehicles up and down main thoroughfares and set them on fire. Thick black smoke puffed over the city from the burning rubber. The fighters also torched abandoned cars. They raised their weapons above their heads and fired into the air, shouting demands via loudspeakers. The Christians and other infidels could stay only if they converted to Islam. Otherwise, the militants shouted, they had to leave—now.

Before dawn perhaps hundreds of thousands of the city's residents had made their way out in cars, others on foot, all of them taking refuge in the towns of Nineveh Plains or wherever they could get to first. Sinan and his family waited for the sun to rise before departing. Just after 4 a.m. they started out on foot for the town of Qaraqosh, twenty miles away. Sinan had an uncle who had moved there in 2006 after receiving threats in Mosul, and the family planned to stay with him.

"We took simple clothing and our identity documents. We didn't have time for more, and we are thinking we are going away only for a while," he later told me.

About two million people lived in Mosul. Overnight and into the next day, 150,000 fled the city. "If this continues, Mosul soon will be emptied of Christians," one departing family said.

In Baghdad, Maliki—who had won a third term in close April elections but had yet to form a coalition government—called on parliament to declare a state of emergency and announced a "general mobilization" of forces. Mosul, he said, would not be allowed to fall "under the shadow of terror and terrorists."[1] But in Mosul, the shadow had already fallen.

Sinan's family walked for seven hours before reaching Qaraqosh. "Everything was burning," Sinan said. They pressed their shirts to their noses to block the stench of burning tires and gasoline. Black smoke appeared like a curtain, and daytime temperatures soared above 100 degrees. At one point Sinan heard a sharp sucking sound and felt a bullet whiz past his shoulder. He and his family were shot at four times, he said, never sure by whom. "Between night and day, everything changed."

Sinan's family, fifteen members from various parts of Mosul, made it to Qaraqosh to spend the night. All of them arrived at his uncle's home, weary from fear and exhausted by the heat, sinking to sofas and the floor. Out in the streets, more families poured into Qaraqosh, piling into homes of friends and relatives by moonlight, some taking refuge in churches and a local convent.

Only when the evening grew quiet, Sinan said, did they begin to think of the future, starting with the very next day. They had brought nothing with them, and they had left their livelihoods behind in Mosul. What would they do now? They had no money, nothing even to sell. As worn out as they were, no one could sleep, thinking what their futures might hold. Sinan said, "We only have waiting."

No one could sleep in Bashiqa either. "We were living in worry and tension," Samah said. "At night in each house, the sons and fathers—even mothers—carried guns to prepare for the fight. We thought, *They will come to us at night like what happened in Mosul.*"

In Kirkuk, about one hundred miles southeast of Mosul, residents heard that ISIS was headed their way, determined to capture the heart of the country's oil fields that lay in between. "Ninety-nine percent of the Christians have left Mosul," said Haitham Jazrawi, the pastor of the evangelical church in Kirkuk. Years ago Insaf's home in Kirkuk had been struck by a missile, and everyone there was familiar with what it was like to live in tension with authorities, ethnic groups, and now Islamic State threats. Haitham was the first pastor I reached by phone just after learning of the ISIS takeover of Mosul. When I talked to him again that same evening, he spoke rapidly and louder than usual. "No one knows what will happen to us in the next days," he said, obviously nervous. "Pray for us. We still believe that our Lord wants us to stay in Iraq."

Over the coming days, it would prove harder and harder to stay anywhere in the vicinity of ISIS. The terrorist organization kidnapped two nuns and three orphans, releasing them two weeks later. Women were restricted from leaving their homes, and when they did, they were ordered to be veiled. ISIS took over forty churches in Mosul, destroying crosses and statuary, turning some into prisons for captured women and girls.

Even as reports emerged of torture and abuse, including rape, some Christians returned to their homes, hoping to reach some accommodation with the ISIS authorities in Mosul. They thought if they lay low, they might keep their property. Eventually shops would open again, and business would resume.

ISIS made quick work of imposing Sharia law and a new Islamic regime. During Friday prayers on July 18, instead of the muezzin's call to prayer going out from the mosques, the loudspeakers demanded that remaining Christians leave. They had until noon Saturday. The deadline and the conditions were unequivocal, familiar to Christians: convert or pay jizya to remain as second-class citizens. For all others, there was nothing left "but the sword."

Duraid Hikmat, a resident, said most Christians were afraid to leave at that point, afraid of being identified as Christians by ISIS, who now had militants staked out everywhere in the city. Some converted to Islam on the spot.

Others left as best they could. Ahlam, a thirty-four-year-old mother of two young boys, said she and her husband carried their boys on their shoulders for twelve miles just to escape before the deadline. They saw hundreds doing the same, including many helping the elderly and disabled. Church leaders said 150 families left Mosul under the deadline threat, and those few who remained, thinking they could negotiate with the militants, had been advised by their churches to flee.

Out in Nineveh Plains, volunteers from Iraqi Kurdistan drove in to await the exiles in safe areas, giving them rides to nearby towns so they could avoid walking in the heat. Ahlam was in tears when she and her family met a ride that way. "I left my home in Mosul, which my family built decades ago. And it was taken away in an instant," she said. "Everything's gone, all our memories. Our home has become property of the Islamic State."

From her home in Toronto, Insaf began connecting families she learned were fleeing Mosul with Christians in the north, in Iraqi Kurdistan, who could help them. The churches in cities like Erbil and

Dohuk prepared packets of water, diapers, formula, and flatbread, drove them to intersections on the roads leading north out of Mosul, and waited. As families like Ahlam's began to arrive, they received a care packet and, in some cases, offers of housing in church classrooms or homes away from the danger.

ISIS wasted no time confiscating property in Mosul, spray-painting homes belonging to Christians with the black Arabic letter *nun*, for *Nasara*, or Nazarene, the name Christians were commonly known by in Arabic. At one gated home belonging to a Christian family, an olive tree spilled its branches over the wall, and below that the militants spray-painted, "Long live the Islamic State in Iraq and the Levant.[2] Muslims are happy with the return of Mujahideen. Allah is Greater."

Outside the city, the Islamic fighters posted checkpoints, mostly to intimidate and extract valuables from those fleeing. They pointed their guns directly at the children while stripping the parents of their valuables. They forced mothers to turn over gold jewelry and fathers to give up their cell phones and cash.

One mother dropped her diamond engagement ring into her baby's diaper, and she and her children made it safely through. In the hasty departure she'd become separated from her husband and had no other resources to buy her family food. An elderly man, arriving in the safety of a church in Nineveh Plains for the night, described how the ISIS fighters entered his house. "They said if you convert to Islam, you can stay in your home; otherwise get out." His voice trembling, he added, "I had a chicken I wanted to take for food, but even that they did not let me take."

Disbelief ruled the moment in the quiet of Nineveh's ancient churches. "We have lived in this city and we have had a civilization for thousands of years," one Christian stammered, "and suddenly some strangers came and expelled us from our homes."[3]

Sinan observed that many of the ISIS fighters he saw were not from Iraq: "They were from Afghanistan, from Saudi Arabia." His family settled in at his uncle's home in Qaraqosh, realizing they would probably never go back to Mosul.

The door-to-door audacity of the Islamic militants shook Mosul residents. ISIS had walked freely on their streets, passed their doorways, and in some cases broken right into their homes, ordering them face-to-face and at gunpoint to leave. And no one had stopped them.

As the Christians congregated out in Nineveh Plains and told their stories, they suspected Muslim neighbors had actually shown ISIS the way to Christian homes—a breach of trust among neighboring Christians and Muslims, whose coexistence in the city had been generations in the making. And the refugees realized, with a sense of doom, that apart from a few fellow Christians, no one had come to help them—not their own army nor the police nor the outsiders to whom they had long looked for protection.

All over the country, Iraqis worried the campaign to expel Christians from Mosul would soon extend throughout Nineveh Province, stretching to the border with Syria and across ancient lands belonging not only to Christians but to Sabaean-Mandeans, Turkmen, and Yazidis. If that happened, warned Juliana Daoud, a professor at Basra University from Nineveh, it would be "the last nail in the Christians' coffin in Iraq."[4]

The Syriac archbishop of Mosul, Nicodemus Daoud Sharaf, was one of the last to leave. He left his home with only five minutes to spare, he said. He could see ISIS militants down the road three hundred yards away. He said, "They take everything from us, but they cannot take the God from our hearts—they cannot."[5]

✦ ✦ ✦

What I'd been told years ago by a NATO adviser turned out to be right. He described a meeting of American and European military commanders where he'd presented a report of the ongoing atrocities and injustices directed at Christians and other minorities. Then he asked one officer after another in the room, Would you intervene if genocide comes to Iraq's Christians?

I would not deploy my troops to intervene, came the American answer.

No, we would not intervene, came the British answer.

Later in London, he asked the chairman of the British government's Joint Intelligence Committee, and the answer was the same. No, we would not intervene.

The adviser said he even reframed the question: Sir, with your history of liberty for all and desire to do what is right, would you not intervene? No, we would not intervene.

The NATO adviser worried then of "a tragedy of unspeakable proportions" and said it would mean, as it had throughout the war years, that some of Iraq's most intellectual and successful citizenry—leaders in culture, academia, and business, not to mention many among its shopkeepers and working masses—would be made destitute, forced to go on the run.

What had been uttered in classified briefings was now playing out in northern Iraq. It was never clearly stated why, given the millions of dollars and thousands of lives the West had invested: the American veterans who had suffered injuries and sacrificed their limbs to IEDs, who were still living with their own trauma, only to see a more lasting, more widely traumatic destruction unfold. All the displaced Christians knew was that there would be no protection unit, no UN peacekeepers, no rapid deployment force to step between them and ISIS. There would be no National Guard–style show of force to protect their streets or their shops or their homes. There would not even be a policeman to direct traffic as they jammed the highways to flee.

For a decade U.S. and British troops, plus coalition forces from twenty-one other countries, had intervened militarily in Iraq. They'd spent tens of billions of dollars on building a "new Iraq" with civic projects and government remodeling at all levels. As Iraq's second-largest city fell into the hands of a foe on the United States' most-wanted-terrorist list, the nonresponse from the watching world was stunning and unprecedented.

Mosul's Christians had survived Persian conquest and Mongol invaders. They had endured the coming of the Arab armies, the early-twentieth-century massacres by the Ottoman Turks, and the dictatorship of Saddam Hussein. But overnight they succumbed to the breakdown following an American-led war—a war launched to battle the kind of extremism that was now their undoing.

+ + +

Sinan snuck back into Mosul three times, dodging ISIS checkpoints and street sentries each time. He wanted to collect family valuables, his mother's jewelry, his father's documents.

"They destroyed everything. All our house was destroyed. In the beginning they don't seem like they will do anything to Christians. They said they came to give us freedom from the government, that sort of thing. I saw them on the street many times when I was there again. You felt even then they would not stay the same."

Sinan's family joined thousands of others from Mosul who left with what they could and lost everything they had. ISIS forced them to relinquish deeds to their homes. In many cases, those documents represented property that had been in their families since the Ottoman era.

Besides looting personal belongings, ISIS moved decisively on Mosul's financial holdings. From the central bank and other banks in the city, fighters stole cash and gold bullion. They seized one billion dollars worth of military vehicles and weaponry—most of it American made—from the military base. Before the summer was out, ISIS would be the richest terrorist group in the world. Incredibly, it had amassed $2 billion in resources. With the territory it acquired, ISIS quickly began earning approximately one million dollars a day in crude oil sales, plus additional millions per month in wheat sales, jizya taxes collected, and ransom from kidnappings.[6] It was soon as wealthy as any small nation.

+ + +

In the heart of Mosul's Old City off Nineveh Street, Abu Bakr al-Baghdadi stepped to the pulpit of the Grand Mosque on July 4 to deliver a sermon as the first caliph of the Islamic State, "the leader of Muslims everywhere."

His appearance caught officials in Baghdad and Washington by sur-prise. He appeared unconcerned that he was a wanted man in both capi-tals. From the towering carved marble platform of the ancient mosque, the heavily bearded Baghdadi proclaimed himself *Amir al-Mu'minin*, "Commander of the Faithful," and he declared the Islamic State to be the first caliphate to function under Islamic law in over one thousand years.

"Lift your heads up high. You now have a state and a caliphate that restores your honor, your might, your rights, and your sovereignty." He told the assembled men, "Terrify the enemies of Allah and seek death."

In the widely broadcast message, Baghdadi called on followers to perform *hijra*, or migration, from the outside world to the caliphate: "Hijra to Dar Al-Islam is obligatory," he said. Sharia law, he added, is "a religious obligation."[7]

Baghdadi cut an imposing figure before his all-male adherents gath-ered in prayer at the start of Ramadan. He never paused, speaking for thirty minutes without notes. He wore the black *abaya* (robe) and turban that recalled the last of the Abbasid caliphs, who were the first to dye their robes black as a sign of nobility (a tradition carried to the West for clergy and judges). He sported a luxury watch—a Rolex or an Omega. This was no grungy guerrilla hiding in a cave. Terrorizing infidels was an important part of a larger agenda. Baghdadi had come to erase the modern borders of the Middle East.

ISIS exploits, the YouTube videos of explosions and shootings in Mosul, and the videotapes of staged beheadings and mass executions all made Baghdadi legit in the eyes of aspiring global jihadists and dis-affected Muslims in Europe and elsewhere. He preached a "pure Islam," or martyrdom on the battlefield, to achieve the greatest reward in para-dise. Doing battle with infidels, in his worldview, wasn't an option only for some; it was an obligation for all. He didn't bother declaring a global jihad as Osama bin Laden had. In a way, he didn't need to. An Islamic State conquest of "Rome," he concluded, simply would be inevitable.

The sermon released a floodgate of jihadists who streamed across the Turkish border into Syria and filtered down the Tigris or Euphrates to

Iraq. Sometimes fifty fighters showed up in a day. They linked up with an organized realm. As caliph, Baghdadi directly supervised a Shura Council of seven men and a Sharia Council of six or more. Beneath the two branches, which represented legislative and legal bodies respectively, were councils governing provincial matters, military intelligence, religious affairs, finance, and media. The caliphate also had specialty offices, including a Coordinator of Guest Houses and Suicide Bombers, a Supervisor of IED Deployment, and a Coordinator of the Affairs of Women and Orphans.

Soon after Baghdadi's sermon, Abu Muhammad al-Adnani, ISIS emir of Syria and spokesman for Baghdadi, issued an unequivocal threat to the West: "We will conquer your Rome, break your crosses, and enslave your women," he declared. "If we do not reach that time, then our children and grandchildren will reach it, and they will sell your sons as slaves at the slave market."[8]

Westerners saw a resurrected Osama bin Laden in Baghdadi. But Osama bin Laden had only dreamed about a future caliphate. Baghdadi carved out the actual territory, and restive jihadists around the world heard an enticing call to arms touting Islamic rule in Iraq and Syria, and beyond.

+ + +

"Tell me what you want," Georges Clemenceau, France's prime minister, said to his British counterpart, David Lloyd George, as the two walked together in the halls of London's French embassy in 1918.

"I want Mosul," Lloyd George replied.

"You shall have it. Anything else?" Clemenceau asked.[9]

For the victorious European powers following World War I, it was that easy to carve up the Middle East. The Ottoman empire had dissolved in defeat, and with a nod from Clemenceau, the imperial province of Mosul went to British control, joining Baghdad and Basra, instead of becoming part of French-controlled Syria under the Sykes-Picot Agreement.

The British installed a monarchy under King Faisal I in newly birthed Iraq. In many ways, life under British influence was a storied time when arts and commerce flourished and the multilingual, multi-layered, multireligious fabric dating to ancient Mesopotamia thrived. But the Allies had created contrived states and had their own geo-political interests to pursue. Petroleum was a heady new mistress.

For Lloyd George and others, the region's human diversity—its deli-cate balances allowing Arabs, Jews, Christians, Yazidis, and Turkmen to coexist—was an afterthought. Tensions simmered between the factions, and in 1932 the British reluctantly agreed to grant Iraq independence amid growing internal strife, while maintaining a hand on the country's military and economy.

Controlling oil interests prompted the British to look the other way when the Iraqi army launched a massacre of Assyrians north of Mosul in 1933. In part, the slaughter was payback for the Assyrians' perceived good relations with the British military during the war. The attacks emptied about sixty-five Assyrian villages and left between six hun-dred and three thousand Assyrians dead. Iraqi soldiers under a Kurdish commander targeted religious leaders, killing eight Assyrian priests, including one they beheaded and one they burned alive. Authorities in Baghdad detained the Assyrian patriarch, Mar Eshai Shimun, then forced him into exile in Cyprus. He found permanent refuge in Chicago, where the leader of the Assyrian Church of the East has been headquartered ever since.

The Assyrians who departed Simele and other towns in northern Iraq fled to Syria, where they established new villages in northern Syria's Hasakah Province. When ISIS overran these same villages and towns, it captured hundreds of the descendants of Assyrians who once had fled from being massacred in Iraq.

As July inched toward August, humanitarian aid groups mobilized to help Mosul's displaced people, but the silence from the United States and Britain, who had long consorted with each other over Iraq, was deafening.

After ISIS took Mosul, two days passed before President Barack

Obama acknowledged Iraq would need "more help" from the United States. "I don't rule out anything," he added.[10]

American warships moved into the Persian Gulf, and the region braced itself for expected Tomahawk missile strikes on ISIS strongholds. But once again, the Tomahawks stayed in their pressurized canisters. In mid-July, Rear Admiral John Kirby told reporters that the Obama administration would be "measured" and "keep an open mind" in its response to ISIS. "Getting this done right," he said, "is more important than getting it done quickly."[11]

What wasn't said had import too. President Obama made no statement in support of Iraq's Christians. Then just as the Iraqi parliament elected a new speaker after weeks and weeks of paralysis over forming a new government, Obama officials signaled that Prime Minister Maliki's time was up. In 2010 they had insisted Maliki take office even though he hadn't won the popular vote. Now they made it clear they wanted him to leave.

Political chaos in Baghdad again overruled the urgent need to act against ISIS. Days of backroom jostling extended to weeks before parliament finally selected a new president, who in turn appointed Haider al-Abadi prime minister on August 11. The patriarch of the Chaldean Church, Louis Sako, warned officials in Baghdad that a sluggish political response to ISIS would bring Iraq "face to face with human, civil, and historic catastrophe."[12]

Sako said Christians and Muslims shared "every sweet and bitter circumstance of life" in Iraq. "Together they built a civilization, cities, and a heritage. It is truly unjust now to treat Christians by rejecting them and throwing them away, considering them as nothing."[13]

From Raqqa in Syria, the Islamic State regime installed its leadership at its second front in Mosul, its fighters leaching into surrounding villages and towns. I would later discover that Mosul's Department of Education, all of it, had relocated to the Kurdish city of Dohuk, and I would realize how comprehensive the ISIS takeover was. Muslim establishments, too, had been ruptured. Every structure that didn't conform to Sharia law and the rule of the Islamic State was being abolished.

ISIS also wasted no time in wiping out physical evidence of Christian life. By late July forty-five churches in Mosul had been destroyed, occupied, or converted into mosques. They included seventeen Syriac churches, seventeen Chaldean churches, two Armenian churches, the city's one Evangelical Presbyterian Church, and others, along with two convents and at least one cemetery. In many cases, the militants posted videos on social media showing their demolition. Around that same time they posted another dramatic clip showing the explosion of Jonah's tomb. Its decimation dealt a symbolic blow to Christians, Jews, and Muslims, as all three religions cite the Old Testament prophet who worked to save the pagan city of Nineveh. ISIS seemed to telegraph even to Muslims that only its brand of Islam would suffice.

By summer's end, ISIS would have dominion over an area larger than Great Britain, inhabited by six million people. It was becoming the dominant jihadi force in the Middle East, and it was ruthlessly cruel, executing even al-Qaeda commanders who would not pledge immediate loyalty. If the Islamic State fighters held their gains and continued without military opposition in Iraq, the realignment stood to be more radical for the Middle East than the Sykes-Picot Agreement a century before.

17

ENLISTED

Nineveh Plains, July 2014

....

Recall the former days when . . . you joyfully accepted
the plundering of your property, since you knew that you
yourselves had a better possession and an abiding one.

HEBREWS 10:32-34

....

Tens of thousands of people fled from Mosul into the harsh mid-summer desert like marbles bouncing over a hard floor, finding a place to rest anywhere they could. Day by day, ISIS fighters launched attacks out of Mosul on surrounding villages. Each time they did, the people scattered.

Nineveh Plains appeared a marginally safe place for exiles from Mosul. The peshmerga forces of Iraqi Kurdistan responded to the ISIS advance by moving into the area, battling the militants in scattered villages while holding most of the territory north and east of Mosul, including important cities like Qaraqosh and Kirkuk, with its vast surrounding oil fields.

As families from Mosul crowded in with relatives, homes that had housed five people now held fifteen or more. Churches far enough outside Mosul took in other displaced residents. The Kurdish regional government provided some protection but no financial or material aid.

Many Mosul residents headed north to Erbil, the capital of Iraq's

Kurdistan region. Less than fifty miles from the front line forming against ISIS, it was at the leading edge of an unfolding humanitarian crisis. Overnight, rent on a modest flat in the city went from $500 to $2,000 a month, putting it out of reach for the majority of those who'd been forced from their homes with nothing.

By the end of June, more than a million Iraqis had been displaced by ISIS.

Shops and businesses remained closed. Families waited indoors, hunkered down against the heat and the danger. In Baghdad and Washington, officials talked of creating a protected area for Iraq's Christians in Nineveh Plains.[1] So the Christians waited, expecting some kind of intervention to restore them to their homes in Mosul or to provide a safe haven with international protection.

✛ ✛ ✛

When I had talked with Insaf in early June, she was in Canada planning conferences for the fall to help women and girls in Iraq. By early July, with the ISIS takeover of Mosul, she was on the ground helping Iraqis survive the Islamic State.

The crisis propelled Insaf to fly from Toronto to Erbil with her red suitcases and $5,000. Her daughter, Nour, and son-in-law, Malath, welcomed her into the home they shared with their two-year-old daughter. Insaf quickly converted their living room into her command center. As on so many other trips to Iraq since our first one together in 2003, she appeared outwardly unorganized, uncertain just what she would do. But as usual she had a plan, plus enough determination and confidence to carry it forward and to enlist others along the way.

The height of summer was upon Iraq. Daytime temperatures, almost always above 110 degrees, sometimes topped 120. In the Nineveh villages, wells ran dry. Electricity, constantly in short supply, failed more often. Wherever they turned up, what the homeless from Mosul needed most was cash—to buy new phones, phone cards, drinking water, and supplies.

Insaf began dividing her funds into envelopes, $80 for each displaced family she would visit. She pooled resources with her longtime friend from Kirkuk, Maher Tawfiq, who ran a charity organization called Life Agape.

They hired a driver and paid $200 for a tank of water, enough to help fifteen families. It was a start. They began morning deliveries to families taking refuge in churches across Nineveh, dispensing water, a basket of food, and an envelope to each family.

+ + +

As the Christians were fleeing Mosul, I was traveling for work in the United States and then planning to join my family for a week's vacation. All the while, I was thinking that I should be on a plane to Iraq. ISIS could split the country in two, in a way similar to Saddam Hussein's actions after the first Gulf War. To see the gains U.S. forces and Iraqis had fought and died for being lost, to watch only from afar while Iraq disintegrated again into the country it had been when I'd had to sneak across the Tigris in a motorboat—that seemed irresponsible to me, not only as a journalist but also as an American and a traveler among the Christians.

On the final day of a conference in Orlando, I spoke about the suffering unfolding in northern Iraq, the growing number of displaced families and their catastrophic losses. Often when I was asked to give a talk about persecuted Christians in the Middle East, a few dozen advocates for their cause would show up. This time about two hundred women filled the room, and the latecomers stood squeezed together along a back wall. I'd spoken on this subject for years, but with ISIS militants actively chasing Iraqis, I didn't have to give an elaborate overview; I simply began by reading off the week's headlines.

I read from a printed edict handed out by ISIS against "the grandchildren of the Crusaders, the Christian infidels" in Qameshli, the Syrian town through which I had traveled on my way into Iraq in 2002. In addition to instructing its adherents to burn down movie theaters and stores selling alcohol and cigarettes, ISIS ordered them, "Empty the city of all Christians: Take their women; they are yours, and behead the Christian men."[2]

Then I talked about Christians I knew and their determination to continue worshiping and serving despite such threats. At Mar Matti monastery, the monks were sheltering about two hundred families from Mosul. They had Kurdish soldiers protecting the area but were cut off from roads to nearby cities. Brother Yousif was dividing dwindling food supplies to share with the families, hoping their provisions would last until the danger was over.

Every word I spoke felt weighted with the very present reality: Even as we were talking about the Iraqi and Syrian Christians in an Orlando conference hall, some of them might be beheaded, burned, or forced out of their shelters again. By the time I'd answered the audience's questions after my talk, I was drained, exhausted from my inability to do more than speak about what was happening.

Two of my daughters had joined me for the conference. They came to hear my talk, though it was a subject they'd heard me discuss for years. Afterward, sensing my weariness, they urged me outdoors for a swim in the Florida sunshine and then for burgers.

The next morning we checked out of the hotel and loaded our bags into a rental car to drive north for a real but rare family vacation. As I steered the car out of the hotel's underground parking garage, a woman with two young children in tow hurried toward our car, flagging me to stop. I pulled up beside her and rolled down my window.

We had never met, but she addressed me by name. "I was hoping to see you this morning," she explained. She told me she'd heard my talk and had been up most of the night, burdened for the families in Iraq and praying for them.

"I have this money," she said, pushing a fat, sealed envelope through the car window to me, "and I would like to give it to you because you will know what to do with it."

For long seconds the envelope sat there between us. She leaned into the window, eyeing me. I could think only of Insaf and her intense gaze at our first meeting in the backseat of a car in Amman, how she had thrust white envelopes at me, daring me to be complicit in her mission. Then, as now, my training and instincts as a journalist were confronted by another woman's level gaze. My habit of being the observer, the outsider, the "objective" witness—the one who took notes while others took action—was giving way in the face of another sudden entreaty from an ordinary mom, like Insaf, like me.

I glanced at my oldest daughter, seated beside me, who looked on but gave no hint of what I should do. Then I looked in the rearview mirror at my youngest. She had been five years old when I made my first trip to Iraq; now she had just graduated from high school. *Lifetimes*, I thought, eyeing my daughter's seventeen-year-old face but seeing the face of a five-year-old. *So many Iraqis have faced lifetimes of conflict; lifetimes of danger; lifetimes made of momentary decisions about staying or going, about risking or protecting their own lives and their families.*

The decisions mothers make are on some level not so different in Orlando or Baghdad or Mar Matti—decisions about how best to protect our children and how best to teach them. Sometimes protecting and preserving involve risk and sacrifice. They require giving something up. One could argue I had sacrificed time and energy to be away from my children so others could better understand what was happening in the Middle East. Here was a mother offering a different sacrifice, but in essence it was the same: She was giving what she had to give. I took the envelope. I would be complicit again.

"I'm not even sure how much money is in here, but I want it all to go to Iraq to help the families," the woman said.

I pushed the envelope back to her and asked her to write her phone number and e-mail address on the outside, so I could let her know where I sent her money. In that moment, I didn't know what I would do with it. She handed it back, we said our good-byes, and I drove away. Our brief encounter was like some underground assignation in a movie: Her urgency in giving money she hadn't even counted was odd and unsettling.

As we eased out into traffic, I passed the envelope over to my oldest. "Why don't you see what's in there?" I asked.

She counted, numbers under her breath, then said, "Five hundred dollars."

It seemed like a lot from one mom. I thought of the families at Mar Matti and of the ones from Mosul squeezed inside small houses with their next of kin. We drove on, talking about what I should do, suddenly agreeing that we shouldn't only talk about the Christians in Iraq—we should help them.

The more I thought about how to help Iraqi families, the more I thought of Insaf as the conduit. The next time I could, I opened my laptop to send a note to her. Clicking on my inbox, I found an e-mail from Insaf already there. She was on her way to northern Iraq.

"Pray that God will grant me wisdom, and spirit of discernment to go where help and comfort is really needed; to be uplifted in the Spirit to aid and comfort others, and pray also for protection," she wrote.

I responded, telling her I had money to send with her. But how could I get it there?

"Banks are too slow and uncertain," she replied, "so wire the money to me with Western Union. I will get it the next day."

In Ankawa, the suburb of Erbil where many Christians lived, the Western Union office listed its address this way: Karez Avenue Opposit To The Church, Arbil. I wondered whether the transfer would really work, but I took Insaf at her word. Ankawa had coffee shops, shopping malls, and fast Internet. It was an oasis of function in a country of dysfunction.

Over the next several days I made morning trips to a Winn-Dixie, which had the closest Western Union desk I could find on vacation. And there beside the lottery tickets, baked goods, and Mylar birthday balloons, I wired money to Insaf. A young man who'd emigrated from Uganda worked the desk and helped me fill out the forms. I handed him fistfuls of cash, first from the mom in the hotel garage in Orlando, then from members of my extended family and an assortment of others, including people in my own church, who called or wrote me. *What can we do?* they asked. Their voices and their e-mails conveyed the helplessness they felt as night after night they watched haunting TV images of terrified Iraqis fleeing for their lives.

In this way, both while traveling and then back at home, I wired thousands of dollars to Insaf from grocery stores over the coming weeks, always to the Western Union office in Ankawa, Opposit To The Church. Sometimes I would e-mail her from my phone as I left the store, telling her money was on its way, and about thirty minutes later she'd send word that she'd received it. I would always breathe a sigh of relief and amazement that it got there at all.

I was hardly alone. Bit by bit, Insaf collected donations from her network all over the world—Iraqi friends and relatives who lived in Toronto, Detroit, Vienna, Melbourne, Istanbul, and elsewhere.

By the end of July, thanks to Western Union, Insaf had received more than $30,000 from her diverse network of donors. It came like manna, a portion every day, enough to buy fans and air coolers for families one day, cooktops for women to set up housekeeping in tent camps the next day, and mattresses the following day when she headed to a church in Nineveh Plains where hundreds were bedding down on hard sanctuary pews. She posted photos of her excursions on Facebook, and she sent me long lists detailing the items she had purchased and the envelopes of cash she had distributed.

Insaf explained how, as she drove from Erbil into the blanched plains, she saw women with babies sitting by roadsides, sometimes under makeshift tents made of what looked like bedsheets suspended over poles stuck into the packed dirt. Empty lots had filled with families, some living out of their cars, some on bare ground. They slept with clothes rolled beneath their heads for pillows. The sanctuaries and hallways of Erbil's churches were lined with families who settled their children to bed on wooden pews or on the ground in the courtyards. Local aid groups and churches set up rows of tent camps anywhere they could, even on busy street corners.

Iraqi churches posted needs and solicited funds on Facebook, collecting money like Insaf did, ad hoc and day by day. Church groups across northern Iraq fanned out to help the displaced, often joined by American aid teams or European charity workers. Large-scale efforts by the United Nations and international aid groups also took shape, but few of these groups knew the terrain of Iraq's persecuted minorities.

The Iraqi pastors—who themselves had spent the war years migrating from safe haven to safe haven, escaping bombing after bombing while keeping track of their parishioners along the way—knew where Mosul's displaced Christians had gone. Every morning they gathered up a few workers like Insaf, loaded vans with supplies and drinking water—always water—and headed for a village out in the plains to drop off supplies and talk with the families before the sun got too hot.

Insaf traveled with Syriac clergy one day, and on another day with a team of evangelicals from the Alliance church in Erbil where her son-in-law was the pastor. She helped carry the supplies to Mar Matti monastery for the families sheltering there. "No one knows where is safe anymore. But prayer is strong, and it is moving the hands of God to help us," she explained to me by phone.

On some of her rounds, American clergy who had showed up to help accompanied her. The teams, laden with cash and valuable goods, had to keep a vigil over their security and their schedule. One clergyman called Insaf "a security nightmare" because she kept disappearing to take tea in a tent or to visit the families camping out on open ground and terraces.

Near the end of July, Insaf and Maher made a day trip to Bashiqa, Samah Anwar's town. They delivered fifty mattresses, a hundred pillows, and food—along with donated TOMS shoes and gift-filled shoeboxes put together by the relief group Samaritan's Purse—to a Syriac Orthodox church, where clergy handed them out to the homeless.

"God is surprising me with his generosity," Insaf told me after receiving more wired money, extending her stay by one week and then two as the money continued to come in.

Exhausted and overwhelmed by needs, Insaf decided to return to Toronto in early August, leaving the remainder of the funds wired to her with Haitham Jazrawi, the pastor in Kirkuk. Like many churches and pastors, he, too, was hosting families from Mosul on the church grounds and also helping Yazidis and Muslims who had turned up in the city. Insaf decided she would return to Iraq in September.

Like most everyone else, Insaf flew out of Erbil wondering what the militants planned to do next. Sporadic fighting had spread from the crossroads at the Syrian border to the oil fields of Kirkuk. The militants were on the move, but few Iraqis realized that ISIS was about to launch another major attack.

18

THE FINAL FALL

Qaraqosh, August 2014

....

We're washed up as a race, we're through, it's all over, why should I learn
to read the language? We have no writers, we have no news—well,
there is a little news: once in a while the English encourage the Arabs
to massacre us, that is all. It's an old story, we know all about it.

"SEVENTY THOUSAND ASSYRIANS,"
A SHORT STORY BY WILLIAM SAROYAN

....

On Friday, August 1, Kurdish peshmerga confronted ISIS outside Sinjar, northwest of Mosul, and overpowered the militants. They killed twenty ISIS fighters and captured thirty without taking casualties themselves. The attack was mostly exploratory: It handed ISIS intelligence on the strength of peshmerga forces guarding the oil fields and the main road leading to the Syrian border.

Two days later ISIS sent an overpowering detachment, along with mortars and rocket-propelled grenades, to drive the peshmerga into retreat. By the end of the day ISIS raised its black flag over government buildings in Sinjar, a city of 300,000.

"We awakened in the morning and heard Sinjar is now filled with ISIS," said Samah Anwar, whose family had been able to remain in Bashiqa. "We heard they killed the young men with swords and exploded old people with bombs." They had kidnapped boys to serve as fighters, she said, and took captive girls "for selling them by cheapest price, about five dollars, ten dollars."

Bashiqa had belonged to generations of Assyrians and Kurds, but now it was home mostly to Yazidis and Sunni Arabs. Its hillsides were dotted with date groves and the sandy-colored, pointed domes of Yazidi temples, a landscape mingled with the crosses and bell towers of Syriac and Chaldean churches, visible for miles around from the distant plains.

Bashiqa was a long way from Sinjar, but all that day the word coming from Sinjar was so grim that Yazidis began to leave Bashiqa, said Samah. Her family had no car, but her uncle encouraged them to leave with his family. His car could hold four. "We pressed seven from my family and eight from his family, and we left home," said Samah. "We were in a miserable state."

Samah's father and two of her brothers stayed behind to guard her house and her uncle's. Each family had decided to post a man to watch over the property, hoping not to lose everything, as had happened in Mosul.

The cars headed down the hillsides as thousands of Christian and Yazidi refugees, including those who had first fled Mosul to Bashiqa, began running again. Some carried the bedding and other supplies delivered by Insaf and others; some forgot them in their haste.

Samah's family car crept along crowded roads. The heat inside the sedan was stifling, with fifteen passengers, including a wailing four-month-old girl. She was hungry, and her mother's breast milk had dried up with fright. The baby cried for hours, as the family headed north, where another uncle and his family lived on the outskirts of Dohuk in the town of Sharya.

"We only took with us our clothes," Samah said. "The future or where we are going or what will happen next, we didn't know."

✝ ✝ ✝

Over the years I had traveled through Sinjar and had once stopped to visit the Yazidi temple complex in the village of Lalish. Inside its cave shrines were massive urns of olive oil and flimsy scarves, loose drapes used in a worship I never quite understood. I entered through a doorway ornately carved with snakes and went barefoot, according to custom, through the dark and damp passageways.

Yazidis reportedly worship an angel some consider Satan, and they claim to have one of the oldest religions in the world; but in fact it emerged in the twelfth century in the mountains northeast of Mosul with a mixture of Zoroastrian, Christian, Sufi, and Muslim ritual. Yazidis may worship the sun, but they also baptize their children.

Nowhere else in the world could you see such Yazidi villages, the conical roofs of their temples appearing like upside-down ice cream cones across the Lalish Valley and into the mountains near Mosul. Yazidis tended to live in remote hillside villages, to marry among themselves, and to accept no outsiders. They were extravagant worshipers, gathering often for weddings, funerals, dances, and prayer services. In 2002 the Yazidis in Bashiqa and other Nineveh villages had come together to pray against the coming war with the United States.

Muslims and Yazidis avoided one another, and violent extremists repeatedly targeted Yazidis, killing five hundred of them in one bombing in 2007. Christians had lived alongside them but had made little progress befriending them. Samah, single and working to be a doctor with full support from her family, showed me that Yazidi communities could be progressive too.

✦ ✦ ✦

Samah's family reached Sharya at nightfall. They unfolded themselves from the car, finding water for the baby and for themselves. Then they saw victims arriving from Sinjar.

"They were in a very bad state," Samah said. "Most of them wore no shoes. They were dirty; they looked very bad, hungry and thirsty."

"My daughter, my daughter," one woman screamed. Another cried out for her son. They had fled Sinjar at gunpoint, they told Samah, and had watched as men and boys were separated from their families and gunned down. Women were subjected to "internal investigations," they said, meaning they had to reveal their pubic area to ISIS militants.

Many of the women and older girls with hair between their legs were rounded up and loaded on buses or taken away in pickup trucks. To Samah, it seemed no one had arrived without a story of horror, without losing husbands or wives, sons or daughters.

As the sun went down and the air cooled, the new arrivals prepared to sleep in the street. They used their clothes to make tents, knowing the sun would rise early and hot. No one had anything else.

"We were crying, and we couldn't sleep that night," said Samah. "As the night passed, I thought I'll hear about the death of my father and my brothers too."

In the eyes of ISIS, the Yazidis didn't require the same treatment as Christians. They weren't "People of the Book." At the outset ISIS gave Christians some pretense of choice—convert to Islam, pay a tax (that was actually a form of limitless extortion), or leave. The Yazidis rated only the first choice—convert to Islam or be killed. Caught in the act of fleeing, many were captured or killed.

The Sinjar families arriving in Sharya were shattered, physically and mentally. In the street one young man vowed to return to Sinjar to take revenge on ISIS for killing his family. Only he and his father remained; ISIS had killed everyone else. The father argued with his son, telling him not to go back. I will kill myself if you go back, he said. The son insisted, and after he got in a car to drive off, the father carried out his promise. As Samah and others watched in disbelief, he pulled out his own gun and shot himself.

ISIS swept Nineveh Province, forcing a massive exodus of Iraqis, including about 150,000 Christians. Overnight these displaced families converged on the cities of Iraqi Kurdistan. More than 25,000 Yazidis showed up in Sharya on August 3, as Samah's family did. Everywhere the outcasts fled, they expected ISIS to show up again.

Seeking safety, about 50,000 Sinjar residents trekked up Mount Sinjar by the cool of night, hoping to elude their attackers. The high desert range, a barren ridge four miles wide and twenty-five miles long, was all rock and scrub, devoid of plant life, water, and shade. Those who climbed the 4,400-foot range thought they had avoided bloody clashes with ISIS in the streets of Sinjar to the south.

Little did they know that ISIS had taken towns north, east, and west of the range as well. Once they scaled Mount Sinjar, those escaping the city were trapped without water, shelter from the sun, or provisions.

With the rising of a direct late-summer sun, forty-five children died of thirst within the first hours of the next day. At least fifty elderly people perished that same day. ISIS fighters who chased them killed 1,500 men, all with wives and children watching. The dead were mostly Yazidis, but those trapped on the mountain included fifty Christian families who had escaped Sinjar as the terrorists took over the Syriac church and covered its cross with the black ISIS flag.

The number of captives killed on Mount Sinjar would quickly rise to 1,500, then to 2,600, and eventually to more than 7,000. Initially the Islamic State fighters selected and made off with more than 500 women and girls, some of whom were Christians. Some would be taken to Mosul and others to Raqqa, where an organized system of trafficking and enslavement was already taking shape.

Kurdish journalist Barakat Issa, in Sinjar to cover the arrival of ISIS, fled with city residents. He described dead bodies lying everywhere among the exposed rock and dust of Mount Sinjar. Parents threw children from the mountain rather than watch them die or be captured by ISIS. After everyone's cell phones had died, he said, runners—mostly young men willing to risk being caught—delivered updates on new deaths. "When we see someone running," Issa said, "we know they are either fleeing or carrying the news of someone's death."[1]

+ + +

Sinan and his family in Qaraqosh, one hundred miles east of Sinjar, realized that it was time to leave. ISIS was pressing toward the largest city in the Nineveh Plains.

"We had by then received no salary for weeks, no money," Sinan said. He already had searched for work in Erbil, a much larger city about forty miles east and out of the danger zone in Nineveh Plains, and hoped to move his whole family there. When ISIS cut off water to the city, then cell towers and electricity as it had done elsewhere, they knew invasion could be imminent. Without a plan or provisions, the family set off for Erbil.

Qaraqosh, its numbers swollen well beyond its normal 50,000 inhabitants with the influx of Christians on the run, had faced threats of an ISIS invasion for weeks. The Islamic State announced its arrival with an explosion. On Wednesday, August 6, the commander of peshmerga forces notified the Chaldean archbishop that his forces were abandoning Qaraqosh. ISIS mortars on the city outskirts were shelling and destroying peshmerga posts. The peshmerga had no reinforcements.

Word spread among clergy of the peshmerga's impending departure, but before they made plans to evacuate, a mortar round struck the heart of a Christian neighborhood. The deafening explosion interrupted children playing in courtyards and women lingering for conversation in the cool morning hours. The blast hurled into the air a thirty-year-old woman who had planned to be married that day. She lay dead in the street. The explosion also struck two brothers and a cousin playing nearby, killing two of them, seven- and nine-year-old boys, and leaving the third, a six-year-old, bleeding—alert but near death. Four other children were also injured.

Family and neighbors gathered, carrying the wounded to the hospital and the dead to a church. With the peshmerga's retreat, any help had to come from church leaders. They held a hasty funeral mass with ISIS mortars exploding all over the area. Parishioners said their prayers over the dead, buried them, and collected their possessions to leave.

At the convent for the Dominican Sisters of St. Catherine of Siena, Maria Hanna, the prioress, woke as she had since June, considering how best to provide for the 510 families displaced from Mosul whom she and thirty other nuns cared for. The nuns themselves knew about displacement: They had been forced out of their convent in Mosul by a 2009 bombing.

Sister Maria Hanna was shocked to see the peshmerga pull out. The Kurdish government had promised to protect Qaraqosh. But the same was happening elsewhere, as the peshmerga fell back in at least fifteen villages across Nineveh Plains.

By 11:30 that night, an exodus from Qaraqosh was under way. The sisters, along with the Dominican priests, paused to celebrate the Eucharist at the altar before departing. They prayed it would not be defiled by ISIS, but they didn't linger long to consider whether it might be the last time a Christian sacrament would be celebrated in Qaraqosh.

At about midnight, thirty-three nuns, joined by two families, wedged themselves into three cars and headed out of town for the main highway. Everywhere they saw people leaving Qaraqosh on foot, men with children on their shoulders, women holding babies, young boys helping older couples. The older women wore long robed garments with scarves thrown loosely around their necks, clutching a few belongings to their chests. The older men wore white dishdashas, robes that stood out like flashes of light in the darkness. Some older children clutched at small knapsacks, pulling them over the rocky paths, while others ran ahead of their parents, unaware of the dangers ahead.

Reaching the intersection for the main highway, Sister Maria Hanna and her party came to a stop. As one they drew in their breaths, stunned. Cars and pedestrians stretched in every direction—men; women, some of them pregnant; children; the handicapped; and the elderly, all pushing their way to Erbil. "The view was beyond describing, as words cannot fully capture it," she said. "There were Christians, Muslim Shiites, Yazidis, and Shabak; some people were on foot, some were riding in the backs of pickups or lorry trucks, or on motorcycles."

Watching humanity crawl across the old Assyrian flatlands, Sister Maria Hanna thought, was like nothing seen since biblical times. She forgot that she herself was part of the exodus, packed into a sedan with a dozen fellow exiles. Two days later she wrote to friends and fellow Dominican sisters of the overnight journey to Erbil:

> There are three checkpoints to arrive in Erbil. It took us five hours, from midnight to 5:00, to pass the first one; we reached the second one at 7:00 and the third one at 8:30. We arrived [at] the convent at 9:30 [a.m.] exhausted emotionally, physically, and mentally. What we saw was unbearable; people were suffering for no reason but because of their sect, religion, and race. We felt like we were in a nightmare, wishing that someone would waken us up or that when the sun comes out, it will be all over. But it was not the case; we were actually living a hard reality. It usually takes an hour and fifteen minutes to drive from Qaraqosh to Erbil, but the day before yesterday, it took us ten hours.

✝   ✝   ✝

Many were killed or maimed in those moments of taking flight. Mortar fire killed a four-year-old boy named David. One ISIS emir abducted a three-year-old girl named Christina, snatching her from her mother, forty-three-year-old Aida Hana Noah, as the family tried to leave town. Aida had sent her sons on ahead out of town, but she stayed behind to care for her blind husband and for young Christina. The toddler was carried away, crying, and never seen by her mother again. Another woman captured from Qaraqosh reportedly cared briefly for Christina in Mosul before the child was sent to live with a Muslim family.

One young mother was in labor with her first child as ISIS attacked. At the Qaraqosh hospital, her doctor feared waiting for a natural delivery and ordered a cesarean section. Jacob Naseer Abba was perhaps the last baby born to Christian parents in the city. Nurses noticed his leg bones turned outward and hurriedly swaddled him in double diapers to set them straight. Then they sent the mother and child on their way. With Jacob barely four hours old and his mother nursing stitches from her C-section, the two joined the throngs of families leaving on foot. A stranger flagged an ambulance and persuaded the driver to ferry the mother and newborn son to Erbil. Insaf, who had returned to Iraq in time to witness the exodus, was at the church where the family was taken. When Insaf greeted them, the weary young mother placed her newborn into Insaf's arms.

By Thursday, August 7, the crawl of humanity was making its way east, south, and north from Nineveh. Most were heading to the cities of Iraqi Kurdistan. Erbil, the capital, along with Dohuk to the northwest and Sulaymaniyah to the northeast, would become the cities of refuge for anyone escaping ISIS.

The monks and displaced families at Mar Matti had to evacuate too. With Brother Yousif, they took a back road over Mount Al-Faf, skirting ISIS checkpoints, to reach Dohuk. For the first time in perhaps a millennium, Mar Matti was empty.

As part of the exodus, the Yazidi families were evacuating Sharya. Samah and her family waited for her father and brothers, who were blocked from reaching Sharya by ISIS militants. Finally, Samah's father and his sons set out for the mountains near Mar Matti, climbing donkey paths. After many hours of hiking, they reached Sharya.

For Samah, the joy of seeing of her father and brothers quickly was overtaken by their announcement that ISIS had entered Bashiqa. "ISIS was in our village, celebrating, enjoying the place we lived in, dreamed in, grew in," said Samah. "We cried a lot over this."

With her father's late arrival, Samah's family were among the last to leave Sharya. They headed for Dohuk, roads jammed just as they were everywhere. On the city's outskirts they discovered a school had just opened its doors, as there were too many displaced people living in the street. It was a small school of only six classrooms off one large hallway. End-of-summer dust sloshed over the hallway and stuck to the walls. But Samah's family had nowhere else to go, and at least the school had a roof.

Samah's family was assigned to a classroom with six other families, twenty-six people she didn't know from different areas of Nineveh. "All of us were sleeping on the floor with no mattress, no pillow. Some slept in the classrooms, others slept in the corridors." They went to sleep without food, not knowing how long they could stay there. When they woke up, they were not sure where they were. Remembering how suddenly their lives had changed, they wondered whether this would be a day for staying put, or another day on the run.

+ + +

The stories of captivity and death, flight and survival, would pile up, reminding me of the stories Americans kept repeating following the 9/11 attacks. They were a way to understand what seemed incomprehensible. Yet these accounts spread across the 1,500-square-mile expanse of Nineveh Plains where ISIS banished more than a million Iraqis. Many Muslims went south. The Christians, Yazidis, and other non-Muslims felt they had no hope of finding haven anywhere but to the north, in Kurdistan.

Predominantly Christian towns like Tel Kaif, Bartella, and Telskuf, which I had visited in 2007 and 2008, emptied like water pouring from a broken cistern. ISIS went door to door, looting homes and shops at will, threatening harm to anyone who tried to stay. In the towns to which Christians and Yazidis retreated, the families slept on the floors of churches or schools and recycled the same water to shower, wash their hands, and use the toilet.

Sister Mary Dominic and the other nuns of Telskuf fled to Alqosh, where they took refuge in a church near the old synagogue of Nahum's tomb. Soon enough, though, the Christians of Alqosh realized they, too, had to leave: ISIS fighters had been spotted less than six miles away. Sami gathered his family, the ancient ledger of Jewish names, and the keys to Nahum's tomb, readying for a nighttime escape.

On Mount Sinjar under the stars, those who had managed to survive to this point could watch as Islamic State fighters torched and plundered their homes in the city of Sinjar below.

+ + +

For weeks Kurdish officials pleaded with the United States for arms and munitions to beat back ISIS. President Obama remained focused on fighting in Ukraine. On August 5 and 6, while the whole center of Iraq was giving way to Islamic jihadists, he attended three sessions of an African leadership summit put on by the White House.

On Thursday, August 7, the United Nations Security Council issued a statement, backed by all fifteen member nations, urging other countries to support Iraq in its fight against the jihadists. White House spokesman Josh Earnest refused to confirm rumors that the United States was preparing to launch air strikes against ISIS, but he warned that the situation could become a "humanitarian catastrophe."[2] In response, the White House ordered supplies air-dropped over the Sinjar Mountain range. An American C-17 and two C-130s dropped seventy-two bundles—enough food and water for about 8,000 of the nearly 50,000 people who remained there. Helicopters followed at lower altitudes to dump more food, water, and diapers. As they unloaded the bundles, desperate men, women, and children raced toward the choppers to climb aboard, parents handing up babies to U.S. military personnel even as gunners on board fired off belts of ammo against ISIS attackers.

"I have never seen a situation as desperate as this," said one veteran journalist accompanying the airdrop, "and a rescue effort as ad hoc and as improvised."[3]

By nightfall the Kurds, lacking resupply from either Baghdad or Washington, feared they might lose Kurdistan. Islamic State militants were reportedly less than five miles from Erbil, the capital. No one doubted any longer the strength and viciousness of ISIS. Late-night newscasts in Erbil said the fighters were close enough to reach the city in ten minutes.

Inside the U.S. consulate in Ankawa, dozens of Americans—diplomats, military personnel, and contractors—were in lockdown mode, communicating by e-mail and cell phones with Washington and with

Kurdish officials. At one point the Kurdish interior-ministry official told the Americans that his office was starting to shred documents. ISIS was that close, and without outside intervention, the Kurdish regional government's downfall seemed possible.

Yousif Matty, the pastor who ran the classical schools in Kurdistan, shifted into emergency mode too. Christians had been the common denominator in all the places ISIS had attacked in June and July, and if the militants entered the Kurdish capital, they were likely to target Christian sectors of the city, such as Ankawa, where Yousif lived next to one of the schools.

Yousif gathered his family, including his wife, Alia; his daughters, Noor and Farrah; his son, Majd; and his son-in-law, Siror. The three men collected all the important records for the three schools, including financial and student information. They boxed the files and moved them to his son's home. They filled their cars' gas tanks in case a quick getaway was needed. They pulled machine guns, which they'd stowed away during earlier years of war, from deep storage. The guns had long been hidden for just this, a worst-case scenario, the one they had hoped would never happen—when Islamic militants came after Christians, and no one stepped in to stop them.

The family gathered at Majd's home and waited as the overnight darkness deepened. The steady noise of cars in the streets never slowed. Sporadic shooting could be heard in the distance. Then somewhere between three and four in the morning, they heard the high-altitude roar of planes in the air, a constant drone overhead accompanied by thuds that felt like small explosions. They were fighter jets breaking the sound barrier.

The first strikes came from two F/A-18 combat jets flown off the aircraft carrier *George H. W. Bush* in the Persian Gulf, dropping five-hundred-pound laser-guided bombs on an ISIS mortar position southwest of Erbil. A drone armed with Hellfire missiles struck another ISIS mortar position. Later, four aircraft dropped laser-guided bombs on an ISIS convoy.

The strikes continued into the next day, putting the United States back into combat in the skies over Iraq barely three years after ground forces had been withdrawn. But the air offensive broke what had been weeks of unchecked advance by the Islamic jihadists. By daybreak ISIS could have been at Erbil's doorstep, Yousif would later recall. Instead, its commandos had been pushed back to a distance twenty-five minutes away. It felt like a victory, even if it was only a reprieve.

Tens of thousands of Iraqis remained stranded on Mount Sinjar. Most who survived nearly a week on the mountain eventually walked twelve miles to Syria for refuge. The Kurdish peshmerga then opened a road, allowing the refugees to make their way back to Iraq, to safety in Kurdistan near Dohuk.

Many elderly and disabled Iraqis, along with their caregivers, were trapped in the cities and towns overtaken by ISIS, beholden to the Islamists' whims and cruelties. Otherwise those cities and towns sat eerily empty, guarded by guns and black-cloaked militants but home to no commerce, no everyday life.

In Qaraqosh, about one hundred Christians had been left behind. ISIS held them hostage inside their homes or churches. One father described being tortured while his wife and two children were threatened after the family refused to deny their faith. When ISIS ordered them back to their home, the family escaped.

✝ ✝ ✝

A few months later I met Najeeb Daniel and his wife, Dalal, both in their seventies. ISIS militants had held them in their Qaraqosh home for fifteen days in August, then forced them to run. The militants loaded them, along with others who had been too old or disabled to leave sooner, onto a bus. They drove them to the edge of town, where they dropped them off and ordered them to cross the Khazir River, located nearly ten miles away. Given the condition of the group, the walk to the river took nearly twelve hours. Already tottering, Najeeb fell into a hole along the way and broke his leg. The armed militants shooed them from behind, yet he couldn't move. Someone—Najeeb said it was a nun—dispatched a young man with a wheelbarrow, who picked up Najeeb and several others and ferried them to the river's edge. The young man carried Najeeb across the river on his shoulders. His wife said the water reached chest height.

Once they made it to the other side, the gunmen left them alone. Learning of their flight, Kurds came in cars to help them, and medics took Najeeb to a hospital in Erbil. When I interviewed Najeeb and his wife, they were living in one bare room on the upper floor of Erbil's downtown shopping mall, where hundreds of displaced families were staying. Like nearly everyone who escaped ISIS, they made a home wherever they could, in this case accessible only by escalator. Najeeb's leg had been set but hadn't healed well, and he couldn't walk. He sat on the floor under a blanket, his chin quivering uncontrollably. When he tried to speak, only fragments of sentences would come. Dalal told me their story.

For years the Iraqi Christians who populated Nineveh Plains had weighed and measured the high cost of staying but felt the tug of blood and history. When al-Qaeda kidnapped their sons and fathers, they thought of earlier Ninevites, the Assyrians who had converted to Christianity, and they remained.

When the Sunni militias made life in their cities a daily hell of roadside bombs, they thought of the Chaldean church fathers and the monastic hermits with their libraries, and they hung on.

When the jihadist death squads in Baghdad and Mosul forced Christians from their neighborhoods, bombed them, and shot at them even while they worshiped, they remembered the life of music, the arts, the gatherings, and the commerce in the once-vibrant Jewish and Christian quarters, and they persevered. They even built new churches to keep faith alive.

And when the politicians overlooked their plight again and again, or when those who'd made it out to other countries told them it was too dangerous to remain in Iraq, they thought of the land, its history, and their fellow believers, and they responded as Insaf had years earlier: "I only hear Jesus saying, 'Feed my sheep.'"

Now Nineveh Plains was empty of Christians, empty of all worship but ISIS worship. The bells of the churches had fallen silent for the first time since the seventh century. Voices for singing had been carried away. The crosses had come down; the worship spaces had been converted to mosques or simply destroyed. The people who would not renounce their faith had been chased out, finally and perhaps irrevocably.

From Sami's cousin Dawlat Abouna in Baghdad, I learned that not only had Sami fled Alqosh but that he had departed Iraq for Turkey, taking the keys to Nahum's tomb with him.

"He is not coming back," Sami's cousin told me.

Would he talk to me? I asked. He was the emblematic keeper of the Jews' and the Christians' legacy, I said. We all need to hear his story.

"No," came Dawlat's reply. "He says he will not speak to any American ever again."

19

FIGHTING ISIS

Nineveh Plains, 2015

....

How lonely sits the city that was full of people!

LAMENTATIONS 1:1

.................,...

"Let your eyes be open on this house day and night," read a ripped fragment in Syriac, a page out of the Old Testament I found atop a tattered heap in an upper room of an ancient church. ISIS fighters had looted St. George's in Baqofa. They pulled communion wine and chalices from a cabinet, strewing them across the stone floor near the altar. They flung vestments out of a nearby closet, overturned altarpieces and furnishings inside the sixteenth-century chapel, then shot at its plaster walls and ceiling lights.

But somehow the militants overlooked the Scriptures. I found them lying in an alcove as I made a short climb up stone steps to the roof of the church. Pausing with me, Assyrian militiaman George Khamis pushed his AK-47 over his shoulder, pulled a flashlight from a padded pocket of his bulletproof vest, and translated the Syriac for me. It came from King Solomon's expansive prayer of dedication as he stood before the Temple in Jerusalem,[1] beseeching God for his presence and protection, even in defeat.

From the rooftop, Khamis and others in the militia patrolled this sector of Nineveh Plains, where Kurdish peshmerga had fought Islamic State combatants door-to-door in August 2014. ISIS had captured twenty-two villages in the flatlands surrounding Mosul. When the peshmerga, with support from U.S. jet fighters, succeeded in routing ISIS from nearby Mosul Dam, they also pushed the Islamic State fighters out of a handful of villages between Mosul and Dohuk. One of those villages was Baqofa, an Assyrian town dating to the seventh century.

The March wind blew and the rain drizzled, pooling at my feet atop the armed lookout St. George's flat rooftop had become. A sudden hailstorm forced the patrol under a crumbling limestone overhang as icy clods pounded us. Then the sky calmed, returning to a persistent wet, dreary gray. The clouds broke only long enough to send shards of afternoon light across Nineveh's greening pasturelands, the long grass blowing to its silvery underside in the storm.

Mongol invaders first attacked Baqofa in 1436, but the town survived. The Persians killed scores of residents in 1743, and a Kurdish attack in 1833 led to hundreds of deaths, plus kidnappings of women and children. But it wasn't until August 2014 that invaders succeeded in completely emptying the town.

ISIS militants cut electricity and cell phone service to Baqofa—as they did in every community taken. They ransacked houses and church property. They forced about five hundred residents from their homes, and at gunpoint hustled them into pickup trucks with the familiar "convert or leave" threat.

Although the Kurds had now secured the town, it wasn't safe enough for residents to return. The front line was less than two miles away, signified by a berm the militants were building in the distance, and beyond it, a row of black ISIS flags fluttering in the wind.

"Kurdistan right here is fighting on behalf of the whole world," said Khamis.

In a sense, he was right. Before U.S. air strikes began, the Kurds had fought ISIS village by village, street by street, house by house, retaking key territory without fanfare, holding a line against their enemies while the Iraqi army melted back toward Baghdad.

After Mosul and Nineveh, the Islamic State moved on Tikrit while holding Fallujah west of Baghdad, which it took in January 2014. It stole headlines with mass beheadings in Libya and Syria. Even as I was in Nineveh Province, ISIS made gains, emptying a dozen Assyrian villages in Syria's northeast, kidnapping 262 Christians in one nighttime raid. But for nearly seven months, Abu Bakr al-Baghdadi's plundering warriors made no progress in northern Iraq. With their local militias, the peshmerga held a 640-mile front, stretching from the Syrian border north of the Sinjar Mountain range across Nineveh and then south to Kirkuk and to the mountains of Kurdistan at the Iran border.

On this wide-open ground, it was a face-off. From the church rooftop, we could hear the earthmovers churning in the distance. Islamic State forces were digging trenches and piling up the earthen berm: fortifications to stave off an anticipated military offensive in which Iraq's army and Kurds would try to take back Mosul. ISIS fighters expected it to begin later in the spring.

The trenches were five feet deep by five feet wide, lined along the bottom with concrete barriers. Inside the trenches, the militants placed 81-mm medium-weight mortars. These could shell within a three- or four-mile radius, putting Baqofa and St. George's within range of damage. That was another reason Kurdish authorities wouldn't allow residents to return, and another reason most residents didn't want to.

We could hear shelling in the distance, plus the hum high overhead of jet fighters and reconnaissance aircraft, obscured by clouds. Air strikes continued, mostly at night, and it was an open question why the Americans hadn't targeted the ISIS unit operating so visibly on the plain so close to the Kurdish front.

We picked up steady radio transmissions, intercepts from ISIS militants dug in a few miles away. They spoke mostly in Arabic but also in Hindi, Urdu, and occasionally English, radioing one another using recognizable call signs like "bin Laden" or "Taliban."

When the intercepts paused, the town was eerie, haunted with quiet. I asked one of the soldiers to ring the church bell. St. George's bell tower rose from a landing above us, the bell itself suspended from a stone archway. It could be seen for miles. One of the soldiers fished through a hole in the wall beneath the tower, pulled out a long rope, and gave it three short tugs. The bell clanged and vibrated, but there was no one to come to its summons. I hoped at least "bin Laden" and "Taliban" and the other militants with them heard it.

+   +   +

By late 2014, the peshmerga turned over patrol of Baqofa and other recaptured towns to Dwekh Nawsha, one of five Assyrian militias. On any given day, about fifty of its soldiers patrolled Baqofa, switching off in shifts. They had to share their weapons: Only about half of the militia's 250 members had guns.

Odisho Yousif, the Assyrian I had met following his 2006 kidnapping, helped organize Dwekh Nawsha. The chain-smoking political activist I'd met years ago now wore regulation desert camo and a bulletproof vest. Odisho had once served in the Iraqi army during the Iran-Iraq war, and the militiamen called him Lt. Col. Odisho Yousif.

Odisho, who was almost fifty-nine, had a receding hairline and graying temples. He remained a coil of energy and a tireless networker. He didn't deny that taking up arms to protect the Nineveh Plains homeland was a controversial decision for Christians. "We don't want to give the militia image to our struggle," he said, but ISIS left Assyrian Christians with no choice. "It's not acceptable to watch our lands taken by terrorist groups and expect Kurds to come to liberate them, and we just watch while Kurds fight. It's our land and our people, so we have to be active."

In Syriac, Dwekh Nawsha means "self-sacrificers," or in effect, "future martyrs." Odisho wouldn't admit that the odds were stacked against his army of irregulars. "We may be few in number, but we are big in faith and in our doctrine," he said.

Rotating daily between the front lines and his rear guard, Odisho was training recruits and seeing to drill exercises, as the commander of any army unit would. The soldiers ranged in age from their twenties to their sixties. Some had military experience; others had none. They trained for combat on open terrain and for house-to-house searches in the villages. In off-duty hours, Odisho made a point to connect with Nineveh's exiled church leaders. Some of them embraced the armed unit; others only tolerated it, either for practical or doctrinal reasons. In part to appease them, Odisho collected some of the ancient manuscripts discovered in the abandoned churches in Nineveh and delivered them for safekeeping to churches in towns that had managed to remain free from ISIS.

Using the pooled resources he had once deployed for ransom payments and funeral expenses, Odisho now bought boots, uniforms, and Kalashnikov rifles. In December 2014, the United States Congress passed a defense authorization bill to allow funding to train and equip local security units like Dwekh Nawsha, but no one had seen actual Washington money or military equipment from it. What Odisho procured, including night-vision goggles and communications capability to call in air strikes, came from elsewhere.

Fighters came from outside as well. George Khamis was an Iraqi who had fled the Saddam Hussein regime twenty-three years before to live in Australia. He left a wife and two children in Melbourne to return and join Dwekh Nawsha. Khamis had come back to Iraq for the first time in 2004 when an explosion destroyed his childhood home near Baqofa. Watching news reports of ISIS, he decided he had to return again.

"These people have been occupied for thousands of years, but to have been torn out by the roots and lose everything? And for months, now, nothing? Someone has to act," he said.

I traveled to the front with Albert Kisso, Odisho's deputy who also served as the militia's spokesman. Albert was someone I'd known over the years too. He had served as my driver crisscrossing Nineveh Plains, and I had learned to trust my life to him. Once when I suddenly became sick with fever and nausea in Kirkuk, Albert stopped to find soda and bottled water, and then he handed me antinausea medicine from I don't know where.

He understood English but spoke only a little. Somehow we got by. I'd draw the outline of a map on my notepad, and he'd fill it in with names and places as a way to confer over our itinerary. I'd ask questions; he would sketch in return.

Albert was about five feet seven, fit and muscular. When I first met him, he reminded me of a young Omar Sharif. His black hair and mustache were trim, as if he'd just left the barber's chair, and his white collared shirts and pants were always pressed. No matter the temperature, he showed up cool and collected, always businesslike and always on time.

Now Albert met me in olive-drab army fatigues, wearing a dark baseball cap and a bulletproof vest, a Kalashnikov slung over each shoulder. He had kept his trim mustache, but he now had a small goatee, and his hair had gone gray.

Albert collected me to travel to the front in a pickup truck loaded with soldiers. He rode in the front with a driver; I was wedged into the backseat with a middle-aged British soldier named Andrew and a young, pretty woman who told me to call her Jenny. Six guys rode high in the bed of the truck, several more Americans among them.

At least six Westerners were serving alongside Albert's regiment, and many others were serving as part of other forces—the Nineveh Plain Protection Units, the Syriac Military Council, or the Sons of Liberty run by American Matthew VanDyke.

I'd already met some of the American soldiers working with Dwekh Nawsha at a house where they were living in Dohuk. With their weapons and ammo spread over chairs and down a hallway, the volunteers sat on sofas watching television or cleaning guns. Only a few made eye contact with me. They'd grown wary of media coverage, and everyone seemed to be there under different, discomfiting circumstances. They had crossed the borders illegally from Turkey to Syria to get to Iraq, or they'd fought with Kurdish militias in Syria, or their families didn't know where they were. Some Westerners who had joined the militias plainly sought the spotlight; most simply wanted to be left alone to fight ISIS.

Louis, a twenty-four-year-old ex-Marine from Texas, was getting out of the service just as Daesh, as he called ISIS, invaded Iraq. He used Facebook to get in touch with Dwekh Nawsha.

"I didn't think we were doing enough," he said, referring to the United States, so he used his savings to buy his own weapon and equipment and fly to Iraq in January 2015. Louis had spent a deployment in Afghanistan fighting the Taliban in Helmand Province, but he said the trench warfare in Nineveh was less like counterinsurgency warfare and more like World War I.

Few of the Westerners had counted on the high cost of living in northern Iraq, where the humanitarian crisis pushed fuel, food, and lodging expenses above comparable rates in the United States. Louis, like others, was burning through his savings. But he wasn't giving up: "I believe in the cause a lot, so I'm willing to sacrifice everything."

Alan Duncan was another foreigner who showed up to fight, a middle-aged soldier from Scotland who had served in the Royal Irish Regiment in Saudi Arabia and Iraq in the 1990s. He called it shameful that Middle Eastern Christians had been left to fend for themselves, but he objected to the idea that this was a religious war.

"Not one of us Westerners is here on some Crusade or other rubbish—that's damaging," he said. "We are working with Sunnis and Shia. It's not some holy war; it's a war against Daesh."

The foreign fighters were a hodgepodge of Christians, atheists, and the religiously indifferent. What they had in common was a conviction that the United States and its allies owed something to the Iraqis and that they themselves had watched too long from the sidelines, waiting on the West to act.

Their efforts were hampered by a lack of sophisticated equipment and difficulty getting to the front lines. Dwekh Nawsha had to defer to the Kurdish peshmerga, and the Westerners had to defer to Dwekh

Nawsha. That often meant translating the peshmerga orders from Kurdish to Arabic, so they could be translated by the Assyrians from Arabic to English.

In the spring Louis told me he spent too much time eating in Dohuk pizza parlors and waiting to see action. But that eventually changed. Odisho moved the skilled soldiers into training Dwekh Nawsha recruits, rotating them to the front lines, where in May the patrol in Baqofa started taking hits.

Mortar fire from ISIS positions increased, and one night eighteen ISIS fighters attacked Dwekh Nawsha positions. By this time the militia had some machine guns, and the Assyrians and Americans repelled ISIS, killing two enemy fighters. Through the summer they thwarted additional attacks against Baqofa and another nearby town, Batnaya.

I learned later that Jenny, with whom I had ridden in the pickup truck, was actually Gill Rosenberg, a Canadian-born Israeli citizen who became one of the first female volunteers to fight ISIS in Syria's civil war. At one point, rumors circulated that she'd been captured in Syria and killed by the Islamic State. She worked alongside the YPG, the leading Syrian Kurdish militia, before making her way across the border to Iraqi Kurdistan. In Baqofa she was the only woman on patrol. Her phone beeped with calls and texts from other foreign fighters seeking advice on how to buy weapons.

Rosenberg, thirty-one, did search and rescue in the Israeli Defense Forces but spent four years in a U.S. prison as part of some phone scam, which she later said she regretted. When I was with Jenny/Gill, she insisted her whereabouts be kept secret and wasn't sure she'd be allowed to return home.[2] But she said fighting ISIS was worth any personal risk. After seeing images of beheadings and crucifixions on social media, she said, "I had to be here and do something. This wasn't some regular war—this was something beyond anything I'd witnessed."

By July she would be back in Jerusalem, where she was questioned by Shin Bet, Israel's domestic security agency. After her release, she spoke to reporters. She said that soldiering with Dwekh Nawsha had become too dangerous and complicated: "I felt that I could come back and give more to the effort not by fighting on the front lines, but by either raising awareness and talking to people about it and my experiences."[3]

During my day at the front, we traveled to Telskuf, the Assyrian town where I'd met Sister Mary Dominic with Insaf in 2007. ISIS had taken Telskuf in 2014 but later abandoned it under a barrage of air strikes. Two bombing runs by F/A-18s targeted and destroyed the headquarters ISIS had commandeered inside a large two-story house. Except for one sheared-off section with an intact upper room, the house and the one next door sat dissolved in heaps of rubble. Inside, a wooden cross leaned against a wall, open to the elements, improbable but emblematic for a town of seven thousand Christians.

As in Baqofa, only military personnel, not civilians, were allowed to stay in Telskuf. The peshmerga permitted residents one-hour passes to collect their possessions, but the shelling made it impossible for civilians to stay longer.

Telskuf was left abandoned, an uninhabited tomb of a town. The bakery with its wheels of baklava where Insaf and I had paused to buy bread and boxes of the syrupy pastry—gone. The busy market selling vegetables and melons—no more. The convent with its school—padlocked, empty. Sister Mary Dominic and the other nuns had taken refuge farther north in Alqosh. No one could say where all the village's poor and displaced people had gone.

"You have probably seen worse than this, but there is nothing worse than a city without people. It is like a graveyard," said Khamis.

It was so eerily quiet I could hear the soldiers' padded boot steps on the streets and the swish of combat fatigues rubbing together as they walked. Every so often the wind out on the plains would saw over the tall grasses that had begun to grow along what had been sidewalks. Ahead of us, two donkeys emerged from a passageway, turned, and walked together down the wet street. They were the only living creatures we would find.

In Dohuk the day before, I had stumbled on St. Peter and St. Paul

Assyrian Church. Like many Kurdistan churches, in 2014 it took in and housed sixty families forced from their homes. I wanted to see if any remained there, and I discovered nine families—about fifty people. Most of them were from Telskuf.

The families lived in one large room, a kind of fellowship hall off the sanctuary. It had one sink and no toilet. They used borrowed sofas to divide the hall into living spaces, and each family had a rug, some thin mattresses, and boxes of donated supplies. The boxes doubled as tables and places to hang laundry.

Some of the fathers had returned to Telskuf on one-hour passes—just long enough to learn they had nothing to go back to. As we talked, they pulled cell phones from their pockets to show me photos: their houses ransacked, doors busted, furniture overturned, drawers emptied, and valuables stolen.

"They stole everything; they did not leave us anything," said Faez Ablahad, a policeman from Telskuf. "And if I go back, I will be killed."

I didn't know when I met these families that a day later I would be walking through the streets of their town, spotting a shoe in a ditch here, a scarf and a family photo there, overturned refrigerators and smashed cars peeking out from so much rubble. Having seen their photos, the destruction felt personal; it had names and faces. Telskuf looked as if it had been hit by an earthquake and a tornado combined, some cataclysmic man-made disaster that left no street corner or residential block unmolested.

I wondered whether Telskuf and nearby Nineveh towns were destined to become like other scenes of genocide I'd witnessed: Srebrenica in the last days of the Bosnian War, when Muslims were the victims; or the torched and empty villages of southern Sudan where I'd first seen the fury of Islamic jihadist cleansing. The sheer vacancy of Telskuf set every one of us on edge. I could see what had happened in Telskuf, but my mind couldn't process it.

Where the nine-month-old caliphate would stop was anyone's guess. Were the lone patrols of Dwekh Nawsha and others enough to hold back ISIS? Hardly, it seemed. The Assyrian and Kurdish fighters had a passion to protect the homeland, and their determination was admirable. But their lack of training and weaponry, plus their limited numbers, made them appear to be no match for the oppressive and bloody rule of the Islamic State.

If the battle was lethal, at some level it was also ludicrous. Twenty miles from where we stood, even now a fighting force was holding classes on proper beheading techniques, training boys as young as four years old. Armed men were chaining women inside Mosul's abandoned government buildings, while their compatriots in Tikrit were executing unarmed army cadets and residents. Yet somewhere in the midst of so many deadly deeds, the jihadists took time to rummage through lingerie drawers in places like Telskuf for a few trinkets. The Christians, confronted with their empty towns and their desecrated churches, could only wonder: Is this the way a two-thousand-year-old civilization has to end?

With an estimated 30,000 militants, ISIS had conquered one-third of Iraq. It drove at least 30,000 Christians from Mosul and another estimated 150,000 from Nineveh Plains. Besides the million-plus Iraqis whom ISIS had driven from their homes, Iraq's army had lost four out of fourteen divisions with the seizure of Mosul. A fifth unit of national police collapsed. The United States had sent a couple hundred military advisers, who graduated thousands of Iraqi soldiers from a resurrected training program, but not one of the U.S.-trained Iraqis had been deployed on any battlefield.

Behind ISIS was financial aid from Saudi Arabia and Qatar, said Richard Dearlove, the former head of Britain's intelligence service MI6. The onetime British intelligence chief believed that most of those finances were funneled through private donors with two pragmatic if contradictory aims—to prevent ISIS from gaining a foothold in the Gulf countries and to use ISIS as a buffer against Shia powers, meaning Iran and the Shiite-led government in Baghdad. Saudis, Dearlove said, are "deeply attracted towards any militancy which can effectively challenge Shia-dom."[4]

Besides outside support, ISIS had another important prop: fear. Unlike previous jihadi groups who often practiced guerrilla warfare tactics, ISIS made no attempt to hide. The militants went to great lengths to publicize atrocities, distributing videotaped accounts and news widely via social media and in many languages. They shamelessly published a glossy magazine called *Dabiq* as a propaganda tool. An analysis by the Brookings Institution found Islamic State loyalists using 46,000 Twitter accounts—mostly from within Iraq, Syria, and Saudi Arabia (which housed almost as many account users as Iraq and Syria combined) and written in English 20 percent of the time[5]—all to spread the word of beheadings, executions, and other conquests.

The very tools Christians in Iraq had first deployed to stay safe in earlier war years, ISIS had now turned against them. Facebook, texting, and Twitter had enabled Christians to alert one another to dangers—an IED here, gunfire there, news of kidnapping and ransom demands. Now, instead, those social-media channels fed their fears with news of the latest ISIS assault. "The fear of the crimes Daesh could commit against the women and children of my family is much greater than the fear of being killed by Daesh," one Nineveh man said.

Few possessed the focused resolve required to resist the rule of fear, but I took notice of those who did. Up Mount Al-Faf, barely four miles from where the ISIS fighters were camped, the ancient Mar Matti monastery no longer sat abandoned. Though the families who had taken refuge at Mar Matti in 2014 had moved (and the ancient Syriac and Aramaic Scriptures and other manuscripts had been carried to safety as well), three monks and six students returned and dug in, determined. As long as any Christians were left in Iraq, explained Yousif Ibrahim, one of the remaining monks, he would stay at Mar Matti: "A shepherd cannot leave his sheep."

The nine men were resolute, a living testimony for all who had before them retreated to the ancient monastery. As student Sahar Karaikos explained, "If a people don't have the history of their past, then they will not have a future because they won't know what their origins are, where they came from."

From their promontory, the Mar Matti brothers watched the tracers of air strikes over Nineveh Plains at night. They saw the brilliance of an explosion, then heard and sometimes felt its thud a millisecond later. They saw mortar launches along the berm outside Mosul before the Dwekh Nawsha militiamen sighted them in their scopes. In the ongoing warfare, said Yousif Ibrahim, "The sky lights up at night, but we of course are not scared. God protects us."[6]

20

CITIES OF REFUGE

Erbil, 2015

....

The people who survived the sword found grace in the wilderness.

JEREMIAH 31:2

....

Mosul hadn't been this clean in thirty years. The Islamic State saw to clearing the streets of trash and cigarette butts. It closed down stalls run by illegal sidewalk vendors and put up new streetlamps. Few journalists or outsiders of any kind could get into the city (if they did, they had to swear allegiance to ISIS and sign a covenant), but reports coming out said that ISIS was working round the clock to repair roads, spiff up public spaces, and refurbish hotels.

Whitewashed tombs are clean too. Beneath the civic refurbishment, Mosul was full of the dead and the despairing. Men had to grow beards. Women had to be fully cloaked in full-length black burqas, including gloves, before they stepped outdoors. Beauty salons and barbershops were closed. Churches in the old city were converted to market bazaars, selling war booty plundered from the homes of Christians. If anyone veered from the rules, the ISIS bureaucracy with its *Fuqahā*, or jurists, was ready to enforce Islamic law.

ISIS suspended flights and closed travel agencies. Residents could not leave the city unless they had a documented medical emergency. They hoarded food and supplies, expecting a siege should the Iraqi army attack. If that happened, they assumed they'd become human shields for escaping ISIS fighters.

Perhaps close to a million people still lived in Mosul. All thirty thousand of the city's Christians—plus all its Yazidis, Turkmen, and other non-Muslims—had departed. So had the Muslim Shia and Kurdish population. Only the Sunni Muslim population, the majority, remained.

Mosul's remnant could attest to strict Sharia law, publicly enforced. Anyone caught stealing had a hand amputated. Anyone caught in adultery was stoned to death or thrown from a building. Enslavement of non-Muslim women and children was legal—in fact, the new decrees for slavery were posted on the walls of mosques throughout the city.

Sexual slavery was far from clandestine under ISIS; it was more like a cottage industry. ISIS had killed or captured thousands of Yazidis and hundreds of Christians. Those in captivity clung to a living death, a hell from which they might never recover.

Badush Prison in Mosul was one stopover. ISIS emptied the prison and executed its six hundred to seven hundred inmates—mostly Shiites, a few Christians, and others—dragging them to a ravine outside of town and shooting them. Over the coming months the militants moved abducted Yazidis, Christians, and Turkmen in and out of the Badush cells. They systematically separated young women and teenage girls from their families. They raped the women and girls, many of them repeatedly, before sending them off to Raqqa, the ISIS headquarters in Syria, or to other "slave markets" under its control.

The stories of two sisters, Jilan and Jihan Barjess-Naif from Sinjar, revealed what happened to many women in captivity. According to eyewitnesses who later managed to escape, seventeen-year-old Jilan was "a beautiful green-eyed girl, with rare blonde hair."[1] Islamic State militants held her with twenty other women and girls in one room. Several in the room were ten to twelve years old. Militants gave them dance costumes and told them to bathe. The women knew these instructions were preludes to sexual abuse.

Islamic State militants separated Jilan from less attractive young women and singled her out for repeated raping. As the rituals were repeated, Jilan grew despondent. The next time she was told to bathe, she went into the bathroom, cut her wrists, and hanged herself. When the militants discovered her, they threw her body in a garbage dumpster.

By then Jilan's family had been split apart, her father and six siblings executed. Her sister Jihan was transferred to Raqqa to be sold. In similar circumstances as her sister, she committed suicide a few days after Jilan.

The girls' mother was pregnant. ISIS transferred her to a remote cave, a holding cell between Raqqa and Mosul, where she gave birth. ISIS was known to free women it no longer had use for, and she was one. But upon her release, she learned of the suicides of her daughters, plus the deaths and disappearances of her husband, sons, and about twenty members of her extended family. Kurdish health workers who tried to help her said she lived on "as a mad woman."[2]

As Samah Anwar reminded me, the Yazidis knew what ISIS was up to. The stories of rapes, forced marriages, and slavery arrived with the first displaced families she met from Sinjar. Early on, women in captivity managed to make phone calls to family members and others. Some hid their phones in the black *abayas* ISIS captors made them wear.

A young Yazidi woman trafficked to Syria managed to phone activists working for a relief organization, Compassion4Kurdistan. "If you know where we are, please bomb us," she begged. "There is no life after this. I'm going to kill myself anyway—some have killed themselves this morning." The woman said she had been raped thirty times, "and it's not even lunchtime."[3]

ISIS members posted updates of their conquests on social media. "Anyone interested got 1 of 7 Yehzidi slave girls for sale $2500 each [. . .] don't worry brothers she won't dissapoint [sic] you," declared Mohamed Elomar, a twenty-nine-year-old ISIS jihadist from Australia on Twitter.[4]

Those who marketed and sold abducted women had the backing of ISIS policy. Islamic State published the glossy magazine *Dabiq* regularly, which was released in several languages. *Dabiq* cited the Quran, saying, "It is permissible to have sexual intercourse with the female captive"[5] and boasted about the "large-scale enslavement" of Yazidis. The Yazidis fell into "the camp of kufr," or disbelief, together with, according to a *Dabiq* article, "the camp of the Jews, the crusaders, their allies, and with them the rest of the nations and religions of kufr, all being led by America and Russia, and being mobilized by the Jews."[6]

In the fall ISIS followed up with a pamphlet in the form of questions and answers about captives and slaves. It read in part:

Question 5: Is it permissible to have intercourse with a female captive immediately after taking possession [of her]?
If she is a virgin, he [her master] can have intercourse with her immediately after taking possession of her. However, if she isn't, her uterus must be purified [first]. . . .

Question 6: Is it permissible to sell a female captive?
It is permissible to buy, sell, or give as a gift female captives and slaves, for they are merely property, which can be disposed of as long as that doesn't cause [the Muslim ummah] any harm or damage.[7]

Human Rights Watch interviewed twenty women and girls who escaped ISIS between September 2014 and January 2015. Half of them, including two twelve-year-olds, had been raped—some multiple times and by multiple ISIS fighters. Nearly all were forced into marriage; they were sold or given as "gifts." Other monitors and local officials were discovering similar stories and statistics.[8]

Kurdish health officers identified hundreds of women who escaped or were freed from ISIS and made their way to Kurdistan. They were living in mostly Yazidi camps or other temporary housing. By May 2015, Dr.

Nezar Ismet Taib, a psychiatrist and director of Dohuk's health ministry, was working with five hundred women and girls in counseling. They were mostly Yazidis but included Christians, Kurds, and Syrians. By August 2015, the number who had escaped or been freed from ISIS had risen to 2,058, just counting those living in Dohuk and its surrounding district alone. Of those, said Dr. Nezar, 770 were victims of rape.

One seventeen-year-old he interviewed said she had lost track of how many times she had been raped but knew how many times she had tried to commit suicide—five. "They had been taken from villages and stayed awhile, taken to nearby towns and stayed awhile, taken to Mosul and stayed awhile, or they were sold or moved to Syria," Dr. Nezar told me.

Dr. Nezar was working closely with peshmerga commanders, he said. At one point he almost begged them to somehow slow any liberation of villages or rescuing of captured women and girls; the health system simply couldn't handle the volume of trauma, medical attention, and counseling required.

He had formed a team of specialists and trauma counselors to assist the rescued women. Several were hospitalized, Dr. Nezar said, "to be protected from themselves."

Most of them were under twenty years old; some were as young as nine. "Last week I talked to a thirteen-year-old girl. She was raped many times. She doesn't know what is going on, what has happened to her." Compounding their trauma, nearly all of them had lost one or more members of their family, including parents, who had been killed or captured or had simply disappeared.

ISIS had killed more than five thousand Yazidis, based on stories from relatives and other witnesses. It had captured seven thousand others. In the first six months after ISIS instituted the systematic rape and enslavement of non-Muslim women and girls, at least 150 of them had committed suicide. At some point in the spring, ISIS banned its captive women from wearing head scarves, even though head coverings were required under Islamic law. Too many women and girls had used them to hang themselves.

By all existing international laws and treaties, the ISIS slave trade constituted international sex trafficking and war crimes. It was taking place in known locations. Escaped abductees could name where they had been held—in houses, hotels, factories, former government offices, schools, prisons, and military bases in Mosul, Tel Afar, Tal Banat, and Sinjar in Iraq; and in Raqqa, Rabia, and other towns in eastern Syria. Women who escaped testified that some buildings housed five hundred young women and girls. World leaders like UN Secretary-General Ban Ki-moon would express "grave concern" over the slave trade,[9] while calling ISIS destruction of ancient sites like Nimrud "a war crime."[10]

Summer would turn to autumn, and autumn to winter, and winter to spring with no strategic effort, beyond the work of local health officers like Dr. Nezar, to rescue the captured women and girls. Normally polished and self-assured, Dr. Nezar sounded like a weary old man as we spoke by phone about his latest cases. He was athletic and, at six feet, tall for a Kurd, but I imagined him, in his usual suit and tie, somehow diminished, sagging inside. The work had grown too big, and he was too alone; but it had to be done.

Dr. Nezar and other officials to whom I spoke noted that the international community seemed to be allowing a robust and likely lucrative trade in humans—against all treaties and laws on trafficking—to proliferate, unchecked. They suspected that some criminal organizations or other groups were profiting from the horror.

+ + +

In such a decimated landscape, it was hard at first for those who managed to survive the cruelty of ISIS to notice much besides the summer heat. The summer of 2014 was unusually hot. Samah and her family lived for two months in the classroom housing twenty-six people. The school was one of about six hundred in northern Iraq converted to housing for displaced families. Samah's family couldn't return to Bashiqa, but they didn't know where to go next.

Officials postponed the start of classes but eventually decided to open some schools in late October. That forced Samah's family to move to an open building under construction in Dohuk. It was like living on the street, Samah tried to explain in her sometimes broken English: "We couldn't sleep due to the cars' voices."

The family decided to move to Erbil, a bigger city with more housing options, while Samah remained in Dohuk to take makeup exams from her interrupted spring term.

When she reached her family in Erbil, she discovered they were living in abysmal conditions. They'd found a corner in a high-rise under construction, where they had stashed mattresses and blankets. The building had only floors and exterior walls. "The place had no water, no electricity, no doors, no windows," Samah said. "It was filled with dust and pieces of glass, plus there were no toilets or bathrooms."

Dozens of families, Christians and Yazidis from all parts of Nineveh and Mosul, had taken up residence on the unfinished floors of the Galaxy Hotel. Vendors arrived some mornings to set up stands, selling fruit juice and snacks, water and ice out of cardboard boxes. Women shared their soap and did laundry in tubs, hanging it to dry on an open, unfinished balcony. They pooled their supplies to cook, setting up small burners in common areas to boil water or heat large pans for cooking. The women mingled and shared their stories as they completed their daily chores.

The experience of Samah's family was typical: The hotel was the fourth place they had lived in the weeks since ISIS had forced them from their home. Each time they moved with next to nothing: just some foam mattresses, plastic bags stuffed with a few clothes, and a few pots, pans, and plastic bowls they'd accumulated since being forced from their home. Each time they learned to share their sorrows all over again.

At the hotel Samah lived on the same open floor with Nidal and her children, a Christian family who had been captured and held by masked ISIS fighters. The militants had told Nidal's husband, "We will take you, or we will take all the family." The father went with ISIS so the family could be released. Nidal had heard nothing more from him.

Sara, a young Christian mother of three from Qaraqosh whose husband had been kidnapped, also lived nearby. She was pregnant when she arrived with her children. Other women in the hotel, all once strangers, were helping her care for the children.

The hotel was far enough on the city outskirts that little formal help reached the families living there. Then one day, "We were visited by a Christian named Najeeb," Samah informed me.

Father Najeeb Michael was a Dominican friar born in Mosul. One day he showed up at the hotel with food, water, clothing, and fans. "He was bringing us everything we need, even money, and then he made many rooms for people. He worked so hard for us," Samah reported.

By the time I met Father Najeeb, he was a legend. He had earned his PhD in Switzerland studying Yazidi writings, discovering along the way that Chaldean monks in Iraq had translated the first written forms of Yazidi teaching into Syriac. His interest in preserving ancient manuscripts never wavered, a passion that was shared by all the Dominicans.

The Dominican order first arrived in Iraq in 1750, and in 1860 they brought in the country's first modern printing press. In addition to preserving centuries of hand-copied texts, the Dominicans printed hundreds of Scriptures and other religious books, textbooks in Arabic, and educational tracts of all kinds.

The Clock Church in Mosul, a landmark site built in 1872, was at the heart of this work. The church was visible above the city's low skyline for miles around. Residents set their watches by its clock, pausing as they passed beneath its tower or upon hearing its brass bell.

In 2006 insurgents set off a bomb at the entrance to the Clock Church, an explosion that ripped through the doors and windows of the chapel where the priests were holding evening prayer. No one was hurt in the blast, but for Father Najeeb, this attack jump-started a quest to save the artifacts of Mosul's ancient Christianity. The church with its monastery and extensive library was at risk.

After the bombing, Father Najeeb began to load a hired car with rare books and manuscripts every evening at sunset. The car would then take these documents to the Dominican mission in Qaraqosh. Eventually he secreted away 55,000 volumes. Besides ancient Scripture and church writings, the collection included dated works on science, astronomy, and medicine.

He and other Dominicans in Mosul already had begun a project to digitize the material: the Digital Center for Eastern Manuscripts. In 2007 they picked up the pace, sending digital files to Minnesota for safekeeping, where most were stored by Dominican brothers at the manuscript library of Saint John's University. Some digitized files also went to the National Archives in Paris.

As ISIS closed in on Qaraqosh in 2014, the Dominican archives had to be moved again. This time Father Najeeb hired a large truck to carry books and manuscripts from Qaraqosh to Erbil.

A displaced man himself, Father Najeeb and the Dominican brothers purchased a four-room house in Erbil, where by 2015 he had stored the physical remains of the vast Clock Church collection. The friar obsessed over care of the documents, but at the same time he grew more burdened to preserve the "live leather," his term for the Christian people.

"Human lives are first, but you cannot protect the tree without the roots. The roots are our history, our heritage. We cannot protect humans alone but must protect our heritage also," he said. "We are trying to save both."

That was how Father Najeeb ended up at the unfinished Galaxy Hotel. He persuaded the building's owners to let the Dominicans turn the construction site into emergency housing. By the time I visited it in early 2015, Father Najeeb had changed its name to Al-Amal Hope Center. He opened another site in an abandoned four-story building in Erbil, calling it "Vine."

With support from Dominican orders in Europe and the United States, Father Najeeb hired a contractor to build out the construction sites, creating cement block interior walls for two-room living units with windows and doors. Al-Amal had electricity but no running water. Hired trucks delivered water tanks, which the young boys then hauled to upper floors in jerricans. Shared toilets and washing sinks were installed at the end of each floor, and women cooked over small single burners in the wide hallways.

Christians and Yazidis lived together at both sites—165 families (750 people) at Al-Amal and 80 families at Vine. On average there were five to six persons per family, and two families usually occupied one two-room unit.

"Now I'm sitting in a building with everything we need in it," Samah told me cheerfully as I visited her at Al-Amal. "It's a real home. And Father Najeeb taught us to be hopeful and patient, even though we don't know what the future is hiding for us."

The trauma lived on in these new dwellings. Children made crayon drawings showing beheadings and rivers of blood. Four-year-old boys were frightened whenever a man with a beard approached them. Yet Yazidis from Sinjar were living alongside Christians from Qaraqosh. Women consoled one another in the cement-block hallways as they patted fat wads of dough into flatbread. A young girl from a Christian family changed the diaper of an orphaned Yazidi boy. Samah taught others English, and in turn she was learning to improve her own skills by speaking English to visitors.

The kindness and hard work of caregivers softened the disappointment and distrust of recent months. Laughter echoed off the corridors as children chased one another up and down the stairs. Men leaned over a row of public sinks at the end of the hallway, helping boys clean up. Conversations hummed as women hung laundry.

+ + +

Insaf made repeated trips to Iraq to help the displaced, and during a visit in March 2015, I joined her there. When I told her I wanted to see Samah and her family, whom I had met earlier, Insaf knew immediately where to find them.

Later, I watched Insaf observing some children of Al-Amal playing on an open carport. When they finished, they were breathless, and she offered to buy each one a bottle of juice from a vendor, also a displaced man, who was selling food and drinks nearby. As Insaf began handing Iraqi dinars to the vendor, the sound of children racing down the staircases grew as they heard about the free treat and came running from all over the building. She put no limit on how many she would buy; she just kept handing over dinars with each new arrival.

No matter where the displaced Iraqis ended up, Insaf developed a knack for locating them. She'd spy laundry hanging from a railing, see boxes stacked at the entrance to a building, and go inside on a hunch that IDPs (internally displaced persons) lived there. She nearly always carried envelopes filled with cash to help friends she went looking for or strangers she stumbled upon. Sometimes she carried scarves, sealed packages of makeup samples, or small toys—the sorts of "nonessential" items aid groups didn't supply.

Insaf still carried money informally donated by others and gave it to displaced families. Instead of tracking details in her spiral-bound notebook, she now kept the roster of who supplied what to whom on one of two cell phones—a Samsung she used for calls in Iraq, and an iPhone from which she made calls to Canada.

By the time I joined Insaf, the displaced Iraqis had weathered the seasons. The summer heat of 2014 had seemed to give way almost overnight to an early winter, bringing new challenges for those in temporary housing. Cold winds, wet rain, and then snow piled against tent flaps or blew through open hallways like those at Al-Amal. Insaf worked with a number of local churches to provide wrapped Christmas presents for displaced families. She and other women organized parties for displaced children to receive gifts. They strung lights across cement-block walls and propped decorated trees outside their doorways. Even the tent camps of the Christians lit up with the season. Churches held special services, even while many still slept in their pews or on mattresses they'd spread in their sanctuaries and hallways.

"Everyone needs others," Insaf said. "You cannot work alone."

One evening Insaf and I attended a Bible study led by her son-in-law,

Malath, in a high-rise apartment building on the outskirts of Erbil. As we arrived, the lights went out, reminding me of the old days of the war. Using our phones for flashlights, we climbed to the fifth floor and entered a spacious apartment occupied by two families who'd fled Mosul in June 2014. Three other families and some of their children had joined them for the study.

A kerosene heater kept us warm as the night chilled, and everyone opened their Bibles, reading by the light of their phones. I couldn't help but notice their eagerness. Some talked about how losing everything had given them the opportunity, for the first time in their lives, to really study their Bibles and spend time in prayer. As they discussed what it means to be humble, Malath told them they could be humble as displaced people without suffering low self-esteem.

Afterward some of the women brought out coffee, sandwiches, and cookies. No one wanted to leave. Hearing their talk and laughter, a stranger wouldn't know they had been chased out of their homes from Mosul or Qaraqosh—some at gunpoint.

These families were better off than most I'd seen, thanks partly to a church in Indiana that had raised $60,000 to assist Malath and his church. He decided to put the money toward rent, providing 80 families (about 250 people) rent assistance for six months. *Multiply the resources of churches in the United States against so simple a need*, I thought, *and American Christians could make a real difference in the lives of ISIS victims.*

As one season gave way to another, Insaf became increasingly convinced that any solution for Iraq would be "not by troops and killing people but by healing." She prayed for healing, she said, not only for those chased by ISIS but for ISIS militants, too. "We are persecuted based on our belief," she said. "We should test our belief now."

In Toronto between trips to Iraq, Insaf decided to pray and fast over the situation. "Usually I don't fast," she said, but she did anyway. "When you fast, the boundaries go. The Spirit moves with fasting and prayer."

She fasted for three days, and each day she found that she could not get her mind off a passage from the Old Testament: the first chapter of Micah. Insaf wanted me to look up the verses and read them over the phone to her as we talked of her fasts. But she couldn't wait until I found them, and she began reciting instead:

> The LORD is coming out of his place, and will come down and tread upon the high places of the earth. And the mountains will melt under him, and the valleys will split open, like wax before the fire, like waters poured down a steep place.[11]

"These high places of the earth are ISIS," she explained, "and they will melt under God's feet."

I reminded her of an encounter years ago, when she first met a victim of Islamic militants: Joanne, the friend in Kirkuk whose husband had been killed by an IED. Insaf had prayed for her—for the fire to become like cold water.

"Yes, that's it," Insaf replied. "ISIS will melt under God's feet, and the fire these people are experiencing will become like water, cooling them, helping them, helping us."

+ + +

Divine help and healing, however, didn't come without sting, especially as ISIS occupation in Iraq entered a second year.

"No person, no country, no humanitarian organization can supply this level of need," pastor Yousif Matty said one day in the spring.

We were having lunch. Yousif's wife, Alia, set a platter of chicken with vegetables and apricots before us, and we were joined by some of Yousif's family, Insaf, her daughter, and her granddaughter. Suddenly I could tell that Yousif and Insaf were arguing in Arabic.

Yousif paused to explain for me in English, "We are fighting here in Iraq for sixty years, fighting for our faith and our homes. We are crying, and there are stories that will break your heart."

Looking at Insaf, he continued: "You cannot come into my home and suggest my sons emigrate or that I should help people emigrate. Out is not really a solution."

For many Iraqis, including old friends, the tensions of recent months brought a reckoning. Yousif planned to persevere, to stay no matter what. He wanted to expand educational opportunities beyond his three classical schools, and he saw an opportunity in all the present chaos to help Iraqis think in new ways. He felt that Iraqi Kurdistan would ultimately become stronger as a result of the ISIS onslaught.

"I want to see Christians biblically educated and a new generation earning degrees locally," he said. "I want to have a university education for them to stay in the region and build our nation again. This is not the first time for Mesopotamian people that Christianity has been oppressed. The movement with ISIS is not going to be the last problem. We have purpose and reason to stay."

At the same time, it seemed that everyone who could was leaving. Insaf, for all her dedication to the people of Iraq, felt that many families had been hurt so much and had lost so much that they should be helped to go.

Others who once longed to return to Iraq were telling me this too. In recent years, Elias Shamuel, the Assyrian accountant who lived in Chicago, had dreamed of retiring with his wife to their home village of Bebede, near Dohuk. Now that area was overrun with displaced people, and village life wasn't what he remembered. The dangers, also, were too great.

"The situation is not only about the eradication of present people," he said. "It's cultural. It is about distinct people groups in the Middle East who won't exist in ten or twenty years."

Elias said he'd never been so pessimistic: "I can see the death of this culture in my lifetime."

Without some change, without outside pressure and support for the Kurds to succeed at the fight against ISIS, he had no hope. "You become like wood to feed the fire," he said.

In the years I had known Elias, he had championed the cause of

Assyrian Christians who remained in Iraq. He had lobbied on their behalf among church leaders and political operatives in Washington. He had helped many people, including Odisho Yousif. Elias was the one they called in the night. He could activate a support network among the Assyrians living abroad. Without that support, it would be harder for many to continue—especially since so many families and churches had been forced to flee and life in Nineveh Plains had, for all intents and purposes, stopped.

Yet in 2015 Elias was among those giving up: "Religiously I am gone. Ethnically I am cleansed. Culturally I am wiped out."

21

A GARDEN BY NIGHT

Baghdad, 2015

....

Return, O LORD, to the ten thousand thousands of Israel.

NUMBERS 10:36

....

The air cooled and the evening grew late, the day's heat settling in droplets over the roses. Earlier one of the women in St. George's Church had carried cups of apricot ice cream out in a cardboard box, and the neighborhood children had run to grab them and then begun a game of chase across the lawn. For Baghdad residents, this was the hour to live for, when the heat lingered but a breeze kicked up to tease out the moisture hanging in the air, the kind of air the date groves love, with warmth and humidity enough to make the fruit grow fat and sweet.

"Have I ever told you what the river is like on a hot summer night?" British diplomat Gertrude Bell wrote home from Baghdad in 1921. "At dusk the mist hangs in long white bands over the water; the twilight fades and the lights of the town shine out on either bank, with the river, dark and smooth and full of mysterious reflections, like a road of triumph through the mist."[1]

With the Tigris murmuring past us two blocks away, I brought chairs into St. George's church garden to sit with Dawlat Abouna, his eyeglasses fogging for a moment in the evening damp. Dawlat was a journalist and a lifelong resident of Baghdad.

"When I came here to St. George's, I figure I am in paradise in Iraq. You feel you are in a secure place. You feel close to God," Dawlat said.

Tell me your story, I said.

"My family has thirty-two archbishops in its family tree," he began.

The Abouna family settled in Alqosh in Nineveh Province sometime in the fourth century. Six early archbishops of the Assyrian Church of the East, all of them from the Abouna family, resided in Turkey. Twenty-six more were in Iraq. From the fifth to the nineteenth century, Dawlat's ancestors held top church offices, shepherding ecclesiastical affairs throughout Persia, India, and Cyprus.

At one time the Abouna dynasty held title to the land from Mosul to Tur Abdin in Asia Minor, now known as Turkey. Patriarch Shimon Farj Albasedi deeded the area to the Ottoman Empire in 1560. "It is unknown until now if he granted it by force or willingly," said Dawlat. Dawlat kept a copy of the deed in his home library; the original documents were stored in the Chaldean patriarchate library in Baghdad.

When Dawlat explained that nine of his family patriarchs are buried in Rabban Hormizd Monastery, I shivered. I thought of the dark passageways leading to their crypts, which I'd explored with Drew and Eder on our visit to the ancient monastery in 2008. There in the quiet of St. George's garden, I felt the long-ago and faraway lineage laid to rest between us, a loop of history now come full circle.

Disciples of Jesus Christ brought their religion to Edessa and Tur Abdin, Turkey, where the Assyrian Church of the East had begun. It took root in churches and monasteries that spread south to Ctesiphon, near present-day Baghdad. From Jerusalem, other disciples carried the Christian gospel westward. It crossed the Mediterranean, spread throughout Europe and tiny England and beyond, circling back in the twentieth century to this spot of ground by the Tigris. Here in a church built by the British, a son of the Eastern patriarchs sat before me. Dawlat the deacon handed out parcels of food to the poor, sat for prayers over his evaporating legacy, and translated the whole saga for Westerners like me who came around again. He seemed like the last man standing—a witness.

+ + +

As 2014 gave way to 2015, the Islamic State continued its march of terror and destruction unhindered. ISIS militants bombed Nimrud's ancient ruins and blew up the fourth-century Mar Behnam Monastery in early 2015. The Dominican Clock Church in Mosul still rose above the city skyline, although ISIS had turned the landmark into a jail. "It's very hard to know what evil is happening there," Father Najeeb Michael told me.

Despite these fresh atrocities, the world took note in May 2015 when Sister Diana Momeka of the Dominican sisters of Qaraqosh took the witness chair on Capitol Hill before the House Foreign Affairs Committee. Qaraqosh remained under ISIS control; her order's convent had been turned into ISIS's headquarters for Nineveh Plains. She described her personal flight with Sister Maria Hanna and others. She pointed out that no government entities had stepped forward with material aid of any kind for Christians. No one had formed a panel of inquiry; no one had brought charges against ISIS to any international court; and no one had a plan for reparations, given how much property had been lost without compensation. "Thankfully, the Church in the Kurdistan region stepped forward and cared for the displaced Christians," she told lawmakers.

"ISIS has and continues to demolish and bomb our churches, cultural artifacts, and sacred places," she said. "We have realized that ISIS's plan is to evacuate the land of Christians and wipe the earth clean of any evidence that we ever existed."

In an emotional appeal, Sister Diana continued, "There are many who say, 'Why don't the Christians just leave Iraq and move to another country and be done with it?' To this question we would respond, 'Why should we leave our country—what have we done?'"[2]

At the hearing, the lawmakers were reminded that President Obama had yet to appoint a special envoy for religious minorities in the Middle East, a position created by Congress in 2014.

While Sister Diana's testimony raised a stir in Washington, forty-three-year-old Karim Wasfi made a name for himself by taking his cello to sites of bombings on the streets of Baghdad, where he would sit down to play, sometimes for hours.

During Karim's first such street performance, he played an original composition titled "Baghdad Mourning Melancholy." Seated with his cello atop a blackened sidewalk, Karim played while behind him survivors were clearing glass and mopping up a bombed shop. Karim's close friend Ammar al-Shahbander, an Iraqi journalist, posted footage of his solo on the Internet. In the video a man in a wheelchair slowly rolls himself next to Karim. Shop owners and passersby gather to watch, some in tears.

The scene formed a montage of the scarred psyches surviving a scarred city and a scarred country. It was beauty rising from ashes, a kindled reminder of the historic vibrancy of Baghdad's cultural scene, supported by Christian, Jewish, Muslim, and other musicians, prevailing in the face of all Islamic State edicts against it.

Only a few days after performing "Baghdad Mourning Melancholy," Karim was playing his cello at another site, where a car bombing by ISIS militants had killed seventeen people, including his friend Ammar al-Shahbander. This time Karim wore a white suit to honor his friend and played for four hours.

"The other side chose to turn every element, every aspect of life in Iraq into a battle and into a war zone," Karim said later. "I chose to turn every corner of Iraq into a spot for civility, beauty and compassion."[3]

Karim directed the Iraqi National Symphony Orchestra along with fellow Iraqi Mohamed Amin Ezzat. The orchestra had launched in 1936, only to be shuttered by Saddam. Following the dictator's fall, it restarted in 2003. I was surprised to learn in 2015 that it was still performing regularly. A March performance in Baghdad began soberly:

A son of one of the musicians had been killed fighting ISIS. That same week ISIS had posted images of its destruction of art and archaeology, including the two-thousand-year-old ruins of Hatra and the three-thousand-year-old remnants of Nimrud. The symphony played Mozart and Brahms in an auditorium seating nine hundred, a performance so well attended that many in the audience had to sit or stand in the aisles. When it was over, the musicians received deafening applause.

The symphony featured seventy-three professional musicians, including "Christians, Muslims, Yazidis, one Baha'i, and even non-believers who do not announce it," Karim said. They played a range of Western classical music and Middle Eastern traditional pieces, joined by forty-three young trainees through a school program Karim launched called Peace Through Art. It taught children not only music but poetry, art, and manners.

In 2015, on the fourteenth anniversary of the 9/11 attacks, Karim and the symphony orchestra performed Brahms's Symphony no. 4, again to a packed hall. The Islamic State, controlling territory just west of the capital, had banned all such music, but Karim followed his own edicts: "I for one refuse to start my day in fear of explosions, and when it does happen I express my refusal through my music."[4]

+ + +

A remnant held on in northern Iraq and Syria as well. The Christians had fled Alqosh in August 2014 when ISIS fought Kurdish forces within five miles of the town, but miraculously, three-fourths of the Christians who had lived there returned.

Alqosh was perhaps the only such town to be reinhabited. Unlike in almost every other town that it targeted in Nineveh Province, ISIS had failed to cut electricity and water to Alqosh during its advance. The tomb of Nahum with its crumbling synagogue might be preserved, as well as many churches, while so many historic sites were being destroyed. Sami, keeper of Nahum's tomb, stayed in Turkey, at least for a while, telling his relatives that life had become too risky for Christians in Iraq.

Those who did return to Alqosh celebrated. Hundreds formed a procession around an Assyrian church to give thanks to God for protecting the village, and they rang the bells of the churches. In an act of defiance against ISIS, a few teenagers took it upon themselves to clean the streets and water city trees. Officials who came back were so grateful, they paid the young volunteers for their work. I couldn't help but wonder whether Eder, our enthusiastic and civic-minded young guide in 2008, wasn't somehow behind it.

As the Puritan church fathers were fond of saying, God works contrary to means. There were people in this long war—men like Pastor Yousif Matty—you simply could not keep down. By early 2015 he had the only school for Yazidis up and running. Shivani Medes School met in fifteen prefab units ringing a central courtyard inside Khanke IDP Camp. Weeks after the school opened, it had grown from 350 to more than one thousand students.

Besides serving displaced Yazidi students, Yousif took in Arab students whose families had been forced from Mosul at the request of the also-displaced Mosul board of education. The new load meant running a second track of classes in the same facilities, one taught by teachers also driven from Mosul. In a way no one could have imagined, ISIS had brought together Yazidi and Muslim students meeting under one roof in a school run by Christians.

In Syria the white-haired Bishop Antoine Audo continued to organize relief for the needy and homeless, which had come to mean nearly everyone. The Christian population of Aleppo had fallen from 400,000 to about 60,000. Aleppo is starving, he warned in 2015, observing from his window that the former shopkeepers and businessmen of the city "run endlessly with bags in their hands, trying to find a bit of bread."

Bishop Audo maintained his determined outlook. "The anarchy of the war allows you to perceive in even stronger terms the greatness of human dignity, just when it seems so humiliated," he said. Aleppo had become a kind of hell, but when I asked the bishop whether he would stay in Syria, he replied, "Of course. It's my country, the place I live, and I have to give a testimony. I respect everybody who chooses to leave. But I will continue."

I tried to fathom the depths of Christian solidarity, watching these believers find water in this desert. The Christians took both earthly and unearthly provisions into the hardest and saddest—and sometimes insanely dangerous—places. Caring for displaced families when they first arrived was one thing, but it was another to help them six months, one year, or eighteen months later. The long years of war and persecution preceding the invasion of ISIS had trained some muscle reflex, only instead of it moving their hands away from the fiery flame, it moved them toward it—and toward one another.

Before the start of Syria's civil war, the Syriac Orthodox archbishop Gregorios Yohanna Ibrahim told me he did not care which churches had the largest attendance, or whether the old-line Syriac churches or the newer evangelical churches held prominence. "These are shark-infested waters," he said. "Survival of the fittest is not an option, and it cannot be spelled out who will come out on top."

Archbishop Ibrahim went missing in 2013, kidnapped on his way back from trying to negotiate the release of other abducted Syrian Christians. I thought of him often, particularly as the old animosities among Christians gave way in a perilous time.

+ + +

In March 2015, I sat in on a Saturday conference on the theme "beauty from ashes" attended by 350 displaced women in Erbil. The attendees included Christians and Yazidis; old and new believers; women born into Assyrian or Chaldean churches and women born again, including some who had come to know about Jesus Christ only since their displacement. The event was arranged by Hope and Peace for Civil Rights, a group working with churches to help the displaced people. The speakers included a Mar Matti brother, the Dominican father Najeeb Michael, and evangelical leaders such as Insaf.

A decade ago, such a gathering would have been unthinkable. Since the coming of ISIS, church leaders—Syriac, Orthodox, Catholic, evangelical—had traveled the countryside together, delivering mattresses, milk powder, and water, texting and talking about what to do next. Together they'd looked for the lost and found them on hot, dusty hillsides, in caves, sleeping under pews and in back lots, and sometimes dead by a near-forgotten roadside. What united these Christians had become greater than what divided them.

The conference hall was full of women all looking their best in glittery sweaters or fitted jackets and wearing carefully applied makeup that highlighted their dark eyes and glossy hair. Most of them did not move from their chairs throughout the program, which lasted from ten in the morning until two in the afternoon. They came from homes they were improvising in shopping malls, high-rises, trailers, and tents. Most of the women wore donated clothes and would return to a donated home to fix a meal with donated foodstuff.

Insaf told them, "Daesh destroyed our culture, our churches, and our lives. But women have life-giving power within them, and Daesh cannot destroy the God who made us; they cannot kill our God-given dignity."

No one seemed ready to answer the question *What happens next?* In the chaos of Iraq, I had learned, you had to look not only at what was happening but what was *not* happening. After the onslaughts by Islamic militants, the Muslims would return to their homes and reopen their stores. The Christians could not. Even their sanctuaries—the churches—ISIS had obliterated. As human rights activist Mark Lipdo pointed out to me, "The world's reluctance in confronting ISIS in northern Syria and Iraq gave minority ethnic and religious people to a monstrous holocaust."[5]

Sufficient military action to dislodge ISIS from Mosul and elsewhere would be long in the making, if it could be mustered at all. Without support from Baghdad, the Kurdish regional government risked bankruptcy. It could not indefinitely bear so great an influx of needy homeless people. Humanitarian groups already were pulling back, unlikely to continue to risk serving under the precarious conditions.

In so vast a state of paralysis, the Western powers talked of a safe haven for Christians, perhaps in Syria by the Turkish border, in Turkey itself, or in Nineveh Plains. Many Christians I spoke to in Iraq didn't want that. A safe haven sounded like another prison, a bigger jail than the churches in Mosul had become. They had known so much more.

+ + +

In the garden, night descended over Dawlat and me like a shroud, the scent of roses rising beneath the cloister of St. George's hedged blast walls. From nearby mosques, the calls to prayer commenced, the muez-zin's voice low and warbling, his verses echoing off the Al-Mansour Hotel and the ministry buildings. Not far away, a harmony of footfalls met pavement amid a drill sergeant's clipped orders. Troops were work-ing through military exercises, taking advantage of the cool night air.

Dawlat was born in Baghdad in 1948 and grew up off Haifa Street near the Central Railway Station in a neighborhood of Christians and Muslims not far from St. George's. Dawlat went to church-run schools and studied English literature at Baghdad University. Most of his life he worked as a journalist, becoming managing editor of the *Baghdad Observer*, an English-language newspaper.

The Baghdad press enjoyed a period of independence and freedom before the Baath Party came to power. At one time forty-five news-papers were published in Baghdad, some of them run by prominent Christian editors. With the Baathist takeover, independent-minded journalists began to emigrate. Some were executed as enemies of the state. Under Saddam, the papers became propaganda machines, their staffs required to join the Baath Party. Dawlat rode all the waves of revolution and compromise, then found himself forced out with the 2003 U.S.-led liberation. Under the Americans' de-Baathification poli-cies, he and many others lost their jobs, and his paper closed. Journalists were treated as if they had been mouthpieces for the Saddam regime, Dawlat said, "despite the fact that the occupation was well aware that the journalists who related closely to Saddam were few."

Dawlat grew increasingly bitter over U.S. occupation, retreating to his extensive library, where he labored over translations of church and family history. But the reopening of St. George's Church revitalized his faith, and he and his wife began attending there. When Canon White took over the regular preaching, Dawlat served as his translator.

The war years were difficult for Dawlat's family, as for everyone. His sister was a senior bank officer and was kidnapped twice during the war. Each time the family found money to pay the ransom, but after the second time she was afraid to stay. She left for America with their mother. A brother already lived there.

"My two sons don't want to leave, and I don't want to leave my family tree," he said. His sons, one married with twin boys and a daughter, had jobs in Baghdad. They all lived close by, in Baghdad's al-Mansour district. They spent many evenings together, eating dinner and watching the news or television shows, talking over the latest events and the future of Iraq. "We have a family life here you Americans once had," Dawlat said.

I told him he was right.

With the coming of ISIS in 2014, Dawlat struggled to hold fast to the centuries of ties binding him. By 2015 his sons had left Baghdad for Erbil, fearing ISIS would overtake Baghdad. They never came back. I thought often of Dawlat at home alone with his library, translating memorabilia from his history books for people like me when what he most wanted was to be talking over the news of the day with his sons gathered around him.

Most of Dawlat's relatives fled Alqosh, many saying they would never return. Much of the family land, once given to the church and then transferred to the Ottoman Empire, now fell to ISIS—a legacy set down in the fifth century, lost.

The worship and work of St. George's continued, increasingly without Canon Andrew White. For a time in 2014, the vicar of Baghdad worked on behalf of displaced Christians in Kurdistan, but threats against his life soon forced him out of the country. By 2015 his time in the Middle East was spent mostly in Jordan, among Iraqi refugees.

St. George's congregation set up a kitchen and hired widows to make food to sell in the market. It started a workshop employing poor women to knit and sew children's clothes and bedsheets that could be sold.

When I asked Dawlat whether services continued as they had when Canon White was there, he replied, "Oh yes! We have started two new groups here at the church—one to pray for our persecuted brothers in the north, and one to pray for our enemies."

+ + +

More than a decade in, I worried about these Christians I'd come to know. A headline would pop up on my computer screen—"Priest Feared Kidnapped in Syria" or "Family Gunned Down outside Baghdad"— and I would pause, unable to breathe, before clicking to open the story, names and faces racing in my brain.

While most Americans continued to wonder at the oddity of Christians hanging on in Iraq, many of them had become somehow like family to me. Insaf, the first, was like a sister. I had watched her give up one dream after another for Iraq, yet still return to serve and spend herself. Even so, I kept losing sight of the sturdiness, the sheer will to survive, arising from the ashes of so much misery. The Christians confronted face-to-face and door-to-door by ISIS had run, yes, but they had run only when to stay meant giving up their faith. The sublime, nearly forgotten reality in all their hardship and loss was this: In losing everything, they had held on to the one thing that mattered to them most.

The Islamic militants had a strategy, and they had pursued it relentlessly for more than a decade in Iraq. Blowing themselves up inside a suicide vest or being killed were acceptable costs, which made them the most ruthless kind of foe. The Western powers would go to war, withdraw, and go to war again, staccato movements without cohesion, lacking lasting meaning.

I had come and gone too. One time I carried home in my backpack a rug bought in a Kurdish flea market. Another time I brought back one of Maher Dakhil's booklets, just to be reminded of his smiling face as he handed them out against Saddam's orders. I took home orange rocks from the Nineveh Plains. I pressed a wrapper from Canon Andrew White's favorite candy shop into a notebook. And I still held on to a turquoise key chain Insaf bought for me in the Baghdad airport gift shop. "Someday you'll want something to remember me by," she had said with a laugh. How we remained friends and traveling companions through so much grief and disappointment can only be explained by her mirthful spirit and her daily, practiced devotion to others.

In Iraq were no guarantees, as Muthafar would say, and every time I closed my notebook and boarded a plane out, I would look long at the endless plains, the desert going white into the distance, and wonder whether I'd ever return, ever see these people I cared about again. I'd wonder where the end of the story was.

With self-protection comes a small compass, I'd learned in the early years of the war. When the perimeters of life are close, we may avoid danger, but we miss the world's greater treasures. In these later years I had to confront how little I'd offered in all my comings and goings in this wider world, how much I'd taken and learned in return.

With the coming of ISIS, the Christians needed more help than ever—they needed rent money, concrete floors, schools, and back-packs. Insaf taught me that they needed dignity, too, which was why makeup and the means to give gifts to their children were also impor-tant. After meeting the woman who handed me the envelope of cash in the Orlando garage, I helped more, but I was a fitful, irregular giver. Like most Americans, I had so many resources but so little time to focus them wisely.[6]

Christianity at its truest stretched and recast harsh realities, turning them upside down, inside out. Its people took mustard seeds and with them moved mountains, which I learned as I watched Insaf, Yousif Matty, Father Najeeb Michael, and many others. Destruction brought comfort, in the words of the prophet Nahum; impossible hardships became possible to endure, and death became life-giving. Augustine said it well: "For God judged it better to bring good out of evil than not to permit any evil to exist."

Dawlat, left to muse among the roses and his library of ancient manuscripts, was a witness, perhaps to something dying, something that might one day live again. In a few short years of war, his nation had been brought to the brink of collapse, in danger of becoming not only a failed state but a failed civilization. Dawlat, for his part, was still sitting in a garden by the Tigris and calling it paradise.

In the middle of so profound a crumbling, there would be exiles and witnesses, pilgrimages to commence and strangers to usher in, stories ended just as new ones were beginning.

My calls and visits would be welcomed, day and night. I would remain the journalist with too many questions, the American whose manners were too abrupt, getting down to business before the rounds of greetings were complete. But I was beckoned, even sung to, in the midst of a life-and-death struggle, this journey to find water in the desert.

I never arrived anywhere without finding I had a seat at the table, with food always waiting: a spread of fatoush, a plate of kebab, and bowls of mezza. The darkest forces still came by night, angling toward death and destruction. But other times someone would carry a tray of tinkling tea glasses into a room where the lights had just gone off, and on the hardest day I could feel the smile and the welcome in it.

Acknowledgments

I crossed the Tigris in a motorboat in 2002 with the help of Qubad Talabani, now deputy prime minister of Iraqi Kurdistan, and Tanya Gilly-Khailany, who went on to become a member of the Iraqi Parliament. Before the war, these two manned a sometimes thankless outpost for the Kurds in Washington, DC, and I remain grateful for the door they opened for me to begin a voyage of discovery in Iraq.

Douglas Layton introduced me not only to the Kurds but to the Christians, and I am grateful for his tutoring and willingness to talk, e-mail, and network no matter where or when. Persecution has its own landscape, and I thank tireless religious freedom scholars Nina Shea at the Hudson Institute, Allen Hertzke at the University of Oklahoma, and Thomas Farr at Georgetown University for their expertise and compassion. The folks at Barnabas Fund in Coventry, England, went out of their way to connect me to persecuted Christians in the Middle East, especially to clergy in Syria. Judith Mendelsohn Rood, professor of history and Middle Eastern studies at Biola University, has been a traveling companion and a friend ready to lend her expertise in Arabic.

An American expat living in Jordan wrote me a letter because she took issue with a magazine article I wrote on the Middle East, not knowing she was about to become my friend and her family my oasis. I am forever grateful to Wendy and Dennis Merdian for introducing me to Insaf Safou, for helping me with lost luggage and Arabic nuances, and for their steadfast example and devotion to the lives of so many in the Arab world.

I was privileged to have a memorable breakfast in 2008 with Gregorios Yohanna Ibrahim, Syriac Orthodox archbishop of Aleppo, who was patient and soft-spoken as we ate alone in his vestry. Over eggs with bread, yogurt, and cucumbers and tomatoes, he explained the vibrancy of the ancient churches in ways a modern evangelical Christian like me finally could grasp. Since his kidnapping in April 2013, he has not been heard from again. He is a martyr, emblematic of the many Middle Eastern clergy devoted to their flocks unto death.

I have encountered in Iraq and Syria many a martyr, both in the Old English meaning of the word—a witness—and in the modern usage, one who has laid down his or her life for the faith. My debt to living witnesses is vast, but most especially to Elias Shamuel, now living in Chicago, and Father Emanuel Youkhana, who divides his time between Germany and Iraq as the director of the Christian Aid Program Northern Iraq (CAPNI). Under Saddam Hussein, Elias was beaten in prison and Father Emanuel was blacklisted, and both were forced to leave their homeland. Like so many Iraqis, they left their hearts behind and contribute in countless ways to preserving a Christian presence in Iraq. These Assyrians guided me into the history and hardships of their people, took my middle-of-the-night calls from Iraq, and made straight my paths.

Iraqi pastors Yousif Matty and Haitham Jazrawi and Syrian physician Jany Haddad sacrificed inordinate amounts of time and hospitality on my behalf. Their wives, too, embody sacrifice and wisdom.

Other news organizations spent their treasure on high-priced security teams, but I had drivers who in skill and character were worth their weight in gold. Albert and Martin in Nineveh Plains, Anglebert in Baghdad, Ramazan along the borderlands of Syria and Turkey, Rami in Damascus, and Fadhil in Kurdistan, plus others, all have my thanks.

In a male-dominated world, they protected me as a sister. I don't want to know all the ways they kept me from perishing, or from just making dumb mistakes.

Wounds from a friend can be trusted, the proverb says, and for trustworthy guidance and much-needed sharpening in this writing business, I thank my former *World* magazine colleague and author Lynn Vincent; my agent, Chris Park; and my editor, Kim Miller. Skill, hard work, and kindness abound in these women, and they went more than an extra mile with this first-time book writer.

Every writing and reporting opportunity that has come my way I owe to Joel Belz, my brother-in-law and the founder of *World* magazine. Nick Eicher and Marvin Olasky, extraordinary editors, took the long odds in asking me to be a reporter and then an editor, becoming steadfast door openers, critics, and friends through years—now decades—of deadlines and stress, enough to defeat lesser men. This book would not be here without them.

My special thanks, also, go to colleagues Tim Lamer, Jamie Dean, David Freeland, Rob Patete, and Kristin Chapman, who contributed research for this book.

My children came to love Mom's trips overseas because trips meant Daddy making breakfast, renting an Xbox, and throwing down sleeping bags for a slumber party at his office. Nat Belz gave years of encouragement that is singular and undeserved for the travel and reporting this book represents. Then he gave months and months of support and wisdom in its writing. He keeps life in perspective for us all, always.

My daughter Emily turned four years old the day Saddam Hussein invaded Kuwait. Neither of us could know how that action would shape our future and bring us into contact with Iraq's people. Now a journalist in her own right, she is a trusted counselor and critic, a role model with a tender heart.

Of my son, Drew, what more is there to say of a junior in college who cut classes for a trip with his mom, who risked a grade point average for an odyssey in a war zone? Drew has gone the distance with me, in countless ways and at all hours, time and again lending his considerable gifts and outsized passion.

My third-born, Naomi, tended the home fires, gave me steady assurance things could run smoothly in my absence, and helped my reentry with reports of all I had missed. As war in Syria exploded, she translated from French firsthand reports from Homs and elsewhere. My work has been sped forward under her encouragement and observant eye.

Sara, my youngest, learned life with a mom making trips to far places, and from the beginning has engaged me with a vivid imagination, challenging questions, helpful insights, and a hand to hold.

To this squad, add the encouragement of my daughter-in-law, Kate Harrison Belz, and my son-in-law, Scott Schindler. They enriched the writing process beyond measure.

My first and earliest encouragement to write anything at all came from my mother, a wordsmith who taught me early on the value of noticing and describing the smallest details of a wide world. While I tended this book, she tended a raging cancer, my writing chapters interrupted by our daily trips to radiation, yet somehow she motivated me still. I am grateful for months and months of her cloistered life in our home, her steadfastness, and the way her dignity amid daily suffering reminds me of the courage of Middle East Christians.

Making one and then more trips to Iraq with Insaf Safou introduced me to a community little known outside Iraq, where some chanted in Aramaic inside chapels made of cut stone while others sang American praise songs in Arabic to the accompaniment of a Yamaha keyboard. Over and over, Insaf showed me patience and kindness, and sprinkled hard days with the laughter and joy that come from having a real and lasting confidence in the world that is to come. *Marhaba*, the traditional Arabic greeting "hello," originated in Syriac, meaning "God is love," as the way the early Christians received one another. *Shukran jazeelan*, my friend, *marhaba*. We have miles to go.

Time Line of Key Events in Iraq and Syria

1920–2015

1920: The modern states of Iraq and Syria are created following World War I. The United Nations puts Iraq under British administration and Syria under French administration.

1932: Iraq achieves independence.

1946: Syria achieves independence.

1968: The socialist Baath Party stages a successful coup in Iraq, and Saddam Hussein becomes deputy to Iraq's new president, Ahmed Hassan al-Bakr.

1979: Saddam Hussein becomes president of Iraq.

1980–1988: Iran-Iraq War

1991: The United States and UN coalition forces launch their first offensive in the Gulf War, following Iraq's seizure of Kuwait.

2000: Bashar al-Assad becomes president of Syria, succeeding his father, who led Syria for thirty years.

September 11, 2001: Nineteen militants associated with al-Qaeda hijack four commercial airplanes and carry out suicide attacks against the Pentagon and New York's World Trade Center.

December 2001: Several jihadist militants come together under the name Ansar al-Islam (Supporters of Islam) and set up a base of operations at the Iraq-Iran border.

October 2001: The United States invades Afghanistan to drive out the Taliban and end its sheltering of al-Qaeda leadership.

March 2003: After Saddam Hussein refuses to relinquish power, the United States begins bombing Baghdad, launching the Iraq War.

April 2003: The Coalition Provisional Authority, led by Paul Bremer, is established as the transitional governing authority following Saddam Hussein's ouster.

December 2003: Saddam Hussein is captured by American military forces.

2004: Abu Musab al-Zarqawi establishes al-Qaeda in Iraq (AQI).

January 2005: Iraq holds a national election to select a National Assembly tasked with writing a constitution and legislating until the new constitution is approved.

September 2005: Maher Dakhil (the lay pastor of St. George's Church in Baghdad), his wife, son, and other church leaders disappear on their drive home from a church conference in Amman, Jordan.

October 2005: Iraqis approve a new constitution in a national referendum.

December 2005: Iraqis elect members for a newly created parliament, which will select a president who will appoint a prime minister.

January 2006: American Jill Carroll, a reporter for the *Christian Science Monitor*, is kidnapped by Sunni Muslim insurgents in Baghdad.

April 2006: Nouri al-Maliki is selected as prime minister.

June 2006: Zarqawi, leader of AQI, is killed in a U.S. strike. Abu Ayyub al-Masri succeeds him.

July 2006: Odisho Yousif and his driver are kidnapped by Muslim insurgents on their way to deliver money to churches in Iraq.

October 2006: AQI leader Masri announces the creation of Islamic State of Iraq (ISI).

December 2006: Saddam Hussein is executed by the Iraqi government.

January 2007: President George W. Bush announces the formulation of a "surge," an increase in the deployment of U.S. troops to support and stabilize the Iraqi government against insurgents.

May 2010: Abu Bakr al-Baghdadi becomes leader of ISI after Abu Ayyub al-Masri is killed in a joint U.S.-Iraqi operation.

March 2011: Civil war breaks out in Syria as popular uprisings are squelched by Assad's government.

May 2011: Syrian government forces begin battling opposition fighters, whose members include jihadist groups, in the city of Homs.

August 2011: Abu Bakr al-Baghdadi is designated a terrorist by the United States.

December 2011: All American troops, except those connected with the U.S. embassy, are brought home from Iraq.

March 2012: American teacher Jeremiah Small is killed by a student in his classroom in Iraq.

March 2013: The Islamist militant group al-Nusra Front seizes Raqqa, Syria.

April 2013: ISI declares its absorption of the al-Qaeda-backed militant group in Syria known as the al-Nusra Front. Baghdadi says that his group will now be known as the Islamic State of Iraq and Syria (ISIS).

January 2014: ISIS takes control of Fallujah, Iraq.

January 2014: ISIS battles al-Nusra Front and other militant groups to establish its headquarters in Raqqa, conquering the city and claiming victory over competing rebel and Islamist militant groups.

February 2014: After months of infighting, al-Qaeda renounces ties to ISIS.

June 10, 2014: ISIS seizes Mosul.

June 11, 2014: ISIS takes control of Tikrit.

June 29, 2014: ISIS announces the creation of a worldwide caliphate, or Islamic state, making Baghdadi the self-declared authority over the world's 1.5 billion Muslims.

July 4, 2014: ISIS leader Baghdadi makes a rare public appearance and delivers a sermon at Mosul's Grand Mosque, declaring the Islamic State to be the first caliphate to function under Islamic law in over one thousand years.

July 24, 2014: ISIS destroys the tomb of the Old Testament prophet Jonah and in the following week destroys or occupies forty-five Christian churches and institutions in Mosul.

August 2014: The militia Dwekh Nawsha is created to defend Assyrian Christians from ISIS.

August 3, 2014: ISIS fighters storm the northern Iraqi town of Sinjar, home to the Yazidis, a minority group. Thousands of fleeing residents are stranded in the Sinjar Mountains.

August 7, 2014: President Obama authorizes targeted U.S. air strikes against the ISIS militants. ISIS seizes Qaraqosh, the largest Christian city in Iraq, along with many nearby villages.

August 17, 2014: Iraqi Kurdish forces recapture Telskuf and other villages, and they retake the Mosul Dam from ISIS.

August 19, 2014: Two years after U.S. journalist James Foley's capture in Syria, ISIS releases a video showing his beheading, the first of many such executions videotaped and then broadcast by the terrorist group.

November 14, 2014: The UN Independent International Commission of Inquiry on Syria concludes that ISIS has committed war crimes and crimes against humanity.

January 28, 2015: ISIS destroys the walls of ancient Nineveh.

February 2015: ISIS abducts more than 260 Assyrian Christians—including men, women, and children—from thirty villages raided in northeastern Syria along the Khabur River, and forces 1,400 families from their homes.

April 2015: Iraqi government forces regain control of Tikrit.

May 17, 2015: ISIS seizes control of Ramadi, Iraq.

September 23, 2015: ISIS executes three Assyrians, part of a group of Christians from villages along Syria's Khabur River it continues to hold.

Notes

PREFACE: PAY MONEY
1. Quran 9:29
2. Acts 2:9
3. An Assyrian priest, whom I've not named out of concern for his safety, told me this in 2005.
4. Yereth Rosen, "Former Coast Guard Chief to be U.S. Arctic Representative," *Arctic Newswire*, July 16, 2014, http://www.adn.com/article/20140716/ former-coast-guard-chief-be-us-arctic-representative.
5. Jeffrey Goldberg, "Not All Bombing Victims Are Created Equal," *Atlantic*, June 4, 2012, http://www.theatlantic.com/international/archive/2012/06/not-all-bombing-victims -are-created-equal/258029/.

CHAPTER 1: INSAF'S JOURNEY
1. Geoff Manaugh, "Saddam's Palaces: An Interview with Richard Mosse," *BLDGBLOG*, May 27, 2009, http://bldgblog.com/2009/05/saddams-palaces-an-interview-with -richard-mosse/.

CHAPTER 2: RIGHT OF RETURN
1. Jeremiah 29:10-14, NIV
2. Genesis 2:8
3. Genesis 32:10

CHAPTER 3: NO GUARANTEES
1. Mark Bowden, *Road Work: Among Tyrants, Heroes, Rogues, and Beasts* (New York: Penguin Books, 2004), 14.
2. Thomas Friedman, "The Chant Not Heard," *New York Times*, November 30, 2003, http://www.nytimes.com/2003/11/30/opinion/30FRIE.html.
3. Bing West, *The Strongest Tribe: War, Politics, and the Endgame in Iraq* (New York: Random House, 2008), 13, 18.

CHAPTER 4: FIRE LIKE COLD WATER
1. C. E. Bosworth et al., eds., *The Encyclopaedia of Islam* (Leiden, The Netherlands: E. J. Brill, 1980), 10.
2. Taken from S. K. Malik, *The Quranic Concept of War* (Lahore, Pakistan: Associated Printers, 1979).

CHAPTER 5: THE WAR BEFORE

1. "Iraqi Kurds Fear New Islamist Group," *BBC News*, October 2, 2001, http://news.bbc
.co.uk/2/hi/middle_east/1572478.stm.
2. Krekar lectured in Pakistan in the 1980s and joined jihadists in Peshawar before Norway
granted him asylum. Only months before 9/11, Mullah Krekar told reporters that
Osama bin Laden was the "jewel in the crown of the Muslim nation."
3. "Iraqi Kurds Fear New Islamist Group," *BBC News*.
4. "The People of the Kurdistan Region," Kurdistan Regional Government, www.gov.krd/p
/page.aspx?l=12&s=050000&r=304&p=214.

CHAPTER 6: WINDOW OF OPPORTUNITY

1. The sixth-century *Chronicle of Arbela* recounts the appointment of a bishop for the
district, then called Adiabene. Arbela, or Erbil, was its capital. By AD 100 a bishop
named Mar Peqida presided over a church in the city, and he was followed by bishops
named Shemshon, Ishaq, Abraham, Noch, and Habel—all Jewish names suggesting that
the first Christians were converted Jews.

CHAPTER 7: VANISHED

1. Eckhard J. Schnabel, *Early Christian Mission* (Downers Grove, IL: InterVarsity Press,
2004), 123.
2. Jehoiachin, the captured king of Judah, built a synagogue in Nehardea, a city by the
Euphrates, using stones carried from Jerusalem. According to rabbinic tradition, Ezra
the Old Testament scribe opened a synagogue and an academy.
3. Recorded variously by Philip Jenkins in *The Lost History of Christianity* (New York:
HarperCollins, 2009), Robert Louis Wilken in *The First Thousand Years* (New Haven,
CT: Yale University Press, 2012), and Schnabel in *Early Christian Mission*.
4. Edessa and the surrounding Upper Euphrates valley were at the easternmost reaches
of the Roman Empire, and for a time came under the rule of the Sassanids of Persia.
The city's population was largely Aramaean, but it was a cosmopolitan mix of traders,
merchants, peasants, and scholars. They spoke a potpourri of languages—Greek, Latin,
Aramaic (also known as Syriac), and Hebrew.
5. Suha Rassam, *Christianity in Iraq* (Herefordshire, England: Gracewing, 2010), 28.
6. "At Least 85 Killed in Iraq Triple Car Bombing," *Agence France-Presse*, http://reliefweb
.int/report/iraq/least-85-killed-iraq-triple-car-bombing.
7. "Entire Lay Leadership of Anglican Church in Iraq Feared Dead," *Christian Today*,
September 29, 2005, http://www.christiantoday.com/article/entire.lay.leadership.of
.anglican.church.in.iraq.feared.dead/4101.htm.
8. Speech made by Amir Faisal to the Jewish Community of Baghdad on July 18, 1921,
quoted in Mindy Belz, "The Edge of Extinction," *World*, May 17, 2014, https://www
.worldmag.com/mobile/article.php?id=30034.

CHAPTER 8: CRUSADERS AND THE MUJAHIDEEN

1. Mark Bergin, "Best and Brightest—'He Died Well,'" *World*, August 27, 2005, http://
www.worldmag.com/2005/08/best_and_brightest_he_died_well.
2. Jill Carroll and Peter Grier, "The Jill Carroll Story," *Christian Science Monitor*, August 2006,
http://www.csmonitor.com/Specials/Hostage-The-Jill-Carroll-Story. See also Howard
LaFranchi, "Remembering Allen: A Tribute to Jill Carroll's Interpreter," *Christian Science
Monitor*, March 6, 2006, http://www.csmonitor.com/2006/0306/p01s03-woiq.html.

3. "Unmaking Iraq: A Constitutional Process Gone Awry," International Crisis Group Report, September 26, 2005, http://www.crisisgroup.org/en/regions/middle-east-north -africa/iraq-iran-gulf/iraq/B019-unmaking-iraq-a-constitutional-process-gone-awry.aspx.
4. See "Iraqi Deaths" table on iCasualties: Iraq Coalition Casualty Count, http://icasualties .org/Iraq/IraqiDeaths.aspx. Total Iraqi civilian deaths for 2006 were 16,564, as calculated by the sum of monthly totals.
5. Mindy Belz, "Binding Up the Wounds of War," *World*, September 29, 2007, http:// www.worldmag.com/2007/09/binding_up_the_wounds_of_war/page3.
6. *CNN Late Edition with Wolf Blitzer*, August 20, 2006, http://www.cnn.com /TRANSCRIPTS/0608/20/le.01.html.
7. Mindy Belz and Jamie Dean, "End of a Ruthless Era," *World*, January 13, 2007, http:// www.worldmag.com/2007/01/end_of_a_ruthless_era.

CHAPTER 9: PLACES OF EXILE

1. "Justice for Saddam," *Wall Street Journal*, November 6, 2006, http://www.wsj.com /articles/SB116277023020113971.
2. Hadeel al Sayegh, "Baghdad Cemetery Provides Window into Iraq's Past," *The National*, August 26, 2013, http://www.thenational.ae/thenationalconversation/comment/baghdad -cemetery-provides-window-into-iraqs-past.
3. "Two Assyrian Baghdad US Embassy Employees Killed by Al-Qaeda," Assyrian International News Agency, June 2, 2007, http://www.aina.org/news/20070602131612.htm.
4. Ibid.
5. "Gen. Petraeus: 'We Are Just Getting Started,'" *USA Today*, April 26, 2007, http:// usatoday30.usatoday.com/news/washington/2007-04-25-iraq-vote_N.htm.
6. The Christian Aid Program-Nohadra Iraq (CAPNI) and Ghassan Thomas, whose church was housing some of the families, gave me this estimate during my interviews with them in Iraq in August 2007.
7. CAPNI, an Iraqi Assyrian aid group, was taking surveys of families arriving in Nineveh for food distributions there.

CHAPTER 10: THE KEEPER OF NAHUM'S TOMB

1. Yael Mizrahi-Arnaud, "The Evolution of Displacement: A Jew in Iraqi Kurdistan," *International Policy Digest*, October 12, 2015, http://www.internationalpolicydigest.org /2015/10/12/the-evolution-of-displacement-a-jew-in-iraqi-kurdistan.
2. Nahum 1:15
3. 1 Chronicles 9:1, KJV. This verse points to genealogical lists, such as the one found in Genesis 46:8-27, that appear in the Bible's first five books.
4. *The Itinerary of Benjamin of Tudela: Travels in the Middle Ages* (n.p.: NightinGale Resources, 2004), 98–101.
5. Ibid. See also I. Abrahams and C. G. Montefiore, ed., "The Itinerary of Benjamin of Tudela (continued)," *Jewish Quarterly Review*, vol. 17 (London: Macmillan and Co., 1905), 524.
6. Rachel Aspden, "A Lost World," *New Statesman*, July 17, 2008, http://www.newstatesman .com/arts-and-culture/2008/07/baghdad-iraq-music-kojaman.
7. For more on life for Jewish Iraqis in the first half of the twentieth century, see Marina Benjamin, *Last Days in Babylon: The Exile of Iraq's Jews, the Story of My Family* (New York: Free Press, 2006).
8. Ibid.

CHAPTER 11: A CHURCH OF MARTYRS

1. Bing West, *The Strongest Tribe: War, Politics, and the Endgame in Iraq* (New York: Random House, 2008), 12.
2. Cameron McWhirter, "Chaldeans Desert Iraq for Promise of Metro Detroit," *Detroit News*, October 28, 2002, see http://www.chaldeansonline.org/telkeppe/Telkeppe-DN /Chaldeans%20desert%20Iraq%20for%20promise%20of%20Metro%20Detroit%20 -%2010-28-02.htm.
3. John R. Krueger, ed., "The Siege of Mosul and Ottoman-Persian Relations 1718–1743," Indiana University Publications Uralic and Altaic Series, vol. 124 (Bloomington, IN: Indiana University, 1975), 175.
4. Mindy Belz, "Pay Money," *World*, November 15, 2008, http://www.worldmag.com/2008 /11/pay_money/page2.
5. Anthony O'Mahony, "Archbishop Paulos Faraj Rahho," *The Guardian*, March 31, 2008, http://www.theguardian.com/world/2008/apr/01/catholicism.religion.
6. Suha Rassam, *Christianity in Iraq* (Herefordshire, England: Gracewing, 2010), 2–3.
7. Ibid., 3.

CHAPTER 12: FASTING AND FLIGHT

1. The "sons of martyrs" is a reference to the Armenian Genocide, which affected Assyrian Christians as well. The churches in Aleppo grew from those escaping that genocide one hundred years ago.
2. Sandro Magister, "The Last Mass of Father Ragheed, a Martyr of the Chaldean Church," May 6, 2007, http://chiesa.espresso.repubblica.it/articolo/145921?eng=y&refresh_ce.

CHAPTER 13: THE COMING OF A NEW CALIPHATE

1. Al-Quds al-Arabi website, London, in Arabic, May 17, 2010, reported by BBC Monitoring (retrieved via Lexis-Nexis).
2. Ned Parker, "Al Qaeda in Iraq Rises Again," *Los Angeles Times*, September 13, 2010, http://articles.latimes.com/2010/sep/13/world/la-fg-iraq-qaeda-20100913.
3. Ibid.
4. "Interview with Vice President Joe Biden," *Larry King Live*, February 10, 2010, http:// transcripts.cnn.com/TRANSCRIPTS/1002/10/lkl.01.html.
5. Emma Sky, *The Unraveling* (Philadelphia: PublicAffairs, 2015), 311.
6. Emma Sky, "How Obama Abandoned Democracy in Iraq," *Politico Magazine*, April 7, 2015, http://www.politico.com/magazine/story/2015/04/obama-iraq-116708_full .html?print#.Vi-H5v4o7cs.
7. Ibid.
8. Christoph Baumer, *The Church of the East: An Illustrated History of Assyrian Christianity* (London: I. B. Tauris, 2006), 146.
9. Robert Louis Wilken, *The First Thousand Years: A Global History of Christianity* (New Haven, CT: Yale University Press, 2013), 292.
10. "Iraq History: The Arab Conquest and the Coming of Islam," Arabic Media, http:// arabic-media.com/arab_conquest.htm.
11. Suha Rassam, *Christianity in Iraq* (Herefordshire, England: Gracewing Publishing, 2010), 80–81.
12. Anthony Shadid, "Church Attack Seen as Strike at Iraq's Core," *New York Times*, November 1, 2010, http://www.nytimes.com/2010/11/02/world/middleeast/02iraq.html?_r=0.
13. Ibid.

14. "Thousands of Christians Have Fled Iraq Since Church Massacre," Open Doors, April 14, 2011, https://www.opendoorsusa.org/take-action/pray/tag-prayer-updates-post /Thousands-of-Christians-Have-Fled-Iraq.

15. Richard Barrett, *The Islamic State* (New York: The Soufan Group, 2014), 9, http:// soufangroup.com/wp-content/uploads/2014/10/TSG-The-Islamic-State-Nov14.pdf.

16. Eric Linton, "20 Killed, 80 Wounded in Bombings across Iraq," *International Business Times*, July 22, 2012, http://www.ibtimes.com/20-killed-80-wounded-bombings-across-iraq-730088. See also "Iraq's al-Qaida Leader Announces New Plan of Attacks," Xinhua News Agency, July 22, 2012, http://news.xinhuanet.com/english/world/2012-07/22/c_131731465.htm.

17. Harald Doornbos and Jenan Moussa, "The Fugitive," *Foreign Policy*, October 3, 2013, http://foreignpolicy.com/2013/10/03/the-fugitive/?wp_login_redirect=0.

CHAPTER 14: THE DEATH OF ONE AMERICAN

1. Mindy Belz, "A Rush of Life," *World*, March 24, 2012, http://www.worldmag.com/2012 /03/a_rush_of_life.

2. Kawa Abdulla, "Exclusive Interview with Father of Student Who Shot His American Teacher," *Rudaw*, quoted in "Issues Related with Religion Pushed Kurdish Student to Shoot His American Teacher, Says Father of the Student," *Kurdish Observer* (blog), March 15, 2012, http://kurdishobserver.blogspot.com/2012/03/issues-related-with-religion -pushed.html.

3. Meer Ako Ali, "What It Means to Kill a Teacher: A Tribute to Jeremiah Small," *Kurdistan Tribune*, March 1, 2012, http://kurdistantribune.com/2012/means-kill-teacher/.

4. John Newton, "Young Christian Beheaded in Northern Iraq," *Catholic Herald*, May 19, 2011, http://www.catholicherald.co.uk/news/2011/05/19/young-christian-beheaded -in-northern-iraq/.

CHAPTER 15: THE NEW JIHAD

1. Steph Cockroft, "How to Live as a Christian in Raqqa," *Daily Mail*, December 23, 2014, http://www.dailymail.co.uk/news/article-2885506/How-live-Christian-Raqqa -ISIS-release-seven-rules-followers-rival-faith-including-praying-earshot-Muslims-never -mocking-Islam.html.

2. Susanne Güsten, "Christians Squeezed Out by Violent Struggle in North Syria," *New York Times*, February 13, 2013, http://www.nytimes.com/2013/02/14/world/middleeast /christians-squeezed-out-by-violent-struggle-in-north-syria.html?_r=0. For more on the plight of Christians in Syria, see *Religious Minorities in Syria: Caught in the Middle: Hearing Before the Committee on Foreign Affairs, Subcommittee on the Middle East and North Africa*, 113th Congress (2013) (testimony of Nina Shea, director, Hudson Institute's Center for Religious Freedom).

3. Salma Abdelaziz, "Death and Destruction in Syria: Jihadist Group 'Crucifies' Bodies to Send Message," CNN, May 2, 2014, http://www.cnn.com/2014/05/01/world/meast /syria-bodies-crucifixions/.

4. Nick Cumming-Bruce, "Beheadings in Syria Now Routine, U.N. Panel Says," *New York Times*, August 27, 2014, http://www.nytimes.com/2014/08/28/world/middleeast /syria-conflict.html?_r=0. See also "Under-Secretary-General for Humanitarian Affairs and Emergency Relief Coordinator, Valerie Amos; Security Council Briefing on Syria," United Nations Office for the Coordination of Humanitarian Affairs, December 15, 2014, http://reliefweb.int/report/syrian-arab-republic/under-secretary -general-humanitarian-affairs-and-emergency-relief-13.

5. "Ex-Lebanon Leader: Christians Target of Genocide," *CBS News*, January 3, 2011, http://www.cbsnews.com/news/ex-lebanon-leader-christians-target-of-genocide.

6. Mindy Belz, "What Liberation?" *World*, May 3, 2014, http://www.worldmag.com /2014/04/what_liberation.

CHAPTER 16: EMPTYING MOSUL

1. Liz Sly and Ahmed Ramadan, "Insurgents Seize Iraqi City of Mosul as Security Forces Flee," *Washington Post*, June 10, 2014, https://www.washingtonpost.com/world /insurgents-seize-iraqi-city-of-mosul-as-troops-flee/2014/06/10/21061e87-8fcd-4ed3 -bc94-0e309af0a674_story.html.

2. *Levant* refers to the geographical area east of the Mediterranean, including Syria. The Obama administration often refers to this terrorist organization as ISIL—the Islamic State of Iraq and Levant.

3. Ahmed Rasheed and Maggie Fick, "Ancient Christian Population of Mosul Flees Islamic State," *Reuters*, July 19, 2014, http://www.reuters.com/article/2014/07/19/us-iraq -security-christians-idUSKBN0FO0V520140719.

4. Ibid.

5. Archbishop Nicodemus Sharaf, interview by Lara Logan, *60 Minutes*, CBS, March 22, 2015, http://www.cbsnews.com/news/iraq-christians-persecuted-by-isis-60 -minutes/.

6. Jay Solomon, "U.S., Allies Step Up Efforts to Choke Off Islamic State's Funding," *Wall Street Journal*, September 4, 2014, http://www.wsj.com/articles/u-s-allies-step-up -efforts-to-choke-off-islamic-states-funding-1410307008; and "ISIS Net Worth: How the Richest Organization Acquired Their Wealth," Realtytoday.com, November 24, 2015, http://www.realtytoday.com/articles/54861/20151124/isis-net-worth-richest -organization-acquired-wealth.htm.

7. Y. Carmon, Y. Yehoshua, and A. Leone, "Understanding Abu Bakr Al-Baghdadi and the Phenomenon of the Islamic Caliphate State," MEMRI (The Middle East Media Research Institute), Inquiry & Analysis Series Report No. 1117, September 14, 2014, http://www.memri.org/report/en/print8147.htm.

8. Graeme Wood, "What ISIS Really Wants," *Atlantic*, March 2015, http://www.theatlantic .com/magazine/archive/2015/03/what-isis-really-wants/384980/.

9. Patrick Cockburn, "History Lessons the West Refuses to Learn," *Independent*, May 12, 2013, http://www.independent.co.uk/voices/comment/history-lessons-the-west-refuses -to-learn-8612306.html.

10. Patrick Garrity and M. Alex Johnson, "Obama on Iraq Turmoil: 'I Don't Rule Out Anything,'" *NBC News*, June 12, 2014, http://www.nbcnews.com/storyline/iraq -turmoil/obama-iraq-turmoil-i-dont-rule-out-anything-n129721.

11. Jim Garamone, "U.S. Defense Officials Study Iraq Assessments," U.S. Department of Defense press release, July 15, 2014, http://www.defense.gov/News/Article /602882.

12. "ISIS in Mosul Marks Christian Homes, Patriarch Issues Urgent Appeal," AINA News, July 19, 2014, http://aina.org/news/20140719115241.htm.

13. Ibid.

CHAPTER 17: ENLISTED

1. "A Rock and a Hard Place," *The Economist*, July 14, 2014, http://www.economist.com /blogs/erasmus/2014/07/iraqi-christians-and-west.

2. Katie Gorka, "ISIS Announces Its Next Attack," *Breitbart*, June 20, 2014, http:// www.breitbart.com/national-security/2014/06/20/isis-announces-its-next-attack/.

CHAPTER 18: THE FINAL FALL
1. "Rudaw Reporter: Death Toll on Shingal Mountain Rising by the Minute," *Rudaw*, August 6, 2014, http://rudaw.net/english/kurdistan/060820141.
2. "Press Briefing by Press Secretary Josh Earnest—8/7/2014," https://www.whitehouse .gov/the-press-office/2014/08/07/press-briefing-press-secretary-josh-earnest-872014.
3. Wolf Blitzer, *CNN News*, August 11, 2014, http://www.cnn.com/TRANSCRIPTS/1408 /11/wolf.01.html.

CHAPTER 19: FIGHTING ISIS
1. See 2 Chronicles 6:20.
2. After returning to Israel a few months later, Gill herself revealed details of where she'd served with Dwekh Nawsha to the *Jerusalem Post*, mentioning both Baqofa (spelled *Bakufa* in the article) and Batnaya. See Ben Hartman, "The Curious Case of Gill Rosenberg," *Jerusalem Post*, August 14, 2015, http://www.jpost.com/Middle-East/ISIS -Threat/The-curious-case-of-Gill-Rosenberg-412120.
3. Miriam Berger, "Israeli-Canadian Woman Fought IS to Stop 'Genocide,'" *Associated Press*, July 16, 2015, http://bigstory.ap.org/article/6d8b35d6e0854e42ae522fcaa00f1a7c /israeli-canadian-woman-fought-stop-genocide.
4. Patrick Cockburn, "Iraq Crisis: How Saudi Arabia Helped ISIS Take Over the North of the Country," *Independent*, July 12, 2014, http://www.independent.co.uk/voices/comment /iraq-crisis-how-saudi-arabia-helped-isis-take-over-the-north-of-the-country-9602312.html.
5. J. M. Berger and Jonathon Morgan, "The ISIS Twitter Census," The Brookings Institution, March 2015, http://www.brookings.edu/~/media/research/files/papers /2015/03/isis-twitter-census-berger-morgan/isis_twitter_census_berger_morgan.pdf.
6. Sheren Khalel and Matthew Vickery, "Monks Won't Leave Ancient Monastery amid ISIL Threat," *USA Today*, May 27, 2015, http://www.usatoday.com/story/news/world/2015 /05/27/christian-monastery-islamic-state-threat/27787683/.

CHAPTER 20: CITIES OF REFUGE
1. "150 ISIS Sex Slaves Commit Suicide, Some Fed to Dogs," *Clarion Project*, June 18, 2015, http://www.clarionproject.org/news/150-isis-sex-slaves-commit-suicide-some -fed-dogs#.
2. Ibid.
3. Johnlee Varghese, "ISIS News: 'Raped, Abused' Yazidi Women Beg West to Bomb Their Brothel and Kill Them," *International Business Times*, October 30, 2014, http:// www.ibtimes.co.in/isis-news-raped-abused-yazidi-women-beg-west-bomb-their-brothel -kill-them-video-612643.
4. Mark Schliebs, "Sydney Siege: Depraved Terrorist Mohamed Elomar Puts Slave Girl Up for Sale on Twitter," *Australian*, December 18, 2014, http://www.theaustralian .com.au/in-depth/sydney-siege-depraved-terrorist-mohamed-elomar-puts-slave-girl -up-for-sale-on-twitter/story-fnqxbywy-1227159935170?sv=48908eeb60425c7e4f2dc 97f53cf6ec3.
5. "Islamic State (ISIS) Releases Pamphlet on Female Slaves," MEMRI (the Middle East Media Research Institute), December 4, 2014, http://www.memrijttm.org/islamic-state -isis-releases-pamphlet-on-female-slaves.html.

6. Elliot Friedland, "Islamic State Selling Message with Glossy English Magazine," *Clarion Project*, August 4, 2014, http://www.clarionproject.org/analysis/islamic-state-selling -message-glossy-english-magazine.
7. "Islamic State (ISIS) Releases Pamphlet on Female Slaves," MEMRI.
8. "Iraq: ISIS Escapees Describe Systematic Rape," Human Rights Watch, April 14, 2015, https://www.hrw.org/news/2015/04/14/iraq-isis-escapees-describe-systematic-rape.
9. "UN Chief Voices 'Grave Concern' at Deepening Crisis in Iraq," UN News Centre, June 29, 2014, http://www.un.org/apps/news/story.asp?NewsID=48165#.Vl3-HXarS71.
10. "Calling Attacks 'a War Crime', Secretary-General Strongly Condemns Destruction of Cultural Heritage Sites in Iraq," UN Press Release, March 6, 2015, http://www.un.org /press/en/2015/sgsm16570.doc.htm.
11. Micah 1:3-4

CHAPTER 21: A GARDEN BY NIGHT
1. Georgina Howell, *Gertrude Bell: Queen of the Desert, Shaper of Nations* (New York: Farrar, Straus and Giroux, 2006), 381–382.
2. Diana Momeka, "Ancient Communities under Attack: ISIS's War on Religious Minorities," hearing before the House Committee on Foreign Affairs, May 13, 2015, video recording, http://foreignaffairs.house.gov/hearing/hearing-ancient-communities -under-attack-isis-s-war-religious-minorities.
3. Renee Montagne, "Amid Violence in Baghdad, a Musician Creates a One-Man Vigil," National Public Radio, June 15, 2015, http://www.npr.org/2015/06/08/412284066 /amid-violence-in-baghdad-a-musician-creates-a-one-man-vigil.
4. Hadeel Arja, "Among Wreckage of Bombs in Baghdad, Composer Kareem Wasfi Serenades the Distraught," *Huffington Post*, July 27, 2015, http://www.huffingtonpost .com/2015/07/27/kareem-wasfi_n_7866428.html.
5. Mindy Belz, "Numbers Matter," *World*, September 6, 2014, http://www.worldmag .com/2014/08/numbers_matter.
6. A number of aid organizations have a track record in Iraq and Syria. For links to some of these U.S.- and British-based groups, see "Updated List: Aid to the Needy in Iraq," *World*, August 25, 2014, http://www.worldmag.com/2014/08/aid_to_the_needy_in _iraq; and "In Extremity, Opportunity," *World*, June 13, 2015, http://www.worldmag .com/2015/05/in_extremity_opportunity.

Index

About the Author

MINDY BELZ is senior editor of *World* magazine. Writing for the publication since 1986, she has covered war in the Balkans, Sudan, Iraq, and Afghanistan—and has reported also from Nigeria, Syria, Turkey, Haiti, and elsewhere. Her reporting has been published overseas and in the United States in *The Weekly Standard* and other publications. She has appeared on Fox News, ABC News, and radio talk shows. Mindy is a contributing author of *Sorrow and Blood: Christian Mission in Contexts of Suffering, Persecution, and Martyrdom* and speaks frequently about persecution and survival in the Middle East. She enjoys engaging with younger audiences on a broad range of current events, as well as teaching journalism both abroad and closer to home under the auspices of the World Journalism Institute. Mindy worked on Capitol Hill and attended George Washington University, but for more than thirty years has lived in Asheville, North Carolina, where she is a wife and a mother of four children.

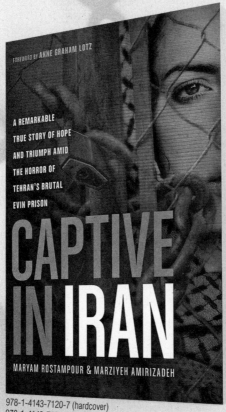